ECONOMIC ACTIVITY AND FINANCE

ECONOMIC ACTIVITY AND FINANCE

Edited by
MARSHALL E. BLUME
JEAN CROCKETT
PAUL TAUBMAN

BALLINGER PUBLISHING COMPANY
Cambridge, Massachusetts
A Subsidiary of Harper & Row, Publishers, Inc.

International Standard Book Number: 0–88410–858–9

Library of Congress Catalog Card Number: 81–20539

Printed in the United States of America

Library of Congress Cataloging in Publication Data
  Main entry under title:

  Economic activity and finance.

  Includes bibliographical references and index.
  1. Economics—Congresses. 2. Econometrics—
Congresses. 3. Finance—Congresses. 4. Capital market—
Congresses. I. Blume, Marshall. II. Crockett, Jean.
  HB21.E24   332   81–20539
  ISBN 0–88410–858–9   AACR2

CONTENTS

List of Figures   vii

List of Tables   ix

Preface   xi
Jean Crockett

The Keynote Address
The Effect of Inflation on Saving,
Investment, and Capital Markets—Irwin
Friend   1

Part I   23

Chapter 1
The Effects of Tax Parameters in the Investment
Equations in Macroeconomic Econometric
Models—Robert S. Chirinko and Robert Eisner   25

Chapter 2
Demographic Variables in Demand Analysis and

Welfare Analysis—Robert A. Pollak and Terence J.
Wales   85

Part II   127

Chapter 3

Some New Perspectives on Tests of CAPM and Other
Capital Asset Pricing Models and Issues of Market
Efficiency—John Lintner   129

Chapter 4

A Framework for the Analysis of Financial
Disorder—Jack Guttentag and Richard Herring   163

Chapter 5

Discussion of "A Framework for the Analysis of
Financial Disorder"—James Tobin   199

Part III   203

Chapter 6

An Analysis of the Predictive Accuracy of
Econometric Models: The Case of the WEFA
Model—Phoebus J. Dhrymes   205

Appendix   233

Index   243

List of Contributors   249

About the Editors   251

LIST OF FIGURES

4–1	Probability of a Shock	166
4–2	Probability of Lender Insolvency	167
4–3	Actual Rate of Return to Lender	169
4–4	Actual Rate of Return to Borrower	171
4–5	Probability of a Disaster	185
4–6	Probability of Lender Insolvency	186

LIST OF TABLES

1–1	BEA Equations, Equipment and Structures	34
1–2	Chase Equations, Equipment and Structures	36
1–3	DRI Equations	39
1–4	Michigan Equations, Equipment and Structures	42
1–5	MPS Equations	44
1–6	Wharton Equations, Total Investment by Sector i	46
1–7	Tax Scenarios.	52
1–8	BEA Simulations, Equipment and Structures	64
1–9	Chase Simulations, Equipment and Structures	66
1–10	DRI Simulations	68
1–11	Michigan Simulations, Equipment and Structures	71
1–12	MPS Simulations	73
1–13	Wharton Simulations, Equipment and Structures Investment	74
1–14	Comparison of Simulations	77
2–1	Summary Statistics	103
2–2	Marginal Budget Shares and Own Price Elasticity by Family Size	107
4–1	Investment Alternatives	174

4–2   Expected Return to Borrower Using $100 of
       Borrowed Funds   175
4–3   Liquidity and Solvency as Determinants of
       Failure   189
4–4   A Go-for-Broke Example   191
6–1   Comparison of PRMSE of Eight-Quarter
       Forecasts: WEFA Model Ex Post. . . .   227
6–2   Comparison of PRMSE of Eight-Quarter
       Forecasts: WEFA Public Forecasts (Post
       Meeting). . . .   228

PREFACE

Irwin Friend is almost unique in his command of the interrelated fields of saving (both personal and corporate), investment (both real and financial), and the behavior of financial institutions and financial markets. He has made outstanding empirical contributions in all three areas and has participated significantly in the cross-fertilization of insights and methodologies that serve to enrich and unify them. Much of his work has been co-authored with a variety of colleagues, but he provides the broad vision that unifies numerous strands into a coherent body of analysis.

His contributions have been predominantly of three types: first, the development and organization of new bodies of economic and financial data that are highly relevant both for hypothesis testing and for policy purposes; second, the implementation of innovative empirical tests of a number of controversial economic hypotheses; and third, improvement of the quality of empirical estimates of important economic magnitudes through better data, careful attention to possible sources of bias, and the cross-checking of alternative methods of measurement.

In the consumption area, Friend directed a major study which was based on the 1950 Bureau of Labor Statistics survey of consumer expenditures and which presented cross-tabulations that permitted much broader analysis of the impact of socioeconomic variables on consumption, saving, and their components than had previously been possible. He pioneered in the use of continuous panel data to augment time series and cross-sectional analysis of the consumption function and in the use of intercountry cross-sectional data. He was deeply involved in the development of a program for the collection of detailed savings data for India, including reinterviews to generate longitudinal data for sample households.

He played a significant role in the testing of the major consumption theories of the postwar era, the permanent income and life-cycle hypotheses, shifting the emphasis from indirect tests which depend on unsubstantiated auxiliary hypotheses, to a more direct approach that attempts to identify reasonable proxies for permanent income on the one hand and clear-cut examples of transitory income on the other. His cross-sectional studies, covering several countries, estimate permanent income either as average income for the individual household over several years or as a function of the income levels representative of various sociodemographic categories to which the household belongs. These studies strongly suggest that the impact of transitory income on consumption is less than that of permanent income but greater than zero. He has also presented cross-sectional evidence that capital gains on stock, which share some of the characteristics of transitory income, have a significant impact on consumption.

In the absence of sufficiently broad samples of continuous panel data, it is probable that cross-sectional studies of the Friend type provide the best available estimates of permanent income effects, although bias due to measurement error cannot be eliminated, nor is it possible to control adequately for the effects of the highly correlated variable, nonhuman wealth, which may have somewhat different effects on consumption than the present value of expected future labor income, particularly in the presence of asset disequilibria. Time-series analysis, on the other hand, presents almost insuperable econometric difficulty if we attempt to disentangle the effect of growth in permanent income from that in nonhuman wealth or from the effects of the long-run adaptations of aggregate consumer behavior that occur in response to changes in the institutional environment or gradual shifts in sociodemographic mix.

A second aspect of the permanent income hypothesis, the constancy of the savings-income ratio for the microeconomic consumption function, is challenged by one of Friend's early works which examines the consumption behavior of different occupational groups. His estimates are drawn from very large samples so that transitory income within groups might be expected to approach zero. In particular, salaries managers and professionals, as well as the self-employed, were found to have a considerably lower average propensity to consume than other occupational groups with lower incomes. It should be noted that these are precisely the groups that predominantly account for households' financial saving. Later work by others, in which homeowning households are further grouped by housing level to control for variation in transitory income, shows that even within the salaried professional and the self-employed group the ratio of consumption to income declines as income rises.

With respect to the composition of personal saving and of the asset portfolios of households, Friend has paid particular attention to the ownership of corporate stock. In two studies, involving a cooperative effort with the Internal Revenue Service (conducted so as to insure full protection of confidentiality), a number of tables were produced from individual income tax data on dividend-paying stocks held. These made possible not only a substantially improved estimate of the over-the-counter component of the aggregate value of corporate stock but also an improved estimate of the distribution of total stock ownership by income class. While distributions of dividend receipts by income class are routinely available from Internal Revenue Service publications, valid inferences cannot be drawn from these as to the income distribution of stockholdings, because high income groups (for tax and other reasons) tend to hold stock with below average dividend payout. In addition, the study provided unique information as to the industry preferences of particular income and occupational groups. The predominance of managers and professionals in stock ownership by individuals was clearly confirmed.

Major findings include the increase over the decade of the 1960s in the proportion of total stock held by persons over sixty-five. Since this group may well have a stronger preference than younger stockowners for dividends relative to capital gains, a shift of this nature and magnitude, particularly if the trend continues, may have implications both for the incidence of the double taxation of dividends and for the optimal financing mix on the part of corporations. Still more significant, the studies show that diversification, even at high income levels, is very much less than might be expected with risk-averse investors in efficient markets. Thus it may be that the total variability of return on individual stocks, and not just the variability due to general market movements, may be necessary to explain required risk premiums. This result is also consistent with the proposition that the desire to postpone capital gains taxes may have locked individual investors into their more successful stocks, to the detriment both of the stock market's role in the efficient allocation of resources and of the optimal balance between risk and before-tax return in individual portfolios. A subsequent survey of over 1,000 individual stockowners in 1975 confirmed both the low degree of diversification and the importance attached to variance of return in evaluating risk.

In the field of investment, Friend is perhaps best known for his role in the development of detailed anticipatory data on plant and equipment expenditures. This series, which is collected quarterly by the Securities and Exchange Commission and the Department of Commerce from a large sample of business firms, has proved an invaluable tool in the forecasting of investment, with a very good record of accuracy. As a byproduct, this survey has provided a number of insights into business decisionmaking and has been particularly useful in generating direct estimates of the magnitude and timing of the impact of monetary stringency on business investment.

A natural outgrowth of this work was the construction of forecasting models for Gross National Product. Friend has developed several models that are characterized by having few equations and by heavy reliance on expectational data. These models are just as accurate predictors for periods up to six months in the future as the much more detailed structural models of the economy.

Another long-term interest in the investment area has been the theory and empirical measurement of the cost of capital, especially equity capital. A paper in the early 1960s provides the most careful regression analysis available of the relative impact of dividends and retained earnings on stock prices. Theory suggests that with perfect markets and no taxes, stockholders should be indifferent between dividends and retained earnings, while with the existing tax advantage for capital gains, they should prefer retained earnings. On the other hand, naive regressions models, which are subject to obvious statistical biases, typically find that a dollar of dividends contributes far more to the market value of a stock than a dollar of retained earnings. To minimize these biases, cross-sectional regressions were fitted within industries, utilizing a sophisticated normalization of retained earnings to reduce measurement error as well as transitory fluctuations in that variable (both of which generally tend to produce downward bias in the coefficient). A test was also made for the possible effects of least squares bias by fitting reduced form equations. The final results indicate that, at least in the late 1950s, dividends contribute somewhat more than retained earnings to market value in nongrowth industries, while the reverse appears to be true in growth industries, although the evidence is not quite so clear. This result is consistent with the proposition that non-homogeneity of tastes among stockholders may be a significant factor in market behavior, supporting a "clientele effect," and further suggests that the relative value placed on dividends and retained earnings is not independent of the availability to the firm of profitable (supra-marginal) investment opportunities, as would be expected in perfect capital markets.

More recent work has utilized the direct questionnaire approach to investigate the effects of inflation and of specific tax policies on the cost of equity capital and on the level of plant and equipment outlays. A group of related surveys was developed, covering individual investors, institutional investors, and nonfinancial businesses. From the combined responses, inferences can be drawn as to the direction, and to some extent the magnitude, of probable impacts on the composition of individual and institutional portfolios, the rate of return on equity required by investors of both types, the financing mix preferred by business, and the volume of business investment. Furthermore, the data derived make it possible to estimate the cost of equity capital for individual firms, based on the current dividend yield and the expected growth rate of earnings or dividends reported by large institutional investors holding the stock. Presumably it is the growth expected by the market, and not the growth subsequently realized, that influences the price of a stock and thus the cost of equity capital at any given moment.

Recent time-series studies provide the most careful statistical analysis to date of the impact of inflation on real economic earnings of business equity (after appropriate adjustments for capital gains and losses and tax effects) and on real required rates of return. Substantive evidence is produced that over the recent past the impact on the first has been negative, on average, while that on the second has probably been positive, presumably in response to an increase in perceived risk.

In a third major area of research, Friend has dealt with the structure of financial markets. Over the decades of the 1950s and 1960s he was the moving spirit in a series of comprehensive studies of capital market institutions. These studies provided a storehouse of factual information that served to correct the preconceptions of casual empiricism and to increase understanding by economists and practitioners alike of the mechanisms at work. In addition, they developed reasonably precise estimates of important financial aggregates not previously available and, perhaps of greatest long-run interest, they presented persuasive and soundly documented, if not definitive, tests of various aspects of capital market efficiency. This body of research has offered an invaluable base for informed policy decisions.

Friend played a major role in the first study to deal in a comprehensive way with the firms composing the over-the-counter market (OTC), a highly complex industry which (even apart from dealings in U.S. government securities) historically exceeds the transactions volume of the organized exchanges and which, through its role in new issues, critically influences the efficiency with which the nation's savings are allocated among potential uses. This study provided the first reliable quantitative information about the extent, nature, and operations of the industry: dollar volume of transactions in securities of various types; number of issues traded both actively and less frequently; number and types of firms; degree of market concentration; capitalization ratios; the variety and relative importance of the different types of services performed; pricing practices for securities traded; inventory practices; and gross margin on services. Data of particular interest for evaluating market efficiency included the size of bid-ask spreads and the total cost for transfers between two public customers; the relationship of prices at which trades with public customers actually occurred to concurrent retail and wholesale bid-ask quotes; and the role of positioning, as inferred from inventory turnover rates, in maintaining price continuity for securities with thin secondary markets.

A subsequent study, directed by Friend in the early 1960s, not only provided a second benchmark from which to determine growth in total OTC volume and compositional and operational changes over the intervening decade but also examined the new issues component of the market in much greater detail than ever before. Trends in corporate new issues were examined historically dating from the establishment of the Securities and Exchange Commission (SEC). Of note were the growth in private placements of corporate debt and in competitive bidding for public issues of such debt, the growth in rights offerings of stock, some modest reduction in concentration within the investment banking industry, and a rather substantial reduction in underwriting compensation. Over the same period, short-term debt increased substantially as a source of corporate funds. All of these trends suggest that by the early 1960s investment bankers were facing considerably increased competition, both within the industry and from alternative mechanisms, in their role as intermediaries in the supplying of funds to business. Increased competition leads, of course, to a presumption of increase in operational efficiency.

Allocational efficiency in the new issues market for stock, an attribute which cannot be ensured by competition among investment bankers, was tested by examining the post-offering price performance of such issues relative to their industry group or to the market as a whole. While secondary offerings, rights issues, and new issues of public utilities appear to perform similarly to the market as a whole, original nonrights industrial issues were found to perform poorly relative to their industry (in the short run of a few months) and relative to the market for industrials as a whole over longer periods of five and ten years. In an efficient market, it would be expected that new issues, particularly unseasoned ones, would bring a higher average return than the market to compensate for their somewhat greater risk. During the 1920s by comparison, prices of new industrial issues tended to be well maintained during the first post-offering year but to decline thereafter (relative to the market) even more substantially than in the postwar period and to show wider variance of performance. The inference may be drawn that new issues of industrials tend to be overpriced relative to their long-run value, but to a lesser extent post-SEC, when regulations required substantially more complete disclosure than in the 1920s.

A study of mutual funds, commissioned by the SEC in response to a congressional directive and directed by Friend, examined these institutions in comprehensive detail over a six-year period in the 1950s. Information was developed on organization and control, investment policy, sales charges and management fees, performance, impact on the stock market, extent of control over portfolio companies, and the relationship of funds to their investment advisors. A subsequent study extended the analysis through most of the 1960s. Three findings presented here are of particular interest.

To an unusual degree relative to other corporations, mutual funds were controlled by management groups having small ownership interest. Typically, the management group was closely affiliated with the outside investment advisor, raising some question of whether shareholder interests were adequately protected by arm's length bargaining in the contract with the advisor. In particular, it was found that for a given portfolio size, advisory fees were frequently quite high relative both to the comparable costs of those funds that did not employ an outside advisor and to the charges made by outside advisors to their other clients. Furthermore, portfolio turnover (at least of NYSE stock) was large relative to the market as a whole, generating large brokerage fees, a portion of which in some cases went directly to the outside advisor and in other cases was used to reward dealers for their success in selling the mutual fund's own shares, thus increasing portfolio size and advisory fees. There was no indication that higher turnover rates produced superior investment returns.

A second major finding was that mutual funds in the aggregate did no better in the performance of their stock portfolios than the market as a whole. Nor was portfolio performance related either to the size of the advisory fee or to the size of the sales charge (front-end load). Since the sales charge reduces the funds available for investment and thus the dollar return associated with any given percentage return, it follows that investors in funds with relatively high sales charges fared relatively poorly. The fact that such funds grew more rapidly than no load funds in term of net inflow from sale of new shares appears to attest to the success of the selling effort inspired by a high sales charge.

With respect to the impact of mutual funds on prices of individual stocks and on the stock market as a whole, it was found that the funds frequently accounted for a high proportion (over 10 percent) of the trading in several favored issues. There was some evidence on a day-to-day basis of an effect that net fund purchases had on overall market price movements. These effects tended to be stabilizing. For individual securities, there was some evidence of month-to-month effects of net fund purchases on price. More important, there is a clear suggestion that the diversion of savings into the stock market associated with the rapid growth of mutual funds (and subsequently with the rapid growth of pension funds and their increasing propensity to invest in stock) may have produced a rise in stock prices (relative to underlying earnings) that could not be maintained once growth rates slowed and portfolio mix stabilized. It appears that temporarily the aggregate demand for stock was shifting much more rapidly from year to year than could be accommodated by aggregate new issues, and this produced continuing upward pressure on stock prices and on the price of a dollar of the underlying equity earnings.

A study of the savings and loan industry of similar scope and detail was directed by Friend in the late 1960s, again under Congressional directive. In addition to developing data on the operating characteristics of the industry and potential problem areas, the study included an evaluation of Federal Home Loan Bank Board (FHLBB) policies and made a number of policy recommendations, several of which have been or are soon to be implemented.

One major conclusion was that a specialized intermediary for financing home mortgages was useful not only because it provides an effective mechanism for the implementation of housing policy but also because large economies of scale exist in evaluating mortgage lending risk and these would not be as fully available to a diversified lender.

However, such a specialized intermediary with long-term assets and short-term liabilities is particularly vulnerable to restrictive monetary policy, as was dramatically evidenced in 1966. In words prophetic for the early 1980s, the report states, "For the savings and loan industry, a prolonged period of inflationary pressure contained mainly by monetary policy and high interest rates could be disastrous."

A number of recommendations were made to ease the impact of a period of rising interest rates on both the savings and loan industry and the home construction industry, which is highly sensitive to changes in the availability of mortgage financing. Not only are the intermediaries' profits squeezed but new funds cannot be attracted (and funds available may actually shrink) because the industry cannot offer deposit yields competitive with other short-term rates. Recommendations relevant to this problem include: increasing the range of permissible assets and liabilities of the savings and loan associations in specific and limited ways; gradually increasing deposit rate ceilings to market levels; holding of part of liquidity reserves in cash and short-term governments rather than long-term governments; having flexibility in liquidity reserve requirements as a first line of defense to net withdrawal of funds; exhibiting, on the part of the FHLBB, greater willingness to make advances to the extent needed in the case of a large scale outflow of funds; pooling the cost of providing such advances by requiring the associations to hold some FHLBB issues; and introducing some long-term debt (with staggered maturities) into the financial structure of the Home Loan Banks, especially in periods of low interest rates.

A second set of recommendations was directed to the improvement of the efficiency of mortgage markets and the liquidity of mortgage instruments by raising state ceilings on conventional mortgages to competitive levels; by adjusting Veterans Administration (VA) and Federal Housing Administration (FHA) ceilings so that new mortgages can sell at par; by strengthening the VA and FHA guarantees to remove the small residual risk to lenders; by issuing government-guaranteed bonds backed by earmarked pools of government-insured mortgages, as authorized in the Housing and Urban Development Act of 1968; and by experimenting with new types of mortgage instruments, including variable rate mortgages, as well as contracts with greater flexibility in the repayment pattern so as to meet more adequately the needs of particular types of borrowers.

In the 1970s Friend's interests turned predominantly to questions relating to the asset structure of household portfolios and to the efficiency of capital markets, particularly the stock market, as measured by conformity to relationships implicit in market efficiency.

A major paper uses detailed data on asset holdings for a large sample of households (the 1962–63 Federal Reserve Board Survey of Financial Characteristics of Consumers) to test the hypothesis of constant proportional risk aversion and to estimate the Pratt-Arrow coefficient for the aggregate household sector, conceived as an appropriate weighted average of individual coefficients of proportional risk aversion. It may be shown that if expectations are homogeneous as to the return and variance of return on the market portfolio of risky assets and if we abstract from human wealth, then in equilibrium the reciprocal of each individual's risk aversion coefficient is proportional to the share of risky assets in his total portfolio times the complement of his average tax rate. Grouping households by net worth class, including equity in homes as a risky asset, and regressing the observed tax-adjusted risky asset ratio against the log of net worth (with dummy variables for age, education, and occupation), the effect of net worth was found to be entirely insignificant. Thus the hypothesis of constant proportional risk aversion at different wealth levels is supported. However, when a crude estimate of human wealth is included for those households with wage or salary incomes, the theoretical development becomes more complex and more tenuous. Empirical estimates show some tendency for increasing proportional risk aversion as income rises, although the rise is not large, particularly if the small group under $10,000 is eliminated. Further, it is argued that biases inherent in the approach probably tend to overstate the increase.

Given that constant proportional risk aversion can serve as a rough first approximation to the facts, the estimation of the magnitude of this constant requires only that the ex ante price of risk, defined as the expected premium on risky assets divided by the variance of return on these assets, can be approximated from ex post data. Using New York Stock Exchange stocks to represent risky assets, the ex post estimate of the market price of risk is found to be well above 1, both for the post-World War II period (through 1971) and for longer periods. Abstracting from human wealth and treating equity in home as a risky asset, the derived estimate for the coefficient of proportional risk aversion is certainly greater than 1 and probably in the neighborhood of 2. Inclusion of human wealth produces a still higher estimate, in the range from 3 to 6.

This finding is of great policy significance. If the household utility functions for wealth are indeed characterized by constant proportional risk aversion with a coefficient in excess of 1, this implies that the positive effect on current consumption of the higher permanent income associated with a rise in the (inflation adjusted) after-tax rate of return on assets fully offsets or outweighs the negative substitution effect of such a rise (although both the saving and the consumption planned for future periods would rise). Such a finding raises serious questions about policy measures that seek to stimulate real investment indirectly by raising after-tax returns on financial assets to increase saving rather than directly by raising after-tax returns on investment and thus permitting investment to bid more effectively against alternative uses for the supply of saving. From the evidence it appears that income tax relief will raise personal saving only to the extent that after-tax income is redistributed from the poor to the rich and then only if the rich have a relatively high propensity to save out of permanent income, a question still open to considerable debate.

A second question of much interest, addressed by Friend in a group of related papers, concerns the feasibility of measuring the risk premiums required on individual equity issues or portfolios as a linear function of covariance with overall stock market returns and of identifying under- or overvalued issues (or portfolios) in terms of deviations from a regression of realized premiums on realized covariances. The capital asset pricing model demonstrates that under rather restrictive assumptions the ex ante or expected values of risk premiums and covariances must be linearly related, with deviations from the line a result of temporary disequilibria. However, several anomalies appear when observed, or ex post, returns are used in fitting empirical relationships and when the return on listed stock is used as a proxy for the return on a market portfolio which theoretically should contain all risky assets available to investors. First, a number of authors, including Friend, find that the intercept of the empirical relationship is significantly different from the observed rate of return on risk-free assets, which under the theoretical model it should approximate. Second, tests by Friend show that deviations from the fitted line are correlated with risk (as measured by covariance with the market) and that the more risky assets and portfolios perform poorly relative to predictions from the regression. This finding is contrary to the model and raises very serious questions about the use of such a fitted line to identify undervalued stocks. Third, the sign of the risk variable is found by various authors to be negative in periods of stock market decline, and this cannot possibly be true of the relationship between the ex ante variables if investors are indeed risk averse (though it is consistent with certain return-generating functions). It must reflect significant differences between ex post values and the ex ante values which they attempt to proxy. Fourth, Friend finds some evidence that residual variance of return, after taking account of the effects of covariance with the market, affects risk premiums. This is consistent with the responses of individual investors in the survey mentioned above and is to be expected in view of the evidence that such investors, for whatever reason, fail to diversify to the optimal degree.

Friend has attempted in a number of ways to mitigate the empirical inadequacies of present tests in order to obtain clearer evidence as to the validity of the model itself. He has utilized random portfolios stratified by risk to reduce the problem of sampling error in estimating risk measures, which tends to be unstable over time for individual securities. He has expanded the proxy for the market portfolio to include corporate bonds, as well as listed stock and long-term governments. He has worked with observed long-term rates of return, which are more likely than observed short-term returns to approximate ex ante returns, given the volatility of stock prices. Finally he has addressed the crucial problem of the inadequacy of any ex post rate of return as a proxy for the theoretically relevant ex ante rate by obtaining, on a continuing basis, data from a sample of large financial institutions on their expectations relating to the long-run return on individual stocks.

While the data base so far available is not large and while the expectations of large institutions are not necessarily representative of all investors, an analysis that utilizes true ex ante data represents an ideal test of the underlying asset pricing model. From the data available to Friend, he finds that the model does not come out well. Intercepts remain much higher than the rate of return on very low risk assets. In spite of the fact that large institutions can be presumed to diversify adequately, residual variance proves fully as useful in explaining risk premiums as the risk measure based on covariance with market return. A new variable reflecting the heterogeneity of expectations among institutions reporting on the same stock performs better than either of the two risk measures previously tested. This suggests that uncertainty as to long-run earnings performance, to the extent than this may be associated with a lack of consensus among knowledgeable investors, contributes significantly to the risk premium required.

The chapters in the present volume carry forward significantly several areas of analysis to which Friend has made major contributions. These chapters were initially presented as papers at a conference in Duck Key, Florida, in March 1981. The volume begins with the keynote address given by Friend in which he summarizes the implications of various aspects of his work for policy in an inflationary world.

In the first chapter, Pollak and Wales implement a new methodology in estimating demand relationships for specific categories of consumption goods within a single time period. In particular, they discuss and test alternative ways of introducing the effects of a demographic variable (in their empirical work, the number of children) into such demand functions. Income, price, and demographic parameters of the several demand functions are estimated jointly in such a way that the additivity constraint is satisfied—that is, the demand functions obtained sum identically to total consumption for all possible values of prices and the demographic variable. The residual variances obtained under the alternative methods of introducing the demographic variable are then compared to determine relative explanatory power. In view of the changes now being experienced in age distribution over time, it would be particularly relevant to extend the Pollak-Wales methodology to age of household head.

It is of some interest to trace the relationship between the model of consumer behavior employed here by Pollak and Wales and that implicit in Friend's work in estimating households' coefficient of proportional risk aversion. Friend's model is consistent with a multiperiod household utility function of the Bergson family, which implies constant proportional risk aversion if we define wealth as the present value of expected future income, including labor income, and define the utility of a given level of wealth as the utility of the optimal consumption stream that can be supported by that level of wealth. Specifically, if

$$U = \sum_t \alpha_t u(C_t) = \sum_t \alpha_t C_t^{1-\gamma}, \gamma > 0 \text{ and } \alpha_t \gtreqless 0 \text{ as } \gamma \lesseqgtr 1,$$

is maximized subject to a wealth constraint, the optimal values of C_t, C_t^*, are proportional to wealth; and the indirect utility function, given the rate of return available on assets, is

$$U(W) = \sum_t \alpha_t (C_t^*)^{1-\gamma} = \sum_t \alpha_t (a_t W)^{1-\gamma} = \bar{a} W^{1-\gamma}.$$

If a function of similar form represents the utility of a particular market basket of goods and services in period t, with quantities C_{it} where i runs over consumption categories, and if the utility of a given level of consumer expenditures in t, C_t, is defined as the utility of the optimal market basket that C_t permits, then the indirect utility function, given prices, is

$$u(C_t) = \sum_i \beta_i (C_{it}^*)^{1-\gamma},$$

where the C_{it}^* are the quantities obtained by maximizing utility subject to the constraint $\sum_i p_{it} C_{it} = C_t$. Since the C_{it}^* are proportional to C_t in this case,

$$u(C_t) = \sum_i \beta_i (b_i C_t)^{1-\gamma} = \bar{\beta}(C_t)^{1-\gamma}.$$

Thus the assumption that the single-period utility function is of the stipulated form, together with the assumption that the multiperiod function is linear in the single-period functions, implies a utility of wealth function characterized by constant proportional risk aversion. Furthermore, the exponent of wealth is identical with that attached to the quantities of individual consumption goods in the single-period function.

It is not possible to piece together from the empirical estimates of Pollak and Wales and those of Friend a complete and consistent picture of household behavior, explaining both the composition of consumption and the composition of wealth. In part this is because Pollak and Wales generalize the Bergson function in such a way that optimal quantities in the single-period solution are linear in total consumption, but not strictly proportional, while Friend utilizes the ungeneralized function. Furthermore, the data sets are drawn from different populations, one American and one British, in somewhat different time periods.

Apart from the limitations imposed by these discrepancies, the two sets of findings potentially complement each other to enlarge the range of household behavior explained. Analysis of the Pollak and Wales type uses household budget data to describe the roles of relative prices and demographic variables. It can provide estimates, not of the parameters of $u(C_t)$ itself, but of a function of similar form, of which $u(C_t)$ must be a monotonic transformation. Most simply, in terms of the basic Bergson function,

$$u(C_t) = d(\hat{b}\, C_t^{\hat{c}})^\delta$$

where $\hat{b}$ and $\hat{c}$ are estimates drawn from single-period analysis of the Pollak and Wales type. Analysis of the Friend type uses household balance sheet data to describe the role of interest rates (the risk-free rate and the premium on risky assets) and provides an estimate of the exponent of C_t, $\hat{c}\delta$, from which an estimate of δ then may be derived.

Logical completeness requires a common model of household behavior consistent not only with the observed choices among consumption categories in a particular time period but also with the distribution of lifetime consumption over a number of periods and with the observed composition of household wealth at various ages. To identify and fit such a model, there is need for longitudinal data providing detail on the allocation of wealth among asset types as well as the allocation of total consumption among expenditure categories. The program of data collection which Friend was instrumental in developing for India has potential for meeting this need but has not yet been extensively analyzed.

It may be noted that the analysis of household portfolios and the analysis of consumption expenditures, whether for good reason or for lack of adequate communication, have taken somewhat different tacks. While both are based on utility maximization, the former has followed a Lancastrian approach, choosing to deal not with individual types of assets but only with the two underlying attributes of return and risk. But are two really enough? Liquidity risk may have a different significance for some investors from risk relating to long-run profitability. Residual variance, as well as covariance with the market, may be of some importance. Dividend payout may be a major consideration for retired stockholders. It is not yet entirely clear that skewness does not matter, though a recent analysis by Friend and Westerfield finds no evidence that co-skewness is significant. Factors such as corporate control and institutional restrictions, to say nothing of specialized knowledge of a particular industry or company, may play a role in the decisions of particular investors. In other words, an individual security may represent a bundle of more than two relevant attributes.

The second chapter, by Chirinko and Eisner, is policy-oriented in that it brings together evidence from the major econometric models as to the magnitude of the impact of tax incentives on business fixed investment, a question crucial to the nation's current economic program. It is methodological in that it tests the sensitivity of the estimated effects to specifications and constraints imposed by the model builders.

The tax variables considered include the investment tax credit and the original present value of tax depreciation, both of which are treated as reducing the effective price of capital goods. The third variable analyzed, the corporate profits tax rate, has a more complex effect. One of the tests made compares investment projections generated by the models for the fourth quarter of 1977 with what these projections would have been if each tax variable in turn were held at its pre-incentive 1953 level, with the other two at their actual levels. A second test compares investment projections for the same quarter (IV/77) based on the 1973 values of the tax variables with the predictions that would have been generated for that quarter under much stronger tax incentives: a doubling of the investment tax credit on equipment and inclusion of a 10 percent credit on structures; tax depreciation based on lives set at half the 1973 level; and a corporate profits tax rate at 90 percent of the 1973 level.

In both tests the effects of tax incentives on investment in equipment were found to be very much greater for the MPS and DRI models than for the remaining models. Both the DRI and the MPS models impose *a priori* constraints on the equipment investment equations. In the first case, the effect on investment of changes in the ratio of output price to the user cost (rental price) of capital goods is constrained to equal the effect of changes in output. In the second case, the constant term in the equation for investment in equipment is constrained to zero. When these rather arbitrary constraints are removed, the effect of the price to user cost ratio is determined to be much less than that of output in the DRI model, while the constant term is significantly different from zero in the MPS model. The estimated impact of tax incentives is reduced in both cases and brought more closely in line with the other models.

Aside from the relaxation of these constraints, the Chirinko-Eisner chapter tests the effect of eliminating variables that depend on stock price (such as dividend or earnings yields). Such variables normally enter into the user cost of capital goods as measures of the cost of equity capital. Stock price is, of course, a highly volatile quantity, and Chirinko and Eisner argue that a decline in earnings or dividend yield, resulting from a rise in stock price, is as likely to reflect an increase in expected earnings or dividends relative to current levels as it is to reflect a decline in the required rate of return on equity. But such a rise in expected earnings is likely to be associated with the availability of profitable investment opportunities and therefore with high investment. A rise in investment because investment opportunities are good is likely to be associated with an understatement of the cost of equity capital if this is measured by earnings or dividend yields, since expected rather than current earnings should properly be compared with stock price in measuring this cost. But then a spurious inverse relationship, without causal significance, will distort the estimated effect on investment of the user cost of capital goods. Since tax incentives enter the investment function through this user cost, their effects also will be misrepresented.

When terms involving stock prices are eliminated and arbitrary constraints are simultaneously removed, the effect on investment in equipment of the large increases in tax incentives that are investigated declines from an average of $7.6 billion, or 8.3 percent of the prediction based on actual 1973 tax law, to an average of $3.5 million, or 3.8 percent. Except for the Bureau of Economic Analysis (BEA) model, which is high, little variation remains among the models. The effect on structures is small in any case, little affected by the changes in specification, and fairly uniform among models.

The next two chapters deal with financial rather than real markets and hidden perspectives beyond the restrictive assumptions that underlie traditional models of market behavior in order to attempt an enriched representation of reality.

The piece by Guttentag and Herring breaks new ground in what may well be a seminal approach to risk in financial markets. They borrow two concepts recently introduced in other contexts and explore their interaction in a dynamic representation of debter-creditor behavior.

The first concept is that of a "disaster"—in their context, a financial disaster—defined as an event or set of events of low probability that would cause losses to occur across a wide spectrum of investment projects. The rough independence that we normally postulate among the outcomes of a large number of projects then fails to hold, with serious aggregate consequences. From the literature of natural disasters, it appears that the subjective probability of a disaster declines with the length of the time since the last event, and further that there is a threshold probability level below which decisionmakers behave as if the probability were zero. The occurrence of losses above normal (though short of a disaster) may cause the subjective probability of disaster to leap discontinuously to a significantly positive level, throwing lenders into disequilibrium. It will be noted that such a model contradicts one of the underlying axioms of traditional capital market theory.

The second strategic concept is that of moral hazard. Since the distribution of returns for the borrower is truncated on the left (at total loss of his capital), while that for the lender is truncated on the right (at return of funds loaned plus the contract rate) and since the lender may not be able to control effectively the riskiness of the use to which the borrowed funds are put, the possibility exists that the borrower may be able to better himself at the expense of the lender by increasing the riskiness of the project he chooses. Given that default occurs, only the lender is affected by extent of the decline in return below the default level. In the absence of default, only the borrower is affected by the extent to which return rises above the default level. Thus the borrower has an unambiguous incentive to shift the return distribution in such a way as to raise the probability of very high returns (at the expense of modest returns) even if at the same time the probability of very low returns is also increased (at the expense of returns only slightly below the default level). If may also pay the borrower to raise the probability of default, but in this case there are some costs to be balanced against the gains.

As long as the borrower's capital exceeds the loan plus the contract rate of return, there is no chance of default and no way that he can gain at the lender's expense by increasing the riskiness of his project. However, if default is possible and if the lender cannot control fully the riskiness of the borrower's use of funds, then he must assume that the borrower will choose the risk level that optimizes his own return, given the contract rate and his capital position. The optimum riskiness for the borrower is positively related to the contract rate and negatively related to his capital position.

The lender may then determine an optimal contract rate, such that any gain from a higher rate in the absence of default would be just offset by the increased probability of default engendered by the fact that a higher risk level becomes optimal for the borrower in response to the higher contract rate. If the optimal contract rate yields a return for a (risk-neutral) lender exceeding his cost of capital, then this rate

represents a sufficient premium over the risk-free rate to induce him
to make the loan. However, if the expected value of return at the
optimum contract rate falls short of the cost of capital, capital
rationing will occur, with the amount of the loan reduced to achieve
a more satisfactory relationship to the borrower's equity position. As
loan value falls relative to borrower's capital, expected losses due to
default are reduced in two ways, causing the lender's overall
expected return to rise. First, for any given return distribution the
range of outcomes over which the lender receives less than the
promised amount is curtailed; and, second, the optimum risk level
for the borrower is lowered and this may lead to a further reduction
in the probability of default.

Returning now to the question of financial disaster, what is the
effect of a shift in the subjective probability of such a disaster, in the
context of moral hazard? If the period is sufficiently long since the last
previous disaster, it is hypothesized that the subjective probability
becomes effectively zero; and both capital positions and liquidity
positions deteriorate accordingly. Creditors can lend to borrowers
with lower capital positions, or permit loans outstanding to rise, or
permit their own capital to fall without increasing the subjective
probability of their own insolvency.

Suppose that an unfavorable event or set of events occurs, short of
a disaster, which causes the subjective probability of a disaster to
become significantly positive. For both lenders and borrowers, the
expected return is immediately and directly reduced. Furthermore, if
the lender's expected return initially equalled his cost of capital at
the optimal contract rate, it is now too low and rationing is in order.
Lenders will cut the aggregate of their outstanding loans as fast as the
maturities of their contracts permit. Borrowers with very short-term
liabilities will be subject to runs. If contract returns were initially set
below the optimal level due to competitive pressures, then there will
be some room for risk premiums to rise. But in any case, some
increase in rationing will occur. Nor can the central bank ease the
situation (apart from providing liquidity to "safe" borrowers as
required), except to the extent that the lenders' cost of capital is
reduced or that direct lending to borrowers is undertaken.

The chapter by Lintner seeks to bring several types of external
information to bear in evaluating the unsatisfactory and ambiguous
evidence produced by tests of the capital asset pricing model based
on regressions among ex post variables (or among estimated ex ante

variables generated from ex post values by some hypothesized process). As previously indicated, the theoretical model refers to ex ante values (and involves a considerably broader market portfolio of risky assets than ordinarily utilized in empirical tests). The imperfect proxies substituted for the relevant ex ante variables make a clear-cut test of the model itself virtually impossible, except through the actual collection of ex ante data that is being undertaken by Friend.

Lintner addresses, in particular, the role of residual variance—that is, variance in the return of an individual security or portfolio not explained by covariance with the market. He offers several items of external evidence that support the existence of an effect of this variable on the required rate of return.

First, the capital asset pricing model necessarily implies the Modigliani-Miller theorems relating the risk (and in particular the systematic risk) of a firm's assets to the market-weighted average of the risk of the firm's levered equity and debt. In the absence of any net tax advantage of debt and any bankruptcy costs, it follows that the value of a firm should be invariant to capital structure. But strong effects on value have been found for "dual purpose" funds, indicating that the failure of assumptions, as to completeness of markets and unlimited short selling, is sufficient to produce significant behavioral departures from the model. In general, if no net tax advantage for debt exists, we would expect the fraction of investment financed by debt to be a random drawing from a rectangular zero-one distribution. Instead distinct patterns, which are fairly stable over time, emerge for different industries.

On the other hand, if the net tax advantage of debt is positive, firms should maximize the utilization of whatever "debt capacity" they have. However, there is very substantial evidence, not only that available supplies of debt are affected by nonsystematic as well as systematic risks of the borrowing firm but also that the present value of bankruptcy costs (again reflecting nonsystematic risks) would serve to restrain firms from maximizing debt even in the absence of lender constraints. Thus the required rate of return on an individual equity will rise above that predicted on the basis of covariance with market return by an amount that reflects risks specific to the individual firm.

A second argument relates to the option pricing model and the use of this model to value the complex contingent claim involved in levered equity. Both the expected rate of return on the levered stock and its covariance with market return are shown to depend logically on the variance of return on the firm's assets. Thus nonsystematic, firm-specific risk plays a causal role, while β serves, at least in part, as a proxy for this risk. To the extent that it is an imperfect proxy, one would expect to find residual variance statistically significant as well as scientifically justified in the market line regression.

Finally Lintner turns to the wide variety of evidence that investors do not and should not hold identical portfolios or have identical expectations, in view of the fact that information is not costless and is differentially available to individual investors. The existence of short positions in risky assets, the profitability of insider trading, the differences among investors in the correlation of nonmarketable assets with traded securities are among the causes of heterogeneity noted. Lintner then cites work by Williams to establish that heterogeneity of expectations and portfolios implies that residual as well as systematic risk will affect required rates of return.

In "An Analysis of the Predictive Accuracy of Econometric Models: The Case of the WEFA Model," Phoebus Dhrymes considers a number of issues to which Friend has made important contributions. These include such questions as, How accurately does an econometric model predict? Does the often used procedure of adjusting constants lead to improved forecasts, and does a large structural equation model yield more accurate forecasts than an autogressive equation estimated by the process of a "time series" model, ARIMA?

Dhrymes uses the Wharton Econometric Forecasting Associates, Inc. (WEFA) III to replicate the five sets of forecasts made beginning in the fourth quarter of 1972 and ending with the fourth quarter in 1973 using the original data available at time of forecast and the actual constant adjustments. Each forecast covers an eight-quarter sequence. Dhrymes repeats the analysis, setting the constant adjustments to zero. He then redoes the analysis using the corrected, revised data (as of 1977).

Dhrymes develops expected relationship of the root mean square error for the four permutations given above and indicates somes hypotheses that can be tested. He presents results for fourteen main variables and finds that data revision in the GNP is not an important element in forecast accuracy. He also finds that that model without constant adjustments but with updated data yields much better forecasts than the one with constant adjustments and original data with respect to nominal GNP and consumption but the opposite with respect to unemployment and investment.

Finally, Dhrymes constructs a fourth order ARIMA model for each variable he studies which he uses to forecast each series. He finds that except for unemployment, the WEFA model using revised data dominates the ARIMA forcasts for all variables but unemployment, and the WEFA public forecasts dominate the ARIMA forecasts for all variables but unemployment and some components of investment.

This volume was planned by Marshall Blume, Paul Taubman, and myself. Two of us are perhaps Irwin's most frequent collaborators in joint research projects. The third is one of Irwin's earliest students and also a collaborator in subsequent research. All of us owe him a large debt of gratitude for what we have learned in our work with him, as do numerous other of his colleagues and students at the University of Pennsylvania.

We wish to express our appreciation to the authors of the articles included here, to James Tobin and Stephen Ross who served as discussants at the initial conference, to F. Gerard Adams and Richard Kihlstrom who served as session chairmen, and to Laurie Cousart whose organizational talents proved invaluable. In addition, we are most grateful to the corporations and funds whose generous contributions underwrote the conference expenses:

American Telephone and Telegraph Company,
Merrill Lynch and Company,
Morgan Guaranty Trust Company,
The Ford Motor Company Fund,
The Proctor and Gamble Fund, and
The Seraco Group.

Jean Crockett
Philadelphia, August 1981

THE KEYNOTE ADDRESS
THE EFFECT OF INFLATION ON SAVING, INVESTMENT, AND CAPITAL MARKETS

Irwin Friend
University of Pennsylvania

In discussing the effect of inflation on saving, investment, and capital markets, it is desirable first to review the theoretical ways in which inflation might be expected to affect these other variables and then to examine briefly the relevant statistical evidence. For purposes of this review, it may be useful to highlight several major misconceptions that unfortunately permeate an important part of the economic program of the present administration in Washington.

SAVING

Abstracting from sociodemographic effects, the main theoretical determinants of the overall propensity to save in the absence of inflation are presumably the discounted flow of expected future wage income or human wealth, initial nonhuman wealth, interest rates on both risk–free and risky assets, the uncertainty of future wage and property income, and the distribution of human and nonhuman wealth among different groups in the population. Such groups would include households in different wealth classes, corporations, and government. Inflation could plausibly affect the overall propensity to save through any of these channels—namely, through changes in the real national income, the real value of nonhuman

1

wealth, the real return on nominally risk-free and risky assets, and the distribution of wealth. Before evaluating the evidence on the actual impact of inflation on saving behavior, it will be helpful to consider the ways in which the different determinants of saving are presumed to operate theoretically and the statistical evidence that has been adduced to test these theoretical presumptions.

The theoretical and empirical literature on the saving-income relationship is too well known to most economists to require much attention here. There is still a significant difference of opinion on whether household saving is invariant to the level of "permanent" labor income. Though my personal judgement is that the saving-income ratio is positively related to any meaningful measure of "permanent" income, the relationship may not be so strong that a moderate redistribution of income would have an important effect on the aggregate household saving-income ratio. However, I have for some time been amused at the implicit change in position of some of the early proponents of permanent income hypotheses who relied on household saving (or consumption) and income data to confirm their theoretical preconceptions. They now seem to believe in complete substitutability between household and corporate saving without reexamining the implications of such substitutability for the earlier statistical tests on which they relied to support the permanent income hypothesis.

Similarly, there is a wide difference of opinion among economists on the substitutability between household and corporate saving and between household and government saving. I must confess that while the rationality and ultrarationality theories (which imply that an additional dollar of corporate or government saving would be offset by a dollar decrease in household saving) make considerable theoretical sense for corporate saving at least in the long run, they seem to me to make less sense for government saving, where among other things, they assume a strange type of intergenerational tax calculation. However, since the proof of the pudding is in the eating, I shall briefly discuss the empirical evidence. My evaluation of that evidence based on the published literature—which includes papers by Feldstein (1973), Feldstein and Fane (1973), David and Scadding (1974), and more recently Howrey and Hymans (1978) and Tanner (1979)—is that there is a moderate degree of substitutability between household and corporate saving but at most only a modest degree of substitutability between household and government saving. The published tests, which are based on time series analysis alone, seem to me quite deficient, especially as they apply to the relationship between household and government saving where I am not convinced there is any appreciable substitutability.

Time series analysis of the relationship between household and corporate saving is subject to the usual deficiency of the inadequacy of the number of independent observations for distinguishing among the effects of a large number of relevant serially correlated variables, while once government saving in addition to household and corporate saving is introduced into the usual time series regression analysis, substantial problems of specification arise. It seems to me essential under these circumstances to carry out cross-section tests both across countries and, more important, across households where possible. Even a casual inspection of cross-country data suggests no substitutability between household and government saving, but the number of independent observations still remains a problem. A much more definitive analysis of the relation between household and corporate saving is possible on the basis of available household survey data, but such an analysis has yet to be carried out.

Before leaving this subject of the substitutability between nonhousehold and household saving, I should point out that net payments into the social security system, rather than a net increase in assets, are reflected in government saving. As stressed by Feldstein (1974), this system, which is essentially on a pay as you go basis, can be considered a governmentally imposed scheme of intergenerational transfers, which he maintains has had a major effect in reducing household saving. Barro (1978) and, more importantly from an empirical viewpoint, Leimer and Lesnoy (in press) have demonstrated the great overstatement in Feldstein's estimated effects, but I believe that a future claim on social security probably does have a moderate effect in reducing household saving.

To summarize my views on the effect of a redistribution of income among the household, corporate, and government sectors, I believe that a rise in the corporate saving-income ratio will probably be partly offset by a decline in the household saving-income ratio, reflecting lower direct saving by stockholders, but except perhaps in the long run as higher corporate saving is associated with higher household wealth, it is unlikely that the offset will be anywhere near complete. Corporations have a substantially higher propensity to save than individuals so that a shift in after tax income from households to corporations, which might be accomplished, for example, by lowering the relative burden of taxes on the corporate sector, would tend to raise the overall propensity to save. Similarly, government (at least in the United States and in other non–centrally planned economies) has a substantially smaller propensity to save than households, so that in view of the low level of substitutability between household and government saving, a shift of after tax income from government to the private sector should markedly raise the overall propensity to save.

The effect on saving of changes in interest rates or, more precisely, after tax rates of return on assets, for many years a subject of interest and controversy to economists, has in recent months been the focus of special attention by government officials concerned with the need to stimulate economic growth. The reason, of course, is that if it is assumed that the totals of government taxes and expenditures are held constant, the primary way that changes in policy may affect saving and investment is through their influence on the after tax rates of return and cost of capital, which also may affect the market value of net worth. However, while the direction of the effect on investment of an increase in the after tax rates of return or a reduction in the cost of capital to business that might be brought about through appropriate policy is unambiguous, this is not true of the effect on saving of a change in after tax rates of return on assets, abstracting from their effect on net worth.

While it has been realized for many years that the effect of a change in real interest rates on saving and consumption depends not only on a "substitution" effect (which is positive for saving and negative for consumption) but also on an offsetting "income" effect, it has only been in the past decade or so that the relative importance of these two effects has been rigorously related to measurable characteristics of households' utility functions. Since there is fairly strong evidence that the assumption of constant relative risk aversion is as a first approximation a fairly accurate description of the utility function of a representative household or of the market place, with a Pratt-Arrow measure of relative risk aversion well in excess of one (Friend and Blume 1975)[1], the implications of such a utility function for the total impact of a change in interest rates on saving (i.e., the combined "substitution" and "income" effects) are of particular interest.

1. The Pratt-Arrow measure of relative risk aversion is estimated in that paper to be in the neighborhood of two, using a model in which investment decisions are not affected by human wealth. Incorporating human wealth, the measure of risk aversion is estimated to be about six.

It has been shown under certain simplifying assumptions by Merton, Losq, Jones and others that with constant relative risk aversion, the relative size of the "substitution" versus "income" effects of changes in interest rates on saving will depend on the magnitude of the Pratt-Arrow measure of relative risk aversion.[2] If it is higher than one, the total or combined effect is negative; if less than one, the effect is positive; and if equal to one, there is no effect.

Since the empirical evidence points to an overall measure of relative risk aversion substantially more than one, theory might seem to indicate that saving is negatively related to changes in real after tax interest rates, with consumption therefore positively related—a result opposite to that implied by classical economics. However, when taxes are introduced into the analysis, the theoretically expected effect on household saving of changes in real after tax interest rates associated with changes in personal income taxes will depend not only on the magnitude of relative risk aversion but also, among other things, on the differential impact of taxation on income from different sources and on whether households consider as part of their wealth the capitalized value of future transfers from the government. Moreover, a change in personal taxes affects personal disposable income and therefore is likely to affect both personal consumption and saving in the same direction so that the relevant question from the viewpoint of the personal sector is how the change in taxes would affect the allocation of personal disposable income between saving and consumption. The nature of this allocation again depends on the magnitude of relative risk aversion and other factors. Thus, the results implied by theory depend on a number of assumptions, and these may or may not be warranted.[3] The underlying theory is referred to here mainly to emphasize that there is no theoretical presumption in favor of the classical result.[4]

Empirical studies of either household or private saving (i.e., household and corporate saving combined) have been inconclusive as to the direct effect of real after tax interest rates or rates of return on the propensity to save, when labor income and initial nonhuman

2. E.g., see Merton (1969), which assumes that all resources come from nonhuman capital or wealth, and Losq (1979), which allows for stochastic wages as well as stochastic returns from nonhuman wealth. See also Jones (1980) and Modest (1981).

3. A number of important considerations not included in these theoretical papers are discussed in Crockett and Friend (1979).

4. Theory does, however, provide a theoretical presumption that saving in specific forms is positively related to relative interest rates.

wealth are held constant. Some studies point to statistically significant negative effects, some to statistically positive effects, and still others to no discernible effect (see Weber 1970, 1975; Boskin 1980; Howrey and Hyams 1978; McClure 1980; Modest 1981).[5] In unpublished research that I have carried out, I experimented with a number of real after tax interest rate series—different periods, different saving specifications, and instrumental variable as well as simple least square solutions—and found that the estimated interest rate effect was at least as likely to be negative as positive. The result obtained depended particularly on the interest rate series used, with no legitimate basis for choosing among them.

Thus, neither theory nor the available data provide a satisfactory basis for determining the sign or magnitude of the direct effect on saving of an increase in after tax real interest rates, which might stem from a decrease in personal income taxes applicable to property income.[6] Yet it is my judgment, on the basis of all the evidence, that the effect is likely to be small. Similarly, in a theoretically rigorous uncertainty model, it is not possible to state with any confidence what effect such a decrease in taxes and the associated change in real interest rates and after tax real rates of return would have on the market value of assets that directly affect savings.[7] On the other

5. Gylfason (1981) finds a significant negative relation between quarterly consumption and nominal interest rates, holding expected inflation constant for the period 1952–78. However, when the years 1965–78, the period of most variation in interest and inflation rates, are analyzed separately, this relation disappears. Tests for serial correlation suggest that the results for this period are more reliable than those for 1952–65. Moreover, the adaptive expectations model used, where expected inflation is determined by inflation of the current and previous quarters, is highly questionable as a basis for inferring the relative long-run interest rate.

6. As noted earlier, the theoretical effect on personal saving of an increase in after tax real interest rates resulting from a decrease in personal income taxes may be somewhat different from the effect of an increase in real interest rates in the absence of taxation. One reason is that reduction in tax rates on property income increases the variance as well as the expected value of after tax return on risky assets held by investors. Another is that the two types of interest rates change may lead to different wealth effects on saving.

7. See Friend and Hasbrouck (1982). Under certain assumptions, notably symmetry of tax effects on property income, including capital gains and losses, theory would imply that a reduction in personal tax rates on property income might decrease the market value of assets and hence increase saving if the real before tax risk-free rate is higher than 0.019 with the reverse effect if the risk free rate is below 0.019 (using reasonable parameter values for the other variables involved). Estimates of the risk-free rate have ranged between 0.01 and 0.03. For a brief discussion of different views of how a decrease in the market value of wealth, distinct from any change in the total future income stream, would increase saving, see Blume, Friend, and Crockett (1978:36–37).

hand, while there is no strong reason for anticipating that higher real after tax interest rates would generate much additional savings, a reduction in personal income taxes might be associated with a positive effect on the cost of equity and therefore a negative effect on the propensity to invest and hence perhaps on realized saving and investment (Friend and Hasbrouck 1982).

The effect of changes in nonhuman wealth or net worth on saving is relatively straightforward. It has been shown both theoretically and empirically that increases in net worth should be expected to and do depress current saving, though the magnitude of the effect would depend on the reason for the change in net worth. A set of simulations by Tobin and Dolde (1971) suggest that under the relevant parameter measures they assume, changes in interest rates and net worth brought about by monetary policy can have fairly substantial effects on saving.

The empirical evidence on the negative relation between saving and net worth is fairly strong, since it consists not only of time series analysis such as that contained in the MPS model but also of household cross-section analysis carried out by Lieberman and myself (1975). However, in view of the current prospect for substantial reduction in personal income taxes, especially on property income, it should be reiterated that we do not know what effect such a decrease in taxes, and the associated change in real interest rates and after tax real rates of return, would have on the market value of assets and hence on saving.

Finally, most economists have seemed to believe that uncertainty of labor or nonlabor income acts as a stimulant to saving. From the viewpoint of pure theory, a number of theoretical analyses (starting with Merton 1969) have shown that added uncertainty in the return on nonhuman wealth would be expected to lower consumption and raise saving if the Pratt-Arrow measure of relative risk aversion is greater than one, which as noted earlier seems to be the case. However, as shown by Losq (1979), uncertainty in labor income as well as in return on nonhuman wealth greatly complicates the theoretical analysis, and the effect of uncertainty in labor and nonlabor income on saving is more difficult to predict. A time series analysis by Modest (1981) finds a negative correlation between saving and price level or real wealth uncertainty, which as he points out is contrary to the prediction of his theoretical model. On the other hand, the higher marginal propensities to save out of transitory than out of permanent income found in most empirical studies could be interpreted as statistical evidence supporting the expectations of a positive correlation between saving and uncertainty of income. Given the predictive deficiencies of existing theory and the relatively weak statistical evidence available, no conclusive judgements on the effect of uncertainty of both labor and nonlabor income on saving seem possible, though I think it is more likely ordinarily to increase than to decrease saving. However, the effect is likely to depend on the nature of the uncertainty, and the nonfinancial components of saving would be expected to be affected differently from the financial components.

To ascertain how inflation affects the propensity to save, I shall first examine how inflation affects the major determinants of saving and then summarize the findings of the empirical studies that have considered the statistical relationships between saving and inflation. Some evidence has been provided by Fama (in press) and by Friend and Hasbrouck (1981) that the real national income and inflation are negatively correlated[8] and by Friend and Hasbrouck (1981) that the real value of household net worth and inflation are similarly negatively related. The income effect would lower real saving, particularly in the public sector, and probably also the aggregate saving-income ratio, while the wealth effect would raise both saving and the saving-income ratio.

It is not clear how the distribution of income among different economic groups has been affected by inflation in the United States. It could be argued that inflation has made it easier for the government to increase effective tax rates and therefore to hold down the government deficit, but the record on the expenditure side raises questions about any such conclusion. A more plausible argument might be that inflation facilitated the transfer of resources from the private sector, which has a higher propensity to save than the government sector, and thus served to depress the overall saving-income ratio. There is no evidence of substantial redistribution of income between households and businesses or between lower and higher income groups as a result of inflation, so that any such redistribution is not likely to have had an important effect on total private real saving.

In view of the absence of any strong theoretical or empirical

---

8. Fama questions whether this represents a causal relationship.

reason to believe that changes in real after tax rates of return significantly affect the propensity to save, it might be considered superfluous to examine the evidence on the relationship between inflation and real after tax rates of return. However, for the sake of completeness, I shall note that evidence to be summarized in the discussion of the effect of inflation on capital markets suggests either no change or some decrease in the expected real before personal tax rate of return on nominally risk-free assets and either no change or some increase in the expected real before tax rate of return on other assets. On an after tax basis, the expected rate on the risk-free asset was probably negatively related to the rate of inflation while the sign of the corresponding effect on risky assets was indeterminate.

The reason for the apparent rise induced by inflation in the risk differential required to hold risky as against nominally risk-free assets seems to reflect the increased uncertainty of returns associated with inflation. Higher expected inflation is also probably associated with greater uncertainty of real labor income. However, as noted earlier, there is no very strong basis for assuming that such increased uncertainty will have any substantial effect on saving.

Special features of the U.S. tax laws have also been cited as contributing to the impact of inflation on saving. Any such tax effects would presumably operate through the determinants of saving discussed earlier, but in any case, it is my judgment that inflation-induced tax effects on saving propensities have been exaggerated.

In addition to the effect of inflation on the inflation-free determinants of saving, economists have historically regarded the incentive to beat price rises, resulting in an intertemporal substitution of current for future consumption, as a major depressant influence of inflation on saving. However, if net investment in consumer durables is considered as saving, it is not clear how the total combined saving in tangible and financial forms would be affected.

On the whole, the sum total of these theoretically expected effects of inflation on the household propensity to save seems quite small. Empirical studies by Juster and Wachtel (1972a, 1972b) and by Howard (1978), based on time series analysis for the United States and four other countries, present mixed evidence on the effect of expected and unexpected inflation on real personal saving, holding constant the real value of permanent and transitory income, unemployment, and the real value of liquid assets. However, for unexpected inflation they provide more evidence of a stimulating than of a depressant effect, while for expected inflation the evidence is more supportive of a depressant effect. The ratio of personal saving to personal disposable income in the 1970s was modestly higher than in the 1960s, when inflation was substantially lower. On the other hand, the evidence is not strong, and the weak performance of personal saving in the past few years during a period of especially intense inflationary pressures suggests that a prolonged high inflation, associated presumably with substantially higher expected inflation, does not raise the saving rate and might act perversely.

For the corporate sector as well, there is no strong evidence of a substantial effect of inflation on the saving-income ratio. The ratio of dividends to book earnings after taxes did decline appreciably from the 1960s to the 1970s, but the corresponding ratio for economic earnings did not show any significant change.

INVESTMENT

In this section of the Chapter, I shall discuss the impact of inflation on the demand for real investment goods, focusing on plant and equipment. The main theoretical determinants of investment in the absence of inflation are the anticipated rate of return on new investment and the cost of capital. The optimal level of investment would be expected to be positively related to changes in the level of real output and the price of output and negatively related to the user cost of capital. The user cost of capital is of course the product of the price of capital goods and the difference between the tax-adjusted gross cost of capital (i.e., including depreciation) and any capital gains arising from changes in the prices of capital goods.

The main channels by which inflation might be expected to affect real investment are mainly through changes in real output, changes in the ratio of capital goods to other prices, changes in the cost of capital, and capital gains from changes in capital goods prices. I pointed out in the preceding section that there is some evidence that the real national income is somewhat depressed by inflation, which, if true, would lower the rate of investment and probably also the investment-income or product ratio. The ratio of plant and equipment costs to other prices as measured by the published indexes has increased modestly in the period of aggravated inflation starting in 1973–1974, which would tend to lower investment in plant and equipment somewhat. The corresponding ratio of housing construction costs to other prices has also increased. However, the substantial rate of capital gains on the housing stock, which has had an important stimulating effect on the demand for new housing, is probably much more important for housing investment.

For investment, unlike saving, it would be expected that changes in the cost of capital would significantly affect demand with an unambiguously negative relation between investment and the real cost of capital. Virtually all the empirical evidence is consistent with this theoretical expectation for plant and equipment expenditures. Thus, econometric models generally show a negative relationship between plant and equipment expenditures and the cost of capital. Similarly, a 1980 survey of nonfinancial corporations listed on the New York Stock Exchange indicated that the respondents considered the high cost and unavailability of external financing as one of the major impediments to business fixed capital formation (Blume, Friend, and Westerfield 1981).

Further light on the effect of inflation on both the real cost of capital and the expected profitability or real after tax cash flow is shed by a 1981 paper by Hasbrouck and myself (Friend and Hasbrouck 1981). That study concludes that inflation has depressed not only stock prices and realized real market rates of returns on stock prices, a finding common to many studies, but also real dividends and earnings per share. However, while the decline in real dividends and in real book earnings per share associated with a one percentage point increase in sustained inflation appears to be of the same general order of magnitude, roughly about 5 percent, the decline seems to be somewhat more than double for real, economic earnings per share. The study also provides strong evidence, although it is not conclusive, that inflation increases the uncertainty of real return on stock investment. This increased uncertainty would be expected to be associated with a significant increase in the risk premium—that is, the difference between the required real return on stock and on a nominally risk-free asset. Somewhat different findings in other relevant studies will be summarized in the concluding section of this chapter, dealing specifically with the effect of inflation on capital markets.

Assuming now that the Friend-Hasbrouck results are correct,

inflation has been associated with a decline in expected profitability of investment and probably with an increase in the expected risk premium. To translate the increase in risk premium to its effect on the real cost of capital to corporations would require information on the effect of inflation on the required rate of return on bonds and stocks and on the relative importance of equity in the capital structure. Empirical studies by Fama (1975), Gibson (1970, 1972), and Levy and Makin (1979) suggest that the expected real before tax rate of return on nominally risk-free assets is either unaffected by inflation, which seems to me most likely, or somewhat depressed. Thus, the real cost of equity has probably either been increased or been relatively unaffected by inflation. Since it might be assumed that the expected real return on bonds would be intermediate between stocks and risk-free assets, and some evidence to that effect has been provided by Jaffe and Mandelker (1975), the real required rate of return on bonds has probably not been appreciably affected by inflation.

With fixed weights in the capital structure, the preceding evidence might lead us to expect either a moderate increase or very little change in the real overall cost of capital resulting from accelerated inflation. However, with an apparent increase in the short-term and long-term debt components of the capital structure, reflecting the effect of inflation both on their before tax cost relative to equity and on the value of their tax deductability, there has probably been little overall change in the weighted real overall cost of capital. This is true in spite of the increased risk to corporations associated with a high and uncertain rate of inflation. As a result of some apparent decline in the real profitability of business investment associated with increased inflation and little change in the real cost of capital, higher inflation would be expected to result in lower investment, other things being equal.

Unfortunately, there does not appear to be any satisfactory statistical evidence on the effect of inflation on investment as a whole or on plant and equipment expenditures. Econometric models have generally not found it useful to incorporate inflation as an additional explanatory variable in their investment functions. On the other hand, the recent survey of nonfinancial corporations conducted by the Rodney White Center (Blume, Friend and Westerfield 1981) indicated that respondents considered inflation as one of the key factors depressing real plant and equipment expenditures. It is interesting to note that of the respondents stating that inflation had an appreciable depressant effect on real investment, about the same number attributed this effect to the impact of inflation on uncertainty of sales, prices, wages, and profits as to its impact on the cost of financing.

My own assessment is consistent with the belief by the business community that investment has been depressed by inflation. I believe this effect is due to the uncertainties associated with inflation and probably also to an increase in the real cost of equity financing, which businessmen were increasingly reluctant to replace with debt. Another possible depressant effect of inflation on investment via the cost of financing is that a number of businessmen may not have appropriately distinguished between the nominal and real cost of financing. This is a point similar to that stressed by Modigliani and Cohn (1979) in attempting to explain the impact of inflation on stock prices and is discussed at greater length in the concluding section of this chapter.

While I am not aware of any satisfactory econometric analysis that has explored the impact of inflation on investment, I should point out that the ratio of business gross fixed investment to gross national product (in either current or constant dollars) did not show any clear trend in the United States over the period of pronounced inflationary pressures beginning with 1973–74. An initial decline in this ratio from 1974 to 1976 was largely offset by a subsequent rise from 1976 to 1979. However, the corresponding ratio for business net fixed investment did exhibit a moderate decline over this period as a whole. The decline is more marked if we exclude government-mandated expenditures, not all of which would have been replaced by nonmandated expenditures in the absence of the relevant EPA and OSHA regulations.

When real plant and equipment expenditures are combined with other real investment, the ratio of investment to real gross national product shows no trend over the 1970s. The apparent absence of an inflation-induced effect on total investment probably reflects a stimulating effect of inflation on investment in housing (except for brief periods of credit stringency) offsetting a depressant effect on plant and equipment expenditures. The moderate increase in the private saving ratio over the 1970s as a whole presumably served to finance an increase in government dissaving rather than an increase in private investment.

CAPITAL MARKETS

Probably the most striking effect of high inflation on capital markets has been the much discussed—and to most economists, surprising—negative correlation between the rate of inflation and stock prices. This negative correlation was found not only in the United States but in most other countries as well (Gultekin 1980). The apparent depressant effect on stock prices, as against the theoretically expected stimulating effect, was found to be associated not only with unexpected inflation, including changes in the rate of expected inflation, but also by some authors with expected inflation.

An analysis by Friend and Hasbrouck (1981) attributes the apparently adverse impact of inflation on stock prices to a depressant effect on dividends, book earnings, and especially economic earnings and perhaps also to a stimulating effect on the real required market rates of return on equity. The effect of inflation on the real required rate of return on equity in turn seems to be attributable to an increase in the uncertainty of real return on stock investment associated with inflation. In the Friend-Hasbrouck study, such uncertainty is measured by deviations in real realized stock returns or in real earnings per share from their expected values both for the market as a whole and for individual stocks.

However, two quite different explanations of the negative correlation between stock prices and inflation have been advanced by Fama (in press) and by Modigliani and Cohn (1979). The Fama explanation is that the correlation is for the most part spurious, with inflation acting as a proxy for economic activity. However, he does not adequately explain the negative correlation between stock prices and unexpected inflation, and it is only when he introduces the monetary base as well as real gross national product that the negative correlation between stock prices and expected inflation becomes statistically insignificant. He considers that the monetary base is acting as a proxy for prospective economic activity, which he cannot measure directly but which the stock market does anticipate. It is not clear to me that the monetary base may not act as a better proxy for expected inflation than for prospective real activity and may not be a better proxy for expected long-run inflation than the treasury bill rate he uses for that purpose. In any case, as Fama acknowledges, his analysis does not provide "an economic explanation for at least part of the documented decline in expected real stock returns during the post 1953 period."

In contrast to the explanation of the negative inflation–stock price correlation suggested by Fama and by Friend and Hasbrouck, Modigliani and Cohn conclude that this relation is due to irrational behavior by investors. Their estimates of real economic earnings per share do not appear to be affected by inflation, unlike the downward trend in such earnings found by Hasbrouck and myself to be associated with the rise in the rate of inflation. With their finding of no signficant relationship between inflation and real economic earnings, they conclude that the downturn in stock prices during the recent inflationary period is attributable either to an understatement of real economic earnings or to the mistaken use of the nominal required rate of return to discount real earnings. The understatement of real economic earnings in their view reflected investors' lack of understanding of the favorable implications of inflation on the real burden of long-term debt.

Since Hasbrouck and I find a significant decrease in real economic earnings, we do not need to interject irrationality to explain a downturn in stock prices, even without an increase in the real required rate of return or investor confusion between real and nominal rates. While like most economists, I prefer to attempt to explain observed economic phenomena without recourse to assumptions of irrationality, I should point out that I would not find it implausible if investors took a very prolonged period of time to appropriately assess and respond to the effect of inflation on real economic earnings and the relevant discount factor. To the large number of colleagues who find such economically "irrational" behavior extremely implausible, I suggest that they attempt to explain the incredibly slow pace of the transition from FIFO to LIFO inventory valuation on the basis of the usual stockholder optimization model. However, although I do not consider the Modigliani-Cohn thesis as beyond the pale, there does not appear to be a need to introduce major irrationality to explain the depressed stock market in recent years.

The increase in risk that appeared to be associated with inflation in the post–World War II period is a tenable basis for explaining an increase in the real required risk differential between common stock and nominally riskless assets and probably for explaining an increase in the real required rate of return on stock, which would in turn be associated with a depressant effect on stock prices. Nevertheless, a similar explanation cannot be used to explain the negative relation between real economic earnings and inflation, found by Hasbrouck and myself to have a substantial depressant effect on stock prices. Part of this earnings impact seems to be caused by a negative effect of inflation on real economic activity. The negative effect of inflation on real economic activity may reflect the adverse effect of increased uncertainty on business planning and productivity, on the level of resource utilization, and on the effectiveness of fiscal and monetary policy, but over the past decade it may also reflect the consequences of the high tax imposed on the U.S. economy by foreign oil producers.

However, the substantial residual negative effect of inflation on real economic earnings has yet to be explained satisfactorily. I believe that part of this effect is attributable to an inflation-induced increase in the effective corporate tax rates as a result of the difference between the book and replacement cost of fixed capital and inventories used up in the production process. On the other hand, I do not believe that this tax effect is as strong as that hypothesized by Feldstein (1973). Fama (in press) and Modigliani and Cohn (1979) both consider it insignificant on the basis of the observed trends in the effective tax rate paid by corporations on their economic income (including interest). Some calculations that Hasbrouck has carried out suggest that only part of the depressant effect of inflation on economic earnings was attributable to the manner in which inflation affects corporate taxes.[9]

A significant part of the depressant effect of inflation on economic earnings, therefore, remains to be explained. There is some evidence that the share of compensation of employees in total cost and profit of nonfinancial corporate business increased slightly in the inflationary period of the 1970s (*Economic Report* 1981:247), but again this does not seem to account for a major share of the inflation effect. I suspect that another part of the explanation over the past decade is attributable to a higher rise in the costs of goods that are purchased

---

9. These calculations also suggest that with a sustained rate of inflation in excess of 20 percent—that is, above the rate we have been experiencing in recent years—economic earnings would have been raised rather than lowered for U.S. corporations as a whole (assuming other things remained equal), since the stimulating effect of inflation in reducing the real burden of the debt would exceed its depressant effect associated with the use of historical cost depreciation and FIFO inventory valuation.

abroad, such as petroleum and other raw material costs, than in those purchased domestically—which, if true, would imply that part of the inflation effect is attributable to the source of inflationary pressure during this period. Of course, much of these effects that operate through the cost of goods might, like tax effects, ultimately be expected to be reflected in selling price.

One other possible explanation that might be adduced to rationalize the observed decline in real economic corporate earnings associated with increased inflation does not appear to be consistent with the empirical evidence. Thus, the effect of real interest payments in reducing real economic earnings of equity was not increased by inflation and may very well have been reduced.

Before leaving this subject of inflation-induced tax effects on stock prices, corporate earnings, and the rate of return required by investors, I should point out that much of this literature seems to me both to greatly exaggerate such effects attributable to personal taxes (i.e., income and capital gains taxes) and to unduly minimize the margin of error involved in the estimates made. As noted in a paper by Hasbrouck and myself (Friend and Hasbrouck 1981), the estimated inflation-induced increase between 1950 and 1978 in the effective rate of personal tax is only about 3 percent. More important, in view of the effect of this increase on the variance as well as expected value of after tax income, this rise in tax rates might induce a modest decrease rather than an increase in the required return on stocks (holding constant the real before tax riskless rate of return). The large inflation-induced effect on stock prices attributed to capital gains taxes may similarly be questioned. Thus, Hasbrouck and I (Friend and Hasbrouck 1982) have recently shown that the use of more reasonable parameter values in conjunction with a model developed by Feldstein (1980) to incorporate tax effects could be interpreted as implying that an 8 percent rise in inflation is associated with a 12 percent increase in stock prices instead of the 14 percent decline that his parameters would imply. I would treat both estimates with a high degree of skepticism.

Because of time limitations, I shall touch only briefly on the effect of inflation on financial assets other than common stock. In view of the poor performance of common stock, it is not surprising to find that no other long-term financial asset was a reasonably satisfactory hedge against inflation. The best financial asset hedge against inflation was short-term, fixed-interest-bearing instruments, notably treasury bills, though even here the hedge for a taxable investor was far from adequate. The longer the term to maturity of a debt instrument, the worse was the inflation experience. Fluctuations in the long-term bond markets were so severe, apparently as a result of changes in inflationary expectations, that at times those markets appeared completely disorganized, with daily movements in yields the largest over the past half century and occasionally a virtual disappearance of bids and offers for a high proportion of the bond issues traded.

It is rather puzzling that in a relatvely prolonged period of high and accelerating inflation such as the United States has been experiencing for many years that there has not been more aggressive development and growth of new financial instruments as a more adequate hedge against inflation. Thus, since homes have been the best inflation hedge among the more commonly held household assets, one might have expected to find the widespread use of financial instruments based on equities in a diversified portfolio of houses or on securities based on a diversified portfolio of variable rate mortgages.

Similarly, a more widespread use of at least partly indexed long-term bonds by corporations and government units might have been anticipated. It is interesting to note that the very small number of bond issues that did incorporate some indexing features had an extremely favorable market reception. A small part of the explanation for the relatively slow development of long-term inflation hedges may be that short-term debt instruments and the accelerated growth of financial futures have served to reduce some of the financial risks associated with inflation. However, I suspect that a more important part of the explanation is that it takes a substantial period of time for potential issuers to assess appropriately the opportunities as well as the risks associated with financial innovations in a radically changed economic environment.

In closing, in view of the difference in the implications of past empirical studies mentioned earlier in this chapter for the effect of inflation on the expected real before tax rate of return on common stock, I should mention a study by Gultekin (1980b) that has just come to my attention. On the basis of forecasts of prices of goods and services and of stock market prices six and twelve months into the future based on the Livingston data, the study relates ex ante measures of expected nominal stock returns to ex ante measures of expected inflation for the period 1946 through 1979. It concludes that a one percentage point increase in the inflation rate was associated with about a one percentage point increase in the rate of return on common stock, though the results presented suggest that expected nominal returns may rise more than expected inflation. The study also concludes that unanticipated inflation as estimated from these ex ante data were significantly negatively correlated with ex post nominal stock returns and that its findings do not support the views of Modigliani and Cohn (1979) that in inflationary periods investors capitalize equity earnings at a rate that parallels the nominal interest rate, rather than the economically correct real rate. Finally, the study concludes that since the 1950s, expected real rates and expected inflation are positively related (Gultekin 1980b). Not surprisingly, I conclude that the study provides support for the Friend-Hasbrouck over either the Modigliani-Cohn or the Fama position.

REFERENCES

Barro, Robert. 1978. *The Impact of Social Security on Private Saving.* Washington, D.C.: American Enterprise Institute.

Blume, Marshall E.; Irwin Friend; and Jean Crockett. 1978. *Financial Effects of Capital Tax Reforms.* Monograph Series in Finance and Economics 4. New York: New York University.

Blume, Marshall; Irwin Friend; and Randolph Westerfield, 1981. *Impediments to Capital Formation.* Rodney L. White Center for Financial Research, Wharton School, University of Pennsylvania.

Boskin, Michael. 1980. "Taxation, Saving and the Rate of Interest." *Journal of Political Economy* 2 (April).

Crockett, Jean, and Irwin Friend. 1979. "Consumption and Saving in Economic Development." In *Research and Finance,* Vol. I, edited by Haim Levy. Greenwich, Conn.: JAI Press.

David, Paul, and David Scadding. 1974. "Private Savings, Ultra-rationality, Aggregation and Denison's Law." *Journal of Political Economy* 82, no. 2 (March-April): 225–249.

Economic Report of the President. 1981. Washington, D.C.: U.S. Government Printing Office, January.

Fama, Eugene. 1975. "Short-Term Interest Rates as Predictors of Inflation." *American Economic Review.* LXV, no. 3 (June): 269–282.

_____. In Press. "Stock Returns, Real Activity, Inflation and Money." *American Economic Review.*

Feldstein, Martin S. 1973. "Tax Incentives, Corporate Saving and Capital Accumulation in the United States." *Journal of Public Economics* 2: 147–171.

_____. 1974. "Social Security, Induced Retirement, and Aggregate Capital Accumulation." *Journal of Political Economy* 82, no. 5 (September-December): 905–926.

_____. 1980. "Inflation and the Stock Market." *American Economic Review* 70, no. 5 (December): 839–847.

Feldstein, Martin, and George Fare. 1973. "Taxes, Corporate Dividend Policy and Personal Saving: The British Postwar Experience." *Review of Economics and Statistics* LV, no. 4 (November): 399–411.

Friend, Irwin, and Marshall E. Blume. 1975. "The Demand for Risky Assets." *American Economic Review* LXV, no. 5 (December): 900–922.

Friend, Irwin, and Joel Hasbrouck. 1981. "Effect of Inflation on the Profitability and Valuation of U.S. Corporations." Working Paper No. 3–81. Rodney L. White Center for Financial Research, Wharton School, University of Pennsylvania.

_____. 1982. "Comment on Inflation and the Stock Market." *American Economic Review* (March): in press.

Friend, Irwin, and Charles Lieberman. 1975. "Short-Run Asset Effects on Household Saving and Consumption: The Cross-Section Evidence." *American Economic Review* LXV, no. 4 (September): 624–633.

Gibson, William. 1970. "Price Expectations Effect on Interest Rates." *Journal of Finance* XXV, no. 1 (March): 19–34.

_____. 1972. "Interest Rates and Inflationary Expectations: New Evidence." *American Economic Review* LX11, no. 5 (December): 854–865.

Gultekin, N. Bulent. 1980a. "Stock Market Returns and Inflation: Evidence from Other Countries." Working Paper No. 48. Center for Research in Security Prices, University of Chicago, September.

_____. 1980b. "Stock Market Returns and Inflation Forecasts: Tests of Fisher Hypothesis with Expectations Data," Working paper No. 50, February 1980, Center for Research in Security Prices, Working Papers/Reprint Series, University of Chicago.

Gylfason, Thoraldur. 1981. "Interest Rates, Inflation and the Aggregate Consumption Function." *Review of Economics and Statistics* LX11 (May): 233–245.

Howard, David. 1978. "Personal Saving Behavior and the Rate of Inflation." *Review of Economics and Statistics* LX (November): 547–554.

Howrey, Philip, and Saul H. Hymans. 1978. "The Measurement & Determination of Loanable Funds Saving." *Brookings Papers on Economic Activity* 3.

Jaffe, Jeffrey, and Gershon Mandelker. 1975. "Inflation and the Holding Period Returns on Bonds." Working Paper No. 8. Rodney L. White Center for Financial Research, Wharton School, University of Pennsylvania.

Jones, Emerson Philip, Jr. 1980. "Intertemporal Financial and Monetary Equilibrium." Ph.D. dissertation, Massachusetts Institute of Technology.

Juster, Thomas, and Paul Wachtel. 1972a. "Inflation and the Consumer." *Brookings Papers on Economic Activity* 1: 71–122.

———. 1972b. "A Note on Inflation and the Saving Rate." *Brookings Papers on Economic Activity* 3.

Leimer, Dean, and Selog Lesnoy. In press. "Social Security and Private Saving." *American Economic Review.*

Losq, Etienne. 1979. "A Note on Consumption, Human Wealth and Uncertainty: Essays on the Theory of Finance." Ph.D. dissertation, University of Pennsylvania.

McClure, Charles E. 1980. "Taxes, Saving and Welfare: Theory and Evidence." Working Paper No. 504. National Bureau of Economic Research, July.

Merton, Robert C. 1969. "Lifetime Portfolio Substitution and Uncertainty." *Review of Economics and Statistics* 51, no. 3 (August): 247–257.

Modest, David M. 1981. "Uncertainty and Optimal Consumption: Theory and Evidence." Massachusetts Institute of Technology, January. Mimeograph.

Modigliani, Franco, and Richard Cohn. 1979. "Inflation, Rational Valuation and the Market. *Financial Analysts Journal* 35 (March-April): 24–44.

Tanner, J. Ernest. 1979. "Fiscal Policy and Consumer Behavior." *Review of Economics and Statistics* 61 (May): 317–321.

Tobin, James, and Walter Dolde. 1971. "Wealth, Liquidity and Consumption." In *Consumer Spending and Monetary Policy: The Linkages.* Boston: Federal Reserve Bank, June.

Weber, Warren E. 1970. "The Effect of Interest Rates on Aggregate Consumption." *American Economic Review* LX, no. 4 (September): 591–600.

———. 1975. "Interest Rates, Inflation and Consumer Expenditures." *American Economic Review* LXV, no. 5 (December): 843–858.

PART
I

1 THE EFFECTS OF TAX PARAMETERS IN THE INVESTMENT EQUATIONS IN MACROECONOMIC ECONOMETRIC MODELS

Robert S. Chirinko
and
Robert Eisner
Northwestern University

INTRODUCTION

Irwin Friend played early and ably in the game of ascertaining business investment plans and what affected them. Increasingly in recent years, and dramatically in the current political debate, large-scale econometric models have been used to predict effects on investment of changes in tax parameters such as depreciation charges, investment tax credits, and business income tax rates. While ultimate results depend upon full model specifications, involving the influence of tax changes on aggregate demand, prices, and interest rates, critical points of departure are the investment equations themselves. We offer here a study of the specifications, estimated parameters, and substantive implications of the existing investment equations and possible alternatives in six models of the U.S. economy—BEA, Chase, DRI, Michigan, MPS, and Wharton.[1]

An earlier version of this chapter was presented to the Fourth World Congress of the Econometric Society in Aix-en-Provence, France, August 28, 1980. It has been made possible by the collaboration and assistance of responsible officers and staff associated with the models under consideration—BEA, Chase, DRI, Michigan, MPS, and Wharton—and personnel of the Office of Tax Analysis of the Treasury, and is being circulated in penultimate form as OTA Paper 47. The authors are particularly grateful to Robert W. Kilpatrick and Allen Sinai for their careful reading of the manuscript but are of course alone responsible for its contents.
    1. An analysis of full model simulations is to be found in Chirinko and Eisner (1981).

A GENERAL VIEW OF INVESTMENT FUNCTIONS

Investment equations in the model under consideration bear a substantial family resemblance. With varying degrees of aggregation and parametric specifications, they generally view investment as a distributed lag response or adjustment of capital to desired or equilibrium levels. These in turn relate to expected demand or output, taken explicitly or implicitly as a function of capital and labor inputs, and the relative prices of output and capital or of capital and labor.

The "rental" price or user cost of capital is in principle the rate of economic depreciation, the opportunity cost in terms of foregone net earnings, and the capital loss (or minus the captal gain) associated with changing prices. These costs are defined as pure decimals, which are then applied to the price of capital goods. A general formulation, which the various model equations only more or less approximate, (cf. Jorgenson 1963; and Hall and Jorgenson 1967) would be:

$$c = \frac{q[(1 - uv)\rho - (1 - u\omega)\dfrac{\dot{q}}{q} + \delta][1 - k - uz]}{1 - u} \qquad (1.1)$$

where

c = the rental price of capital;

q = the supply price of capital goods;

u = the rate of business income taxation;

v = the proportion of the opportunity cost of capital (such as interest, dividends, and foregone earnings) that is tax deductible;

ρ = the opportunity cost of capital, presumably an appropriately weighted average of nominal interest rates and rates of return on equity expected by firms;

ω = the proportion of capital gains and losses effectively taxed;

$\dfrac{\dot{q}}{q}$ = the expected rate of change of prices of capital goods;

δ = the rate of economic depreciation;

k = the effective rate of the investment tax credit; and

z = the original present value of the tax depreciation expected from a dollar of investment.

The investment equations in most of the models include a term such as c but with a number of potentially signficant variations, which we shall note. For one thing, allowance is made in different ways, if at all, for v, the proportion of the opportunity cost of capital that is tax deductible. Second, not all of the models allow for expected capital gains or price inflation, and none recognizes the peculiar tax treatment of capital gains. Third, the rate of economic depreciation is in some instances variable but more usually held constant, at values that differ somewhat from model to model. Fourth, the investment tax credit in equipment equations is variously taken at its nominal rate and the lesser effective rate, which reflects, of course, limitations on its availibility in all or in part. Fifth, the determination of z, the original present value of the tax depreciation from a dollar of investment, is variously defined. It should depend upon the rate of discount, the length of life of capital for tax purposes, and the method of depreciation (straight line, declining balance at 200 percent or 150 percent of straight line rates, and sum of years digits, as well as special provisions for first year allowances). In practice, length of life is sometimes taken to vary by discrete jumps suggested by shifts to guidelines and later to ADR (Asset Depreciation Range) without attention to actual changes in lives over the years. Shifts in methods of depreciation are not always accounted for. Rates of discount, as well as the extent of their variation, differ among models. In one case (Michigan), z does not enter explicitly at all; rather, a tax depreciation rate is used.

In the great bulk of the investment equations, there is no separate estimate of the roles of the rate of business taxation, the investment tax credit, or tax depreciation (however measured). Rather, parameters are estimated for a variable like c, the rental price of capital, or more generally, for a variable in which c is a component.[2]

---

2. The equations are thus vulnerable to criticisms by Eisner (1969a, b, c,), Lucas (1976), and Sargent (1981), among others that they may not prove robust against changes in policy regimes. How the rental price of capital enters investment functions must surely depend on its relation to expected future rental prices. That relation—or "laws of motion" in Sargent's terms—may clearly be different for changes in nontax components such as interest rates and in tax components such as tax depreciation and investment credits or, in general, for changes in variables due to policy and nonpolicy factors. Thus, parameters of investment functions estimated from historical observations subject to particular, perhaps nonpolicy, sources of variance may not describe correctly relations to specified policy-induced changes.

Considerations of cost minimization and profit maximization with output exogenous suggest that desired capital stock will be a function of relative prices and ouput. (This formulation would not apply to a firm operating under perfect competition with no perceived limit to effective demand for product, for then relative prices would be exogenous but output would be endogenous.) We may thus write

$$K^* = f(P, c, Y) \qquad (1.2)$$

where

P = the price of output,
c = the rental price or user cost of capital, and
Y = output.

Alternatively, we may substitute w, a measure of the cost of labor, for P. The assumption of a Cobb-Douglas production function, among other things, was offered by Jorgenson as the justification for a particular description of the desired stock of capital as

$$K^* = \beta \left(\frac{P}{c} \right) Y \qquad (1.3)$$

The assumption of the more general constant elasticity of substitution (CES) production function, with the constraints neither of unitary elasticity of substitution nor of constant returns to scale, would then fit the more general description of the desired stock of capital:

$$K^* = \beta \left(\frac{P}{c} \right)^\sigma Y^r \qquad (1.4)$$

where σ is the elasticity of demand for capital with respect to the relative price of output and capital and r is the elasticity of demand for capital with respect to output. (This last elasticity will be more than, equal to, or less than unity as the returns to scale are decreasing, constant, or, increasing.)

The desired capital stock does not of course in itself tell us anything about investment, which is the rate of replacement of existing capital stock plus the rate of net additions. The rate of replacement may well be a variable depending upon financial considerations and a general set of expectations. The rate of net additions to capital will in principle depend upon costs of adjustment, which will in turn relate to costs of acquiring information necessary to decisions, costs of planning, and again, financial considerations.

All this leads us to a formulation of investment as a distributed lag function of past changes in desired capital stock plus replacement of some of the existing capital. Here, however, we should note that the speed of adjustment of capital to changes in its desired or equilibrium value may not be independent of the causes and the magnitudes of the changes. If, for example, an increase in the demand for output generates an increase in the demand for capital, investment may be expected to be undertaken with all due speed as expectations become sufficiently firm with regard to the performance of the increased demand. If the increased demand for capital is due, however, to a fall in its relative price (due to, let us say, a reduction in the rate of interest), thus generating a demand for more durable and hence more substantial and expensive capital, the rate of investment will be slowed by the availability of existing capacity sufficient for current production. These considerations underlie the "putty-clay" model. A demand for additional housing services will bring on investment in housing as rapidly as cost considerations permit. A lower rate of interest, causing substantial investment in more durable brick houses to replace less durable houses of wood or straw, would cause the rate of investment to increase only as existing houses of wood and straw wear out and are replaced.

This suggests that investment equations should in principle involve separate distributed lag responses to changes in relative prices and to changes in output and should also admit the possibility that the lags are not fixed and may further vary with other economic parameters. We note that our more general expression for the desired stock of capital, equation (1.4), may be written in a logarithmic transformation

$$ln\,K^* = ln\beta + \sigma\,ln\,\frac{P}{c} + r\,ln\,Y \qquad (1.5)$$

The ratio of net investment to existing capital stock is then approximately equal to the change in the logarithm of capital, which may in turn be written as distributed lag functions of changes in the determinants of desired capital, as in

$$\frac{I_N}{K_{-1}} \cong \Delta \ln k = \sigma \left[\gamma_1 (L) \Delta \ln \frac{P}{c} \right] + r[\gamma(L) \Delta \ln Y] \qquad (1.6)$$

where $\gamma_1(L)$ and $\gamma_2(L)$ are lag operators that indeed should be functions of such variables as the rate of interest and the cost of capital.

Finally, since investment equals net investment plus replacement, we may write

$$I = I_N + R = I_N + \delta K_{-1} \qquad (1.7)$$

where δ may vary over time.

The investment equations in the models under consideration most often ignore the possibility that the lag distributions may vary over time and change, in particular as a consequence of changes in other variables. They also ignore in varying degrees the putty-clay hypothesis, either assuming a putty-putty model whereby changes in relative prices can result in a speedy replacement of all of the existing capital stock or assuming that the speed of response of investment to changes in relative prices and output is the same.

TAX PARAMETERS AND PLAN OF ANALYSIS

To the extent that there is no differentiation of lag responses and to the extent that tax parameters do not enter independently, we can anticipate, in general, certain results in investment equations. First, the response to changes in the rate of business taxation, u, or the rate of the investment tax credit, k, or changes in the parameters determining z, the value of tax depreciation, will depend upon the estimated parameters of c, the entire rental price or user cost of capital, of P/c or w/c, the relative prices of output or labor and capital, or of the product of P/c and Y. Further, the response to tax parameters will depend in a number of the models on assumed values of σ, the elasticity of substitution or of the demand for capital with respect to the relative prices of output and capital.

Indeed, what the investment equations of the various models have to say about the effects of tax incentives for investment and what the models have in fact reported for these effects stem very largely from the way the rental price of capital enters the investment equations.

To the extent that a high value of σ is assumed or estimated, changes in tax parameters will appear to have large effects. To the extent that estimated lag functions appear shorter or faster because the estimated speed of response to changes in c, or P/c, or P/c and Y combined are faster, the effects of changes in tax parameters will appear to be more speedy. Conversely, of course, if the speed of reaction to the lagged variables is estimated as less, the implied or reported speed of reaction to changes in tax parameters will be less.

With all of these caveats, and before we proceed to reporting upon our analysis and estimations of specific models, we may note finally what may be expected from changes in the tax parameters designated in equation (1.1). First, if estimated parameters indicate that the partial derivative of investment with respect to c, the rental price of capital, has its expected negative sign, an increase in the investment tax credit will have to increase investment, since the derivative of c with respect to k, the effective rate of the investment tax credit, is obviously negative. How much investment will be increased will depend upon the specification or estimate of σ. How fast it will increase will depend upon the distributed lag function relating to c.

Second, acceleration or other methods of increasing tax depreciation that raise the value of z will have to increase investment and, again, at speeds determined by the distributed lag function on c.

Third, effects of changes in the rate of direct taxation, u, are complicated and ambiguous. Results are affected by assumptions as to what happens to rates of return before and after taxes. Further, the higher the values of k and z and the higher the rate of expected capital gains, the less will decreases in u tend to decrease the value of c. With current high rates of inflation, it is indeed possible, on a priori grounds, that decreases in u, the general marginal rate of business taxation, may raise c, the rental price of capital, and thus, at least in this regard, tend to reduce investment.[3]

3. Effects of other tax parameters, not considered in this chapter, are also determined by the parameters and lag functions for c. Thus, a higher value of v, which could be obtained by making dividends tax deductible to business, would lower the value of c and, if the partial derivative of investment with respect to c has the expected negative sign, will raise investment. The effect of changes in the rate of taxation of capital gains or its rate of inclusion in taxible business income, w, is somewhat tricky. Where expected capital gains are positive, lowering its rate of inclusion in taxable income will lower the cost of capital and hence presumably increase investment. Where capital gains are expected to be negative, if such losses can be deducted from taxable income, lowering the proportion of losses that can be deducted will raise the cost of capital and hence lower investment.

Our general strategy in analyzing the investment equations of the various models is as follows:

1. We shall point out how the tax parameters enter in each set of equations.
2. We shall note the direct effects of tax parameters on business investment indicated by the investment equations as currently specified and estimated. This will be accomplished, as far as feasible, by setting for the entire period, alternatively, the investment tax credit, the lives underlying tax depreciaton, [4] and the rate of business taxation at the values assumed in the last quarter of 1953. We shall then note the differences in the predicted values for investment brought on by these changes. This, of course, is only a very partial exercise. It assumes that other economic variables within the investment equations and feedback from the rest of the system are unaffected.
3. We shall then relax assumptions, altering specifications where appropriate, to better ascertain what the underlying economic data can tell us about the effects of tax parameters on investment without possible biases imposed by a priori hypotheses. This will generally involve several sorts of respecification and reestimation. First, where the elasticities of the response of desired capital or investment to changes in the cost of capital have been preset or constrained, we shall reestimate them freely. Second, where response of desired capital or investment to changes in the rental price of capital has been tied in part or in whole to a measure of the cost of capital based upon earnings-price ratios or dividend-price ratios, we shall reestimate with a cost of capital based on the rate of interest. A low earnings-price ratio on equity may be associated with higher investment not because it reflects a lower cost of capital but rather because it reflects, in stock prices, high expected future earnings. The equity cost of capital to the firm is, after all, the ratio of expected future earnings to current stock prices.
4. We shall estimate the effects on investment of changes in tax parameters as shown by our reestimated equations.

4. Furthermore, tax depreciation is calculated using the straight line method.

TAX PARAMETERS IN THE STRUCTURES OF THE INVESTMENT EQUATIONS

In an effort to facilitate grasping the essential ingredients of the investment equations, we have, with some violence to rigor and detail, set forth equations of each of the models in fairly similar notations in Tables 1–1 through 1–6, supplemented by appendixes with definitions of the rental price of capital and a glossary of variables. (Detailed documentation of the six investment sectors is available in Chirinko and Eisner 1980a: Appendix A.)

BEA

Turning first to the BEA model, we note that the tax parameters enter directly only in the definition of c, the rental price or user cost of capital, which in turn enters into the equilibrium or desired capital-output ratio, $(P/c)^\sigma$. The value of σ is estimated at 0.74 in the equipment equation but only 0.36 in the structures equation. The effects for equipment of changes in tax parameters can then be seen a priori as moderate, at least as against a possible assumed value of $\sigma = 1$. The effects of tax parameters on structures will be small.

The estimated values of σ reflect, among other things, the definition of ρ, the opportunity cost of capital. It attempts to adjust for expectations of inflation by an adaptive function of current and past price changes and also includes as a component a dividend-price ratio. This last, in particular, may bias upward the estimates of σ. Sluggish movement in dividends in response to changes in expected earnings will contribute to a bias in the same direction but significantly larger than that noted above with regard to earnings-price ratios.

The role of the investment tax credit is somewhat muted by recognition of the fact that its effective rate was less than the nominal, statutory rate. The investment tax credit is scaled down by application of a constant factor of proportionality equal to .737379.

The role of tax depreciation is also somewhat muted in the BEA model by using the straight line formulation in calculating z, the present value of the tax depreciation from a dollar of investment.

Table 1-1. BEA Equations, Equipment and Structures.

$$E = \sum_{j=0}^{11} b_{jYE} \left(\frac{p}{c}\right)_{-j}^{\sigma_E} (Y - .87\, Y_{-1})_{-j} + \sum_{j=0}^{8} b_{juE} \left(\frac{p}{c}\right)_{-j}^{\sigma_E} \left(\frac{Y}{UT} - Y\right)_{-j}$$

$$S = \sum_{j=0}^{15} b_{jYs} (1 - .94L) \left(\frac{p}{c}\right)_{-j}^{\sigma_s} \left(\frac{Y}{UT^{.48}}\right)_{-j} + \sum_{j=0}^{15} b_{jus} \frac{p}{c}_{-j}^{\sigma_s} \left(\frac{Y}{UT} - Y\right)_{-j} \quad \text{(Putty-Putty)}$$

$$S = \sum_{j=0}^{15} b_{jYs} \left(\frac{p}{c}\right)_{-j}^{\sigma} \left(\frac{Y}{UT^{.48}} - .94 \frac{Y_{-1}}{UT^{.48}}\right)_{-j} + \sum_{j=0}^{15} b_{jus} \left(\frac{p}{c}\right)_{-j}^{\sigma_s} \left(\frac{Y}{UT} - Y\right)_{-j} \quad \text{(Putty-Clay)}$$

(1)	(2)	(3)	(4)	(5)	(6)	(7)
			Regression Coefficients and Standard Errors			
	Equipment		*Structures*			
			Putty-Putty		*Putty-Clay*	
Variable or Statistic	ρ	ρ'	ρ	ρ'	ρ	ρ'
Constant Σb_{jY} (ELAG1; SLAG1, P-P; SLAG1, P-C)	0.3876 (0.0048)	0.4188 (0.0050)	1.4961 (0.0447)	1.2844 (0.0873)	1.5091 (0.0460)	1.2792 (0.0537)

Σb_{ju} (ELAG2; SLAG2)	-0.0326	-0.0424	-0.1586	-0.1368	-0.1009	-0.0813
	(0.0056)	(0.0057)	(0.0241)	(0.0453)	(0.0278)	(0.0317)
σ	0.74	0.65	0.36	0.27	0.48	0.36
Autocor. coef.	0.675	0.659	0.815	0.945	0.805	0.870
R^2	0.997	0.997	0.979	0.975	0.978	0.976
S.E. regression	1.0748	1.0741	0.8126	0.8799	0.8265	0.8634
DW	2.009	2.007	2.205	2.079	2.039	2.025
n	79	79	71	71	71	71

Means and Standard Deviations

ELAG1, SLAG1	179.103	168.280	32.642	37.517	29.319	34.634
	(51.928)	(48.322)	(9.786)	(7.175)	(3.862)	(4.272)
ELAG2, SLAG2	160.069	151.067	56.850	64.780	48.225	57.368
	(85.092)	(81.185)	(27.903)	(32.380)	(23.524)	(28.583)
Equip. Struct.	60.984	60.984	38.437	38.437	38.437	38.437
	(18.571)	(18.571)	(5.385)	(5.385)	(5.385)	(5.385)

Table 1-2. Chase Equations, Equipment and Structures.

$$E = b_{0E} + b_{1E}(cd + cnd)_- + \sum_{j=0}^{9} a_{jE}\left(\frac{c_E}{p}\right)_{-j} + b_{2E}\, CRED_- + b_{3E}\, NOR_-$$

$$S = b_{0S} + b_{1S}(cd + cnd)_- + \sum_{j=0}^{9} a_{jS}\left(\frac{c_S}{p}\right)_{-j} + b_{2S}\left(\frac{p}{w}\right)_- + b_{3S}\, un_- + b_{4S}\, SP_-$$

(1) Variable or Statistic	(2)	(3)	(4)	(5)	(6)	(7)
	Regression Coefficients and Standard Errors				Means and Standard Deviations	
	Equipment		Structures		Equipment	Structures
	ρ	ρ'	ρ	ρ'		
With Autocorrelation Coefficient						
Constant or Investment	-17.161	-21.548	31.720	38.712	62.486	36.068
	(4.897)	(2.602)	(10.578)	(10.173)	(17.822)	(6.682)
NOR_-	1.290	1.153	—	—	45.680	
	(0.116)	(0.191)			(8.908)	
$CRED_-$	-0.912	-0.572	—	—	-0.0940	
	(0.433)	(0.403)			(0.6868)	
$(cd+cnd)_-$	0.1014	0.0826	0.0549	0.0427	339.715	324.1
	(0.0155)	(0.0221)	(0.0268)	(0.0217)	(64.696)	(71.0)
$(c/p)_-$	-61.381	-30.277	-85.584	-66.539	0.225	0.156
	(19.661)	(13.953)	(39.524)	(29.568)	(0.020)[a]	(0.039)[b]
un_-	—	—	-0.407	-0.483		5.318
			(0.336)	(0.310)		(1.273)

	(1)	(2)	(3)	(4)	(5)	(6)
$(P/w)_-$	—	—	-35.546 (21.612)	-54.083 (21.094)	—	0.2697 (0.0529)
SP_-	—	0.0775 (0.0525)	0.1451 (0.0327)	0.1461 (0.0332)	—	77.102 (21.944)
PRAT	—	0.0711 (0.0278)	—	—	49.912 (22.089)	45.825 (22.208)
PRAT/SP	—	—	—	-1.034 (1.607)	0.574 (0.199)	0.572 (0.183)
Autocor. coef.	0.633	0.552	0.823	0.810		
R^2	0.9965	0.9970	0.9875	0.9875		
S.E. regression	1.0752	1.0057	0.7619	0.7645		
DW	2.023	2.045	2.045	2.035		
n	75	75	90	90		
Structures[b]						
Constant	-14.796 (2.542)	-20.889 (1.490)	33.080 (4.912)	31.777 (6.327)		
NOR_-	1.167 (0.0653)	1.182 (0.1311)	—	—		
$CRED_-$	-1.037 (0.2658)	-0.5343 (0.2835)	—	—		
$(cd+cnd)_-$	0.1155 (0.0089)	0.0827 (0.0165)	3.953 (1.381)	5.013 (1.605)		
$(c/p)_-$	-67.690 (10.500)	-30.110 (9.506)	-45.071 (19.505)	-44.882 (14.711)		
un_-	—	—	-1.119 (0.1812)	-1.033 (0.1767)		
$(P/w)_-$	—	—	-32.790 (9.753)	-33.847 (12.706)		
	—	0.0538	0.1527	0.1438		

Table 1-2. Chase Equations, Equipment and Structures. (continued)

(1) Variable or Statistic	(2)	(3)	(4)	(5)	(6)	(7)
	Regression Coefficients and Standard Errors				Means and Standard Deviations	
	Equipment		Structures		Equipment	Structures
	ρ	ρ'	ρ	ρ'	Equipment	Structures
SP_-		(0.0339)	(0.0212)	(0.0213)		
PRAT	—	0.0714 (0.0214)	—	—		
PRAT/SP	—	—	—	-2.880 (1.833)		
Autocor. coef.	—	—	—	—		
R^2	0.9941	0.9956	0.9689	0.9703		
S.E. regression	1.4034	1.2305	1.2125	1.1924		
DW	0.7429	0.8668	0.4692	0.4934		
n	76	76	91	91		

Note: The "minus" subscript alone ("_"), here and in subsequent tables, indicates a general lag operator of a somewhat varied but usually distributed form, as:

$$(cd + cnd)_- = \Sigma y_j \, (cd + cnd)_{-j}$$

[a] 0.028 for ρ'.
[b] 0.044 for ρ'.

Table 1-3. DRI Equations.

(1) Variable or Statistic	(2)	(3)	(4)	(5)	(6) Means and Standard Deviations	(7)
	Regression Coefficients and Standard Errors				Means and Standard Deviations	
	ρ	$\rho, p/c, Y$	ρ'	$\rho', p/c, Y$	ρ	ρ'
Equipment[a]						
Constant or E	-14.537 (4.130)	-38.863 (10.365)	-15.983 (5.891)	-37.538 (12.940)	63.530 (20.220)	63.530 (20.220)
pY/c (Σb_j)	0.0135 (0.0038)	—	0.0084 (0.0040)	—	3336.7 (952.5)	4186.5 (1065.9)
$(p/c)\overline{Y}$ (Σb_{jb})	—	0.0056 (0.0037)	—	0.0035 (0.0033)	3293.9 (245.4)	4165.3 (223.3)
$Y(\overline{p/c})$ (Σb_{jY})	—	0.0213 (0.0091)	—	0.0180 (0.0066)	3293.9 (767.1)	4165.4 (970.1)
DS (Σd_j)	-48.228 (16.473)	-25.248 (14.876)	-38.789 (18.478)	-14.162 (14.985)	0.2154 (0.0917)	0.2154 (0.0917)
KE_{-1}	-0.1281 (0.0698)	-0.0851 (0.0564)	-0.1337 (0.0798)	-0.0784 (0.0555)	329.3 (91.3)	329.3 (91.3)
$KE_{-1}*UTP$	0.2938 (0.0909)	0.1503 (0.0794)	0.3299 (0.1153)	0.1231 (0.0857)	273.3 (75.0)	273.3 (75.0)
$Y' - Y$	-0.1019 (0.0203)	-0.0959 (0.0192)	-0.1148 (0.0211)	-0.1014 (0.0180)	-60.0 (22.6)	-60.0 (22.6)
$VNWAR$	3.120 (0.888)	2.775 (0.878)	3.164 (0.917)	2.752 (0.886)	0.0930 (0.2922)	0.0930 (0.2922)
Autocor. coef.	0.881	0.748	0.911	0.720		

39

Table 1-3. DRI Equations. (continued)

(1) Variable or Statistic	(2)	(3)	(4)	(5)	(6) Means and Standard Deviations	(7) Means and Standard Deviations
	Regression Coefficients and Standard Errors					
	ρ	$\rho, p/c, Y$	ρ'	$\rho', p/c, Y$	ρ	ρ'
R^2	0.997	0.997	0.997	0.997		
S.E. regression	1.2001	1.1738	1.2447	1.1833		
DW	1.735	1.735	1.647	1.698		
n	85	85	85	85		
Structures[b]						
Constant or S	−0.255	−29.488	−6.074	−31.229	37.788	37.788
	(7.128)	(20.705)	(12.378)	(30.697)	(6.354)	(6.354)
pY/c (Σb_j)	0.0026	—	0.0022		5276.7	7764.8
	(0.0017)		(0.0017)		(750.0)	(831.4)
$(p/c)\overline{Y}$ (Σb_{ip})	—	0.0045	—	0.0029	5427.5	8095.4
		(0.0023)		(0.0021)	(784.1)	(1544.9)
$Y\overline{(p/c)}$ (Σb_{jY})	—	0.0065	—	0.0027	5427.5	8095.4
		(0.0049)		(0.0031)	(1264.0)	(1885.3)
DS (Σd_j)	−45.927	−49.413	−46.623	−38.321	0.2154	0.2154
	(11.745)	(14.796)	(12.035)	(14.826)	(0.0917)	(0.0917)

$KS_{-1}*UTP$	0.1308	0.0948	0.0899	0.0771	352.0	352.0
	(0.0610)	(0.0712)	(0.0862)	(0.0932)	(78.8)	(78.8)
KS_{-1}	-0.0277	-0.0349	0.0125	0.0108	424.0	424.0
KS	(0.0490)	(0.0560)	(0.0698)	(0.0801)	(94.8)	(94.8)
Autocor. coef.	0.871	0.873	0.882	0.880		
R^2	0.979	0.979	0.978	0.979		
S.E. regression	0.9576	0.9575	0.9589	0.9696		
DW	1.917	2.021	1.873	1.951		
n	85	85	85	85		

[a] $E = b_0 + \sum_{j=3}^{9} b_j \left(\frac{pY}{c}\right)_{-j} + \sum_{j=1}^{7} d_j DS_{-j} + f_2 KE_{-1} + f_2 KE_{-1} *UTP + f_3 (Y'-Y) + f_4 VNWAR$

[b] $S = b_0 + \sum_{j=3}^{9} b_j \left(\frac{pY}{c}\right)_{-j} + \sum_{j=1}^{7} d_j DS_{-j} + f_1 KS_{-1} + f_1 KS_{-1} *UTP + f_2 KS_{-1}$

Table 1-4. Michigan Equations, Equipment (Production, Agriculture, and Other) and Structures

$$EX = b_{0x} + b_{1x}\Delta Y_- + b_{2x}\left(\frac{c}{w}\right)_- + b_{3x}S_{-1} + b_{4x}EX_{-1}$$

$$EA = b_{0a} + b_{1a}\Delta Y_- + b_{2a}Y_- + b_{3a}\Delta\left(\frac{c}{w}\right)_- + b_{4a}(\dot{P}_f - \dot{P}_{nf})_{-1} + b_{5a}EA_{-1}$$

$$EO = b_{0o} + b_{1o}Y_- + b_{2o}\left(\frac{c}{w}\right)_- + b_{3o}(i_L - i_s) + b_{4o}\,DASTRIKE + b_{5o}S_{-1} + b_{6o}EO_{-1}$$

$$S = b_{0s} + b_{1s}(Y_{-1} - Y_{-3}) + b_{2s}Y_- + b_{3s}\left(\frac{c}{p}\right)_- + b_{4s}S_{-1}$$

(1) Variable or Statistic	(2) EX, c	(3) EX, c'	(4) EA, c	(5) EA, c'	(6) EO, c	(7) EO, c'	(8) S, c	(9) S, c'
				Regression Coefficients and Standard Errors				
Constant	2.132 (0.759)	2.938 (0.984)	-0.359 (0.239)	-0.084 (0.255)	-2.132 (4.202)	-4.217 (4.867)	1.720 (0.058)	0.635 (1.065)
ΔY_-	0.049 (0.010)	0.054 (0.011)	0.0143 (0.0055)	0.0179 (0.0055)	—	—	—	—
$Y_{-1} - Y_{-3}$	—	—	—	—	—	—	0.0250 (0.0052)	0.0245 (0.0052)

Y_-	—	—	0.00103 (0.00046)	0.00078 (0.00045)	0.0106 (0.0053)	0.0120 (0.0055)	0.0063 (0.0030)	0.0061 (0.0030)
$(c/w)_-$	-4.866 (1.227)	—	-3.775 (2.329)	—	-9.492 (3.485)	—	-32.300 (13.211)	—
$c'_-\overline{(q/w)}_-$	—	-2.771 (2.044)	—	-12.908 (4.341)	—	-12.634 (5.073)	—	-15.158 (19.273)
$(q/w)_-\bar{c}'_-$	—	-16.279 (9.018)	—	64.669 (27.963)	—	1.725 (13.588)	—	-50.072 (19.654)
$\dot{P}_f - \dot{P}_{nf}$	—	—	1.666 (0.454)	1.316 (0.459)	—	—	—	—
$i_L - i_s$	—	—	—	—	1.121 (0.153)	1.101 (0.155)	—	—
DASTRIKE	—	—	—	—	0.665 (0.203)	0.679 (0.204)	—	—
E_{-1}	0.755 (0.049)	0.818 (0.067)	0.807 (0.065)	0.732 (0.073)	0.715 (0.075)	—	—
S_{-1}	0.024 (0.028)	—	—	0.121 (0.053)	0.161 (0.070)	0.882 (0.052)	0.862 (0.054)
R^2	0.982	0.965	0.968	0.993	0.993	0.987	0.987
S.E. regression	0.4079	0.2158	0.2073	1.0897	1.0921	0.8049	0.8025
DW	1.532	1.865	1.960	1.714	1.699	1.995	1.986
	66	66	66	68	68	87	87
Mean and std. dev. of dep. var.	14.922 (2.897)	14.922 (2.897)	4.161 (1.113)	4.161 (1.113)	43.509 (12.570)	43.509 (12.570)	35.928 (6.799)	35.928 (6.799)

Table 1–5. MPS Equations.

(1) Variable or Statistic	(2) ρ	(3) ρ, with constant term	(4) ρ'	(5) ρ', with constant term
		Regression Coefficients and Standard Errors		
Orders for Equipment[a]				
Constant or *ORE*	—	-7.457 (2.260)	—	-20.471 (2.984)
$\left(\dfrac{p}{c}\right)^{\sigma}\Delta Y_{1-j}(\Sigma b_{j\Delta Y})$	25.059 (7.766)	47.768 (12.939)	77.285 (8.442)	152.732 (25.080)
$\left(\dfrac{p}{c}\right)^{\sigma} Y_{1-j}(\Sigma b_{jY})$	1.7350 (0.0598)	2.9832 (0.1615)	2.3545 (0.0721)	6.6801 (0.3106)
$Dk\ (\Sigma d_{jk})$	-26.675	-25.341	-21.129	-19.180
$DP\ (\Sigma d_{jp})$	74.672	69.642	110.06	78.250
σ_E	1.03	0.70	0.71	0.19
Autocor. coef.				
R^2	0.957	0.958	0.927	0.948
S.E. regression	4.6619	4.6072	6.0734	5.1411
DW	1.54	1.63	1.07	1.47
n	83	83	83	83
σ_E by direct estimation	0.164	0.143	0.055	-0.023
Means and Standard Deviations				
$\left(\dfrac{p}{c}\right)^{\sigma}\Delta Y_{1-j}$	0.2515 (0.3853)	0.1616 (0.2498)	0.1586 (0.2667)	0.0810 (0.1306)
$\left(\dfrac{p}{c}\right)^{\sigma} Y_{1-j}$	30.420 (9.049)	19.778 (5.333)	20.036 (5.700)	10.195 (2.378)
Dk	0.0361	0.0361	0.0361	0.0361
DP	0.0723	0.0723	0.0723	0.0723
ORE	58.105 (20.406)	58.105 (20.406)	58.105 (20.406)	58.105 (20.406)
Structures				
Constant	—	-4.676 (4.516)	—	-15.661 (4.911)

Table 1-5. MPS Equations. (continued)

(1) Variable or Statistic	(2) ρ	(3) ρ, with constant term	(4) ρ'	(5) ρ', with constant term
		Regression Coefficients and Standard Errors		
$(p/c)^{\sigma}{}_S Y_{-j}\,(\Sigma b_{jY})$	10.002	8.234	10.650	8.357
	(1.839)	(1.600)	(2.174)	(1.224)
KS_{-1}	-0.1778	-0.1453	-0.1683	-0.1142
	(0.0482)	(0.0409)	(0.0517)	(0.0265)
σ_s	0.22	0.29	0.16	0.27
Autocor. coef.	0.8324	0.8013	0.8792	0.7683
R^2	0.980	0.980	0.980	0.981
S.E. regression	0.8311	0.8345	0.8431	0.8311
DW	2.08	2.03	2.13	1.99
n	63	63	63	63

Means and Standard Deviations

$(p/c)^{\sigma}_S Y_{-j}$	11.6324	12.9682	10.5896	12.5575
	(1.7465)	(1.8642)	(1.5346)	(1.5943)
KS_{-1}	409.935	409.935	409.935	409.935
	(76.657)	(76.657)	(76.657)	(76.657)
S	38.247	38.247	38.247	38.247
	(5.871)	(5.871)	(5.871)	(5.871)

$$^a ORE = \sum_{j=1}^{8} \left(\frac{p}{c}\right)^{\sigma_E}_{-j}(b_{j\Delta Y}\Delta Y_{1-j} + b_{jY}Y_{1-j}) + \sum_{j=1}^{6} d_{jk}D_k + \sum_{j=1}^{6} d_{jp}DP$$

$$^b S = \sum_{j=1}^{17} b_{jY}\left(\frac{p}{c}\right)^{\sigma_s} Y_{-j} + b_{18}KS_{-1}$$

Table 1-6. Wharton Equations, Total Investment by Sector i.

$$(E+S)_i^q = b_{0,i} + b_{1,i}(E+S)_i^1 + b_{2,i}(E+S)_i^2 + b_{3,i}Y_i + b_{4,i}K_{-1,i}$$

$$(E+S)_i^1 = d_{0,i} + d_{1,i}(E+S)_i^2 + \sum_{j=0}^{n_1} d_{jYi}Y_{-j,i} + \sum_{j=0}^{n_2} d_{jKi}K_{-j,1} + \sum_{j=0}^{n_3} d_{jci}\left(\frac{p}{c}\right)_{-j,i}$$

$$(E+S)_i^2 = c_{0,i} + \sum_{j=0}^{m_1} c_{jYi}Y_{-j,i} + \sum_{j=0}^{m_2} c_{jKi}K_{-j,i} + \sum_{j=0}^{m_3} c_{jci}\left(\frac{p}{c}\right)_{-j,i}$$

	(2)	(3)	(4)	(5)	(6)
		Selected Regression Coefficients and Standard Errors[a]			
Variable or Statistic		ρ		ρ'	
	$(E+S)^a$	$(E+S)^1$	$(E+S)^2$	$(E+S)^1$	$(E+S)^2$
Constant	−0.1633	−4.4899	−24.807	−3.1106	−9.1792
	(0.2592)	(2.079)	(6.125)	(1.208)	(6.631)
$(E+S)_i^1$	0.6371	−	−	−	−
	(0.1083)	−	−	−	−
$(E+S)_i^2$	0.2727	0.5797	−	0.6286	−
	(0.0981)	(0.0851)	−	(0.0843)	−
$Y_i, \sum_j Y_{-j,i}$	0.0231	0.0897	0.1578	0.0821	0.1230
	(0.0070)	(0.0198)	(0.0119)	(0.0193)	(0.0159)
$K_i, \sum_j K_{-j,i}$	−0.0202	−0.0354	−	−0.0381	−
	(0.0052)	(0.0128)	−	(0.0110)	−
$\sum_j \left(\frac{p}{c}\right)_{-j,i}$	−	20.168	211.024	12.073	88.115
	−	(20.531)	(58.040)	(12.635)	(70.572)
Autocor. coef.	−	−	−	−	.842
R^2	0.988	0.988	0.979	0.989	0.974
S.E. regression	0.4385	0.4429	0.6003	0.4298	0.6666
DW	1.263	1.890	2.240	2.122	2.137

Note: i = manufacturing, durables

Chase

The Chase model is distinguished by an equation for new orders that feeds into the equipment equation. The new orders equation permits independent estimation of the tax parameters, u, k, and z, with which we are concerned. In both the equipment and structures equations, the tax parameters enter again in c, the rental price of capital. In both equations the opportunity cost of capital, ρ, is based upon averages of interest rates and earnings-price ratios, with the latter more heavily weighted in the equipment equation. Estimates of the elasticity of response with respect to the rental price of capital are not constrained, however, and are not assumed constant.

Economic depreciation is taken as a constant, at a rate of 0.181 for equipment and 0.095 for structures. In BEA it was apparently 0.38 for equipment and 0.16 for structures. The present value of tax depreciation is a function of the kind of depreciation—straight line, sum of years digits, or double-declining balance—with the length of life varying. The equipment tax credit, k, enters at its nominal statutory rate.

The Standard and Poor's index of 500 stocks enters independently in the structures equation. Thus, it possibly dilutes the effect of the earnings-price ratio.

DRI

The DRI model enters the expression PY/c as a single set of lagged terms in both the equipment and structures equations. Thus, elasticities of response are constrained to be identical for prices of output,[5] rates of output, and the rental cost of capital variable. If accelerator and replacement effects dominate and the long-run elasticities of demand for capital with respect to output are unity, this will have the effect of biasing to unity the estimated elasticities of demand for capital with respect to its rental price.

A second major strategic element in the DRI model is the debt service variable, DS, which is the ratio of interest obligations to gross cash flow, where the latter equals depreciation plus profits after taxes

---

5. Defined as final sales less government purchases and imputed housing services, with an adjustment for pollution abatement equipment spending.

plus inventory valuation adjustment minus dividends. One may expect negative coefficients to the debt service variable not merely (or at all) because of liquidity constraints but also because investment will tend to be high in cyclical booms when profits are high. Variation in gross cash flow will be dominated by variations in profits after taxes, quite aside from variations in tax parameters. The DRI model will, however, imply that changes in tax parameters will have the same association with investment as the perhaps spurious association of profits and investment. If no feedback is allowed in terms of lower prices or pass-through of changes in taxes affecting profits before tax, the effects of changes in tax parameters will be particularly exaggerated.

The opportunity cost of capital, ρ, is an average of interest and equity costs, weighted by the proportions of each in business financing. The equity costs consist of a dividend-price ratio plus an estimate of the expected rate of growth of earnings per share.

The rate of economic depreciation is taken from BEA series on depreciation and capital stocks and hence varies through time. The present value of the tax depreciation from a dollar of investment, z, takes into account straight line and sum of years digits depreciation.

The DRI model may be expected to indiciate particularly large impacts of changes in tax parameters because in three key areas the tax parameters are constrained to enter with coefficients equal to that of other variables expected to have a close association with investment—output, profits after taxes, and dividend-price ratios.

Michigan

The Michigan model divides equipment investment into three categories—production, agriculture, and other. It is unique in having the lagged value of structures enter the equation of production investment in equipment. It also contains in the "other" equipment equation—a variable measuring the difference between long-term and short-term interest rates, presumably embodying the effects of expected changes in long rates.

Tax depreciation is taken in the Michigan model as a rate that varies periodically, apparently with changes in allowable lives. The present value of the tax depreciation for a dollar of investment is not calculated.

In the structures equation, the rental price of capital is taken simply as the price of structures time 0.06, presumably economic depreciation, plus the rate of interest. Hence, no tax parameters enter. In the equipment equations, tax parameters enter through the assumed rate of tax depreciation and the assumed nominal rate of investment tax credit, k. Economic depreciation is taken at a constant rate of one-sixth in the equipment equations.

The Michigan model uses interest rates minus a price change expectations term as its measure of the opportunity cost of capital. The rental price of capital variable enters as a ratio of labor costs in the equipment equations and as a ratio of prices in the structures equation. In none of the equations is its coefficient otherwise constrained.

The Michigan equations hence offer less a priori support for the role of tax parameters. They do not enter at all in the structures equations. In the equipment equations they are constrained to have effects similar to those of other components of the rental price of capital.

MPS

The MPS investment equations rest heavily on a third equation for orders for equipment. This in turn involves distributed lag functions of output and changes in output, each multiplied by (P/c). The value of σ is constrained at $(P/c)^{\sigma}$ unity in the equation for orders for equipment, from which actual investment expenditures follow fairly directly. This constrains the rental price of capital to have whatever effect on investment in equipment is indicated by the coefficients of the combined terms $(P/c)\ \Delta Y$ and $(P/c)\ Y$, reflecting accelerator and replacement investment. The value of σ, taken identically equal to unity, is apparently derived from a search procedure indicating this to be appropriate for a particular form of the equation estimated. In the structures equation, however, an estimated value of σ equal to 0.18629 was used, thus implying a much lesser role in structures for the rental price of capital and any tax parameters entering into it.

The value of the tax depreciation from a dollar of investment, z, takes into account the varying proportions of depreciation by straight line and accelerated methods. The investment tax credit is taken at its "effective rate."

In the forms specified, tax parameters can be expected to have a large role in the MPS equipment equations because of the constraint that σ equals unity. It will have a much lesser role in the structures equation because of the relatively low estimated value of σ.

Wharton

The Wharton investment sector involves equations for eight separate industry groups, each estimating the sum of equipment and structures invesment. Aggregate investment is then allocated as between equipment and structures.

The nonagricultural industry investment equations are functions of current output, the one-quarter and two-quarter ahead investment anticipations, and in some cases, the current capital stock. The cost of capital affects investment by its impact on investment anticipations variables. These are generally functions of industry output, the price of industry output relative to the cost of capital, and in some cases, the capital stock. The length of the lags for these explanatory variables varies by sector. No cost of capital term enters the equation for regulated transportation.

The industry costs of capital are based on effective industry income tax rates and the statutory rate of the investment tax credit. The value of z is calculated on the assumption that all tax depreciation was sum of years digits using industry tax lives.

The lack of constraint on the coefficients of the rental price of capital, where it does appear, implies relatively little presumption in favor of a major role for tax parameters in the Wharton investment equations.

TAX SCENARIOS: ESTIMATES OF DIRECT
EFFECTS OF TAX PARAMETERS

One measure of the relative direct effects of tax parameters in the different models may be derived by setting the three tax parameters with which we have been concerned at their essentially "preincentive" values of 1953 and noting the differences in investment indicated by the investment equations. Such a measure is of course very partial, abstracting from feedback effects on the variables in the investment equations. It hence does not offer a reliable measure of the total effects of the tax parameters on investment. It should nevertheless give us a good preliminary indication of the sensitivity to tax parameters of the investment equations currently specified and used in the models. We do not have such estimates for Wharton. The contrasts among the five other models (BEA, Chase, DRI, Michigan, and MPS), as shown in Table 1–7, are striking.

First, we set the investment tax credit at a rate of zero. Second, we put the investment tax credit back at whatever values it entered the equations and set the tax depreciation variable at a value that assumes continuance of straight line depreciation at the tax lives used or specified in 1953. (In the Michigan model the tax depreciation rate was held at the constant value of 0.08 for agriculture and 0.05 for "production" and "other.") Third, we left the investment tax credit and tax depreciation variables at whatever values they entered the equations but set the corporate profits tax rate at the value of 0.52 that existed in 1953. All comparisons were made for the fourth quarter of 1977 for which we had data for all of the models.

Setting the investment tax credit equal to zero but taking all other variables entering the investment equations as unaltered, the predicted values of investment in equipment showed a huge range of results. The low, for Michigan, was a reduction of investment by $1.4 billion. Chase indicated a reduction of $4.3 billion. BEA came in with a reduction of $7.3 billion; and MPS and DRI, as we might have anticipated from the specification of the investment equations, indicated a reduction in investment of $10.9 and $12.9 billion, respectively.

On accelerated depreciation, Chase is low with an effect of $5.2 billion, with Michigan and BEA not far behind with estimated effects of $5.8 and $6.3 billion, respectively. MPS and DRI are again high, with investment losses of $14.7 and $16.5 billion, respectively.

The corporate profits tax rate, as we have pointed out, does not enter as unambiguously in the rental price of capital and consequent impact on investment; and here the differences across the models, while still relatively great, are not quite as large. In fact, the results for Michigan indicate that, by holding the corporate profits tax rate equal to its value in the last quarter of 1953, investment expenditures on equipment would have been higher by $0.94 billion as compared to the baseline values. All of the other models record declines in investment. Chase indicates an effect of $1.4 billion, but this time BEA ranks ahead of MPS, $2.5 against 1.8 billion, respectively. Again, DRI shows the strongest effects, with an estimated decline of $5.7 billion.

Table 1-7. Tax Scenarios. Direct Effects on 1977–IV Investment of Tax Credit, Accelerated Depreciation since 1953–IV, and Corporate Tax Rate Less than 52 Percent. Investment Equations Specified in Models, Billions of 1972 Dollars.

	BEA	Chase	DRI	Michigan	MPS
Equipment, predicted, 1977–IV	92.103	92.125	92.149	93.903	83.720
Predicted difference due to:					
ITC $(k) = 0$	-7.339	-4.281	-12.876	-1.406	-10.877
No accelerated depreciation[a]	-6.346	-5.227	-16.483	-5.830	-14.745
CPT $(u) = 0.52$	-2.539	-1.359	-5.720	+0.940	-1.753
Structures, predicted, 1977–IV	40.255	40.332	43.509	b	42.749
Predicted difference due to					
No accelerated depreciation[a]	-0.473	-1.060	-5.068	b	-0.729
CPT$(u) = 0.52$	-0.810	-0.539	-4.194	b	-0.621

[a]Straight-line depreciation, 1953–IV *lives*. In the Michigan model, tax depreciation *rates* held at values in 1953–IV. In the BEA and Chase models, the tax *lives* for structures did not vary from 1953 to the present. In our simulation we increased them in proportion to the increases that occurred in the DRI and MPS models.

[b]In the Michigan model, no tax parameters enter the structures equation.

Tax parameters do not enter the Michigan structures equation. As for the other four models, DRI is much higher, both on accelerated depreciation and on the corporate profits tax rate, owing to the constraint that movements in the cost of capital or output have on investment through the same set of distributed lag coefficients. The disparities among the remaining models are relatively small, presumably because of the lower estimated value of σ in the MPS structures equation.

It is of course important to be aware that Table 1–7 offers no comparison of the relative effects of variation of different tax parameters, even the direct partial effects in the investment equations. To measure these we would, at the very least, have to compare changes in tax parameters that involve equal losses of tax revenues—in fact, equal present values of losses in tax revenues—since the time patterns of changes in tax revenues will be different for the investment tax credit, tax depreciation, and the corporate profits tax rate.

ESTIMATED EQUATIONS

Differences in results among the models have been related generally to explicit or implicit differences in the more or less constrained values of σ, the elasticity of capital with respect to its rental price.

The investment tax parameters were most frequently imbedded in variables measuring that rental price of capital. Specifications of the components of the rental price of capital variables as well as constraints imposed upon their relations with other variables were of major importance.

We focused our attention, in reestimating the model investment equations, on the coefficients of the rental price of capital variables and on the specifications that affected them. In our new equations we have loosened the constraints on variables embodying tax effects and compared estimates of the original model equations (or our representations of them, sometimes trivially different) and our new equations. We then proceeded to comparable simulations of the old and new equations with specified alterations of the investment tax credit, the tax lives of depreciable assets, and the general rate of corporate taxation. We thus were able to verify the apparent implications of the various estimated parameters of the originally specified equations and our new equations and to quantify the results.

A major focus of our revised equations has been the isolation, as far as possible, of variables presumed to embody the effects of tax parameters. This suggested that in a number of the models, we revise the definition of ρ, the cost of capital, which is a key variable component in the rental price of capital into which the tax parameters enter. In particular, we excluded from ρ the ratio of profits after taxes to stock prices or the ratio of dividends to stock prices. High current ratios of profits after taxes to stock prices may relate less to the current cost of capital than to the state of the business cycle and the relation between current profits and expected future profits, and the latter may play a major role in the value of stock prices. High current profits may, in fact, stimulate investment through liquidity effects and lower the effective cost of capital.

A low ratio of profits after taxes to stock prices may, however, reflect high expected future profits, which would be positively related to investment and yet not be indicative of a low equity cost of raising capital. This is true, a fortiori, with regard to the ratio of dividends to stock prices. The negative relation between investment and this presumed component of the cost of capital may rather reflect a positive relation between current investment and the expected future returns on this investment, which will also be positively related to current stock prices. If we are to measure the effects of tax parameters on investment in terms of their contribution to the rental price of capital, we must avoid tainting our measure of the rental price of capital with spurious measures of ρ, its cost of the capital component.[6]

---

6. Problems remain in the measure of ρ, relating to effects of inflation and risk. It is the real rate of interest—the nominal rate minus expected inflation or capital gains on assets—that should be relevant. The available ex post variables are likely to prove poor proxies for expectations, particularly when the rate of inflation changes rapidly. Among the models, Chase an DRI do not adjust nominal rates of return for inflation. Our exclusion of dividend-price and earnings-price ratios also eliminates the measure, however imperfect, of the risk premium firms may pay in raising equity capital.

Under certain conditions, we could view the measure of the real rate of interest as highly correlated with the true opportunity cost of capital and an excellent proxy for it. These conditions would include introduction of a correct measure of expected inflation and relatively constant risk and debt-equity ratios, which would in fact be affected by the interaction of inflation and taxes. To the extent that these conditions are not met, our formulation of ρ eliminates one source of error but blows up another, which may also bias the estimates of the effects on investment of changes in the rental price of capital, c.

A further major revision we have undertaken relates most importantly to the DRI model, where the effects of changes in relative prices and of output have been constrained to be equal in the combined variable, pY/c, where Y is a measure of output, p measures the price of output, and c denotes the rental price of capital. Our new equations for DRI involve estimates of the separate effects of changes in p/c and changes in Y. Our hypothesis is that, since a strong positive relation between capital and output is well established, estimating the effects of changes in c, whether brought about by changes in tax parameters or changes in other components, will be exaggerated by estimates of a coefficient of pY/c. We might note as a corollary that if the coefficient of p/c is really lower than that of Y, estimating a coefficient for the combined variable may well lead to understatement of the effect of Y. Analogous issues of perhaps lesser substance occur with regard to constraints that impose similar consequences from changes in the relative price of capital goods and output or wages and or changes in relative prices due to other changes in the components of c. We have explored this with an additional set of equations in the Michigan model.

BEA

Critical elements in the BEA model investment equations were the definition of the rental price of capital, c, the associated estimates of the elasticity of capital with respect to the rental price, σ, and the putty-putty form of the structures equation. In this equation, the entire capital stock, not merely net investment and replacement, was specified to change its magnitude with changes in the relative values of the implicit price deflator of GNP and the rental price of investment in structures.

We have undertaken two changes in specifications of the BEA equations. First, we have altered the definition of ρ, the cost of capital entering the rental price, c. The BEA model defines ρ as a weighted average of an expected interest rate term extrapolated from the past change in the rate of interest and current and past levels, and a dividend–stock price ratio. Interest costs are apparently partially adjusted for their tax deductible component. We have defined a new ρ', modifying the definition of ρ by excluding the dividend–stock price ratio and blowing up the resultant ρ' so that its mean is equal to that of ρ. Second, we have added a new structures equation with a putty-clay specification, as indicated in Table 1–1.

Changing the definition of ρ had only a modest effect in the equipment equation. Our estimated value of σ changed from 0.74 to 0.55, suggesting a slightly lower effect for investment tax parameters than in the original equation.

In the structures equation, our new definition of ρ resulted in lowering the estimate of σ from 0.36 to 0.27 in the original putty-putty specification. It should be noted that the standard error of the regression based on the ρ' specification was somewhat larger than that with the ρ specification, however.

The putty-clay specification yields higher estimates of σ in both the ρ and ρ' versions, but again a lower estimate of σ in the ρ' equation. We may anticipate, though, that the higher values of σ in a putty-clay specification will not translate themselves into higher short-term effects of tax parameters on investment.

Chase

In the Chase model, direct effects of investment tax parameters are measured in an equation for new orders in all manufacturing. Here the values of the corporate tax rate, u, of the investment tax credit, k, and of the present value of tax depreciation from a dollar of investment in equipment, z_E, divided by $1-u$, all enter linearly. The new orders variable in turn enters the equipment investment equation but the tax parameters enter this equation again as components of c_E, the rental price of equipment. The structures equation does not contain the new orders variable, so that the only effects of the tax parameters there are as components of c_s, the rental price of investment in structures.

The rental price in both cases includes the cost of capital, ρ. For equipment this is an average of the interest rate on newly issued Aa utility bonds and the ratio of profits after taxes in billions of dollars to the Standard and Poor index of 500 common stocks. The value of ρ is calculated from a similar average in the case of structures, but with a lesser weight for $PRAT / SP$, the ratio of profits to the stock price index. The structures equation also enters a set of lagged stock price indexes as a separate variable.

Our estimates of the equation involving ρ', in which the stock price index and profits after taxes are taken out of the c/p variable and enter separately, indicate a striking reduction in the absolute value of the coefficient of c/p, from 61.4 to 30.3, as shown in Table 1–2. While leaving intact the estimated effects of tax parameters in the curiously specified equation for new orders, the reduction in the coefficient of c/p as we move from the ρ equation to the ρ' equation suggests that an "untainted" estimate of the coefficient of the rental price of capital will indicate lesser effects of tax parameters on investment in equipment.

In the structures equation, the coefficient of c/p is again reduced in absolute size, from 85.6 to 66.5 as we move from the ρ to the ρ' equation. This reduction is less in absolute magnitude and still less relatively than the corresponding reduction in the case of equipment. The structures equation, one may note, has a significantly positive coefficient for the stock price index but a relatively small and insignificant coefficient for the $PRAT/SP$ variable.

DRI

Tax parameters enter the DRI investment equations through c in the pY/c variable and in the debt service variable, DS. The specification is implicitly putty-putty, with direct adjustment of equipment investment to a change in rental price completed over a total of nine quarters. Any reasonably substantial coefficients of the pY/c variables will hence imply a substantial effect on investment.

The debt service variable, defined as the ratio of interest payments to gross cash flow, may also have a substantial effect, because cyclical increases in profits, closely related to cash flow, are likely to be positively associated with cyclical movements in investment. Since cyclical movements of interest payments are much less, we may expect a considerable negative relation between investment and the debt service variable, reflecting essentially the positive relation between investment and profits. This positive relation of investment to profits will come through all the more greatly if the role of output is misspecified. The merging of Y in a combined pY/c variable may then have the effect of lowering the constrained coefficient of Y even as it raises the constrained coefficient of p/c and the absolute value of the coefficient of the debt service variable.

The DRI model uses for ρ a weighted average of interest costs and the sum of the dividend stock price ratio and a measure of the expected rate of growth of earnings. To the extent that the measure of expected earnings growth captures the earnings dilution cost of selling new equity as perceived by firms, the DRI measure of ρ may be robust against the criticisms we have advanced earlier. To the likely extent that it is an inadequate measure of these costs in terms of expected future earnings, the DRI measure of ρ may also be defective as an indicator of the cost of capital.

We have thus undertaken two kinds of revisions in the DRI equations, both separately and in combination. First, we have split the pY/c variables into their separate relative price and output components, p/c and Y or, more precisely, $(p/c)\bar{Y}$ and $Y(\bar{p}/\bar{c})$. Second, we have redefined ρ′ as the DRI measure of the interest rate, blown up to have the same mean as the originally defined ρ (thus $ρ' = i\,\bar{ρ}/\bar{i}$). We are hence able to offer four sets of estimates—(1) the original DRI equations, with the combined pY/c variable and the original ρ and hence the original c; (2) equations with the original ρ, but with $(p/c)\bar{Y}$ and $Y(\bar{p}/\bar{c})$ entered as separate sets of variables; (3) the original DRI specification, but with ρ′ substituted for ρ; and (4) equations with ρ′ substituted for ρ and with $(p/c)\bar{Y}$ and $Y(\bar{p}/\bar{c})$ substituted for pY/c.

The results for equipment appear very much in line with our hypotheses. Splitting the pY/c variable lowers the constrained coefficient of 0.0135 to 0.0056 for p/c and raises the coefficient to 0.0213 for Y. Further, the absolute size of the coefficient of the debt service variable was reduced from 48.2 to 25.2. Splitting the pY/c variable thus points to a reduction in the implicit effects of all tax parameters in the order of more than 50 percent in the DRI equipment equation.

Substituting ρ′ for ρ in itself reduces the estimated coefficient of pY/c and the absolute value of the coefficient of the debt service variable. The combined effect of both alterations—substituting ρ′ for ρ and splitting the pY/c variable—is most dramatic. The coefficient of the separate p/c variable is reduced to 0.0035, little more than one-quarter of its constrained value in the original DRI equation; and the absolute size of the coefficient of the debt service variable is reduced to 14.2, again less than 30 percent of its amount in the original DRI equation.[7]

---

7. An F test reveals that the improvement in fit resulting from the separation of p/c from Y in the ρ′ equation for equipment is clearly significant; $F(2,76) = 4.83$, which is just about at the 0.99 probability level. The F statistic for the ρ equation was 2.74, corresponding to a probability level of 0.93.

The DRI equations for structures, however, reveal no such dramatic differences. This may relate to the generally poor fit of the DRI structures equations. The sum of the coefficients of pY/c was not significantly greater than zero in the original DRI equation, and neither the corresponding pY/c sum nor the sums of coefficients of the separate p/c and Y variables were significantly different from zero in our equations. In our revision incorporating both ρ' and the separate p/c and Y variables, the absolute size of the highly significant debt service variable was somewhat reduced, from 45.9 in the original DRI structures equation to 38.3. Our revisions have not, however, made very much difference in the structures equations.

Michigan

The Michigan model, it may be recalled, generates the smallest effects of tax parameters on investment. Indeed, there is no direct scope for them at all in the structures equation.

We have used the Michigan model to examine a further split of the relative price variable in which tax parameters affecting investment are usually imbedded. What we have done is to break out of the relative price of capital and labor term, c/w, the price of capital goods and the wage rate. This leaves as the residual variation in the rental price of capital, c, the interest rate in the structures equation and in equipment, in addition, a price change term and the tax factors of depreciation, the corporate tax rate, and the investment tax credit.

Results were mixed in the three equipment equations—production, agriculture, and other—and in structures. In "production" investment, which had a mean value of almost $15 billion, the split lowered the absolute value of the coefficient of the rental price of capital component, including the interest rate and tax parameters. In the small agricultural component (mean investment about $4 billion), the absolute value of the coefficient of the rental price of capital residual variable was raised considerably, and the relative price term showed a significant "wrong" positive sign. (This may have related to interaction with the variable measuring relative price changes of farm and nonfarm products.)

In the equation for "other" equipment investment, the mean value of which was $43.5 billion, the split brought little change in the coefficient of the rental price of capital variable. In structures, this split did cut the coefficient of the residual rental price of capital variable roughly in half in absolute value and also showed a very substantial and significant negative coefficient of the new variable measuring the relative price of capital goods and wages. This may suggest a better formulation of the structures equation but is not directly relevant to our current work since tax parameters do not enter here.

MPS

In the MPS equations we have reestimated both equipment and structures equations with focus on the values of σ, the elasticity of demand for capital with respect to the relative price of output and capital. In the MPS model equation for orders for equipment, σ is specified as having a value of unity. When we reestimate this equation with the MPS specification of ρ and no constant term, we do indeed get a maximum likelihood estimate of σ of 1.03. When we estimate σ without constraining the constant term to be zero, however, we find that the constant is significantly negative, the estimated value of σ falls to 0.70, and the accelerator coefficients generally rise.

Variance in ρ in the MPS equations relates chiefly to variance in the dividend–stock price ratio and to interaction of the corporate tax rate and the proportion of capital costs that is tax deductible. There is general allowance for an interest rate component, but the current MPS model equations constrained its coefficient to be zero.

In accordance with our general approach, we have defined ρ' so that the interest rate is included and the dividend–stock price ratio is excluded. Estimates of the equipment equation with ρ' substituted for ρ yield considerably smaller estimates of the value of σ. In the equation with no constant term, as specified in the MPS model, our estimated value of σ falls from 1.03 to 0.71. In the much better fitting model, with the constant term, the estimated value of σ in the ρ' equations falls from 0.71 to 0.19. This last value of σ would suggest a vastly smaller role for tax parameters in affecting investment in equipment.

In the MPS structures equation, the value of σ provided in the model is 0.18629, thus implying only modest effect of tax parameters on investment in structures. Our own estimate of the structures equation as originally specified including the MPS definition of ρ yields a value of σ of 0.22. The dramatic differences seen in equipment do not appear in our different equations in structures. The equation using ρ with a constant term here gives a value of σ of 0.29; that using ρ' yields a value of σ of 0.16; and that using ρ' with a constant term gives a value of σ of 0.27.

Wharton

In the Wharton model, our only modification to the original equations is to alter the definition of ρ. The opportunity cost of capital is defined as a fixed-weighted average of an estimate of the real rate of interest and the dividend–stock price ratio. As argued above, this latter term may be a poor proxy for the true equity costs that the firm faces, and we have reestimated the Wharton equations with ρ' equal to the real rate of interest, scaled appropriately to insure that the means of ρ and ρ' are equal.

The number of equations that were reestimated with the new definition of the cost of capital is rather voluminous; in Table 1–6, we present a representative set of equations for durable manufacturing. In both the one and two quarter ahead anticipations equations, the sums of estimated coefficients are significantly lower for the relative price term, and somewhat lower for the output term. This pattern holds for the majority of the reestimated equations, although in some cases the sums of coefficients increase relative to the original estimates. Given the interrelationships that exist in the investment sector of each industry, it is somewhat difficult to determine from an examination of the coefficients the responsiveness of aggregate investment to changes in parameters. The simulation results presented in Table 1–13 provide a convenient means by which to assess the differences between the original and modified equations.

We may indicate in general that, particularly where the original models suggested major effects of tax parameters on investment, our revised equations, free of what have seemed to us to be critical constraints generating the results, have produced parameter estimates suggesting considerably lesser effects of tax variables on investment. That story can be developed much more clearly and precisely in simulations of paths of investment with varying values of the key tax parameters of the investment tax credit, tax depreciation, and the corporate income tax rate. It is to these simulations that we shall now turn.

SIMULATIONS

We report on four basic sets of simulations, similar as far as possible for each of the six models. The first is a long-run simulation in which the relevant tax parameters are held at their fourth quarter, 1953 levels. This means setting the investment tax credit at zero and the corporate tax rate, effective or statutory as defined in the models, at its 1953-IV rate, and applying tax depreciation by the straight line method at the length of lives assumed by the models to exist in the fourth quarter of 1953.

Second, we have alternatively changed the investment tax credit, the corporate tax rate, and the tax depreciation lives in the first quarter of 1973 and followed the resultant path of investment for generally a five-year period through the fourth quarter of 1977. For the investment tax credit, we have doubled the rate for equipment beginning in the first quarter of 1973 and have introduced a credit for structures at 10 percent (an effective rate of 8.1 percent in the DRI model and 8.5 percent in the MPS model). We have set the corporate tax rate at 90 percent of its historical rate beginning in the first quarter of 1973. And we have set the tax lives for depreciable assets at 50 percent of their historical rates beginning in the first quarter of 1973.

We have then mapped baseline paths for investment in equipment and structures for the original model equations (or our approximate rendition of them) and noted the effects upon investment indicated by each of the specified sets of changes in tax parameters. Next, we have constructed similar baseline paths for each of our modified equations and noted the indicated effects on investment of the changes in tax parameters in these equations. Thus we are able to note not only how indicated changes in tax parameters of the original model equations will affect investment but also how the indicated effects are dependent upon model specification and how they change with the new, less constrained, and in our view, better specified equations that we have estimated.

To simplify the presentation, we shall offer in our tables and concentrate in our discussion on the results for the fourth quarter of

1977, in billions of 1972 dollars and as a percent of baseline. To anticipate in summary fashion the simulations offered generally— and particularly in the results for equipment—a striking confirmation of the hypotheses we have expressed and of the implications of the estimated equations indicated above.

BEA

The BEA equipment equations, it will be recalled, were only moderately modified by our respecification of ρ as ρ'. The rather substantial effects of tax parameters on investment indicated in the BEA model are hence only moderately reduced with our new specification. With none of the "investment incentives" introduced since 1953, the BEA equipment equation indicates that investment in equipment would have been some $15.6 billion in 1972 dollars less in the fourth quarter of 1977, some 17 percent of the baseline. Our revised ρ' equation lowers that effect only to $14 billion, or 15.1 percent of the baseline.

Making the equipment tax credit twice its historical value beginning in 1973 would have increased equipment investment by $9 billion, or 9.8 percent of baseline according to the original BEA equation. According to our ρ' equation, it would have increased equipment spending by $8 billion, or 8.6 percent of baseline.

The relative magnitude of effects shown in the original and modified equation are similar for reductions in the corporate tax rate and in the lives for tax depreciation, as may be seen in Table 1–8. The ρ' equations show modestly smaller effects on investment.

The BEA structures equation, with its distinctly smaller value of σ, shows markedly smaller effects of changes in tax parameters. Using the original BEA putty-putty model, the introduction of a 10 percent investment tax credit for structures would have increased structures investment by only 3.48 percent of baseline by the fourth quarter of 1977. Our modified ρ' equation reduces that effect to 2.64 percent of baseline.

The putty-clay specification that we have introduced generates higher estimates of σ, as might be expected, and hence greater long-run and also greater medium-run effects on structures investment. By the fourth quarter of 1977, the increases in structures investment was some 30 to 40 percent greater in the putty-clay equations than in

Table 1-8. BEA Simulations, Equipment and Structures, Change in Investment, 1977-IV.

(1) Tax Parameters	(2) Equipment	(3)	(4) Equation — Structures — Putty-Putty	(5)	(6) Putty-Clay	(7)
	ρ	ρ'	ρ	ρ'	ρ	ρ'
Billions of 1972 Dollars						
All always at 1953-IV levels, SL dep.	-15.639	-13.992	-0.810	-0.581	-1.035	-0.747
Changes in 1973-I: $k'_{et} = 2k_{et}; k'_{st} = 10\%$	+9.032	+7.955	+1.399	+1.132	+1.927	+1.485
$u'_t = 0.9u_t$	+2.752	+2.421	+0.886	+0.624	+1.135	+0.806
$L'_t = 0.5L_t$	+9.025	+7.931	+1.912	+1.518	+2.576	+1.981
As Percent of Baseline						
All always at 1953-IV levels, SL dep.	-16.98	-15.08	-2.01	-1.36	-2.56	-1.79
Changes in 1973-I: $k'_{et} = 2k_{et}; k'_{st} = 10\%$	+9.81	+8.57	+3.48	+2.64	+4.77	+3.56
$u'_t = 0.9u_t$	+2.99	+2.61	+2.20	+1.46	+2.81	+1.93
$L'_t = 0.5L_t$	+9.80	+8.54	+4.75	+3.55	+6.38	+4.74

the putty-putty equations. The putty-putty result for a 10 percent investment tax credit in structures was $+\$1.13$ billion in our ρ' equation for 1977-IV as against $\$1.49$ billion in the putty-clay ρ' equation.[8] But in the putty-putty equation, the indicated added investment in structures had reached a peak of about $\$2.30$ billion as early as the third and fourth quarters of 1974, and the amount of added investment then began to decline. In the putty-clay model, the amount of additional structures investment rose throughout the five-year period, but was apparently pretty much at its equilibrium level by the fourth quarter of 1977.

Both the putty-putty model for structures investment and the results flowing from it are really implausible (as discussed earlier in the chapter). The putty-clay models indicate that a reduction in tax revenues equal to 10 percent of structures investment would tend to increase that investment by some two-thirds of the lost tax revenues according to the ρ equation and some one-half of the tax revenues according to the ρ' equation. All of these estimates, we must remind ourselves, are based only upon the single investment equations, without feedback from the rest of the model. Higher interest rates resulting from higher investment demand, for example, would tend to reduce the effects of these tax incentives. Effects from changes in aggregate demand would depend, of course, upon what assumptions are made about other offsetting taxes, as well as whether the economy is or is not at or near full employment.

Chase

The original Chase equations do not indicate as large effects of tax parameters on equipment investment. The simulations with our revised ρ' equations reduce those estimated effects further. Thus, the long-run no tax incentive simulation indicates that equipment investment would be less by $\$11.7$ billion in 1977-IV, or 12.8 percent of baseline. Our ρ' equation reduces this estimated effect to $\$8.2$ billion, or 8.9 percent of baseline. The effects of doubling the investment tax credit were only 4.6 percent of baseline, less than half of that indicated in the BEA equations. Our ρ' equation reduced the effects substantially further, to just over 3 percent of baseline. Thus

8. The BEA model is specified so that a 10 percent statutory investment tax credit is transformed into a 7.37 percent effective rate.

Table 1-9. Chase Simulations, Equipment and Structures, Change in Investment, 1977-IV.

(1) Tax Parameters	(2)	(3)	(4)	(5)
	Equipment		Structures	
	ρ	ρ'	ρ	ρ'
From equations with autocorrelation coefficients				
Billions of 1972 dollars				
All always at 1953-IV levels, SL dep.	-11.736	-8.094	-2.547	-1.962
Changes in 1973-I: $k'_{et} = 2k_{et}; k'_{st} = 10\%$	+4.218	+2.804	+2.584	+1.990
$u'_t = .9u_t$	+1.806	+1.480	+1.037	+0.799
$L'_t = .5L_t$	+3.192	+2.211	+2.380	+1.833
As percent of baseline				
All always at 1953-IV levels, SL dep.	-12.80	-8.74	-6.29	-4.86
Changes in 1973-I: $k'_{et} = 2k_{et}; k'_{st} = 10\%$	+4.60	+3.03	+6.38	+4.93
$u'_t = .9u_t$	+1.97	+1.60	+2.56	+1.98
$L'_t = .5L_t$	+3.48	+2.39	+5.88	+4.54
From equations without auto-correlation coefficients				
All always at 1953-IV levels, SL dep.	-11.768	-8.213	-1.341	-1.323
Changes in 1973-I: $k'_{et} = 2k_{et}; k'_{st} = 10\%$	+4.281	+2.840	+1.361	+1.342
$u'_t = .9u_t$	+1.699	+1.513	+0.546	+0.539
$L'_t = .5L_t$	+3.197	+2.244	+1.253	+1.236
As percent of baseline				
All always at 1953-IV levels, SL dep.	-12.77	-8.86	-3.33	+3.29
Changes in 1973-I: $k'_{et} = 2k_{et}; k'_{st} = 10\%$	+4.65	+3.07	+3.37	+3.34
$u'_t = .9u_t$	+1.84	+1.63	+1.35	+1.34
$L'_t = .5L_t$	+3.47	+2.42	+3.11	+3.08

a dollar of lost tax revenues from an increase in the investment tax credit would generate not much more than 30 cents in additional equipment investment, again without feedback from the rest of the model.

The effects in structures were considerably less in the original Chase equation—the 10 percent investment credit, for example, raising structures investment by only 3.37 percent of baseline. Our ρ' equations here made very little difference, as shown in Table 1–9—and as might have been anticipated from Table 1–2, which reported the estimated equation.

The Chase equations were estimated without the Cochrane-Orcutt autocorrelation correction. When we introduced the correction, the results were about the same in equipment but changed somewhat in structures. Here we find simulation of the original Chase equation estimated with the autocorrelation correction yielding a somewhat higher structures effect—6.38 percent of baseline for a 10 percent investment tax credit and similarly greater figures for changes in other tax parameters. Simulation of our ρ' equation, as in equipment, yields a lesser effect, however—only 4.9 percent of baseline.

DRI

The DRI simulations, shown in Table 1–10, offer the most dramatic confirmation of sensitivity of predicted results to equation specification and estimation. The original DRI model equation, with ρ containing its dividend–stock price component and with the combined pY/c variable, indicates that the setting of all tax parameters at the levels that existed in 1953-IV would have resulted in $36.8 billion 1972 dollars less equipment investment in 1977-IV, some 40 percent of baseline.[9] Simulation of the equation estimated with separate p/c and Y variables cut this effect by fully three-quarters, to $8.5 billion only 9.3 percent of baseline. The ρ' equation with separate p/c and Y reduced this smaller simulated effect by half again, to $4.5 billion or 4.9 percent of baseline.

9. The debt service variable in the DRI model makes it extremely difficult to simulate effects of changes in depreciation lives. The algorithm that DRI may have used in such simulations not proving available, we constructed our own. For computational convenience, we used constant tax lives for equipment and structures in performing the simulations, which began in 1954. The reported results in 1977–IV would have been changed slightly if historic tax lives had been used.

Table 1-10. DRI Simulations, Change in Investment, 1977-IV.

(1) Tax Parameters	(2)	(3)	(4)	(5)
		Equations		
	ρ	$\rho, p/c, Y$	ρ'	$\rho', p/c, Y$
Equipment				
Billions of 1972 dollars				
All always at 1953-IV levels,	-36.769	-8.518	-26.013	-4.475
Changes in 1973-I: $k'_{et} = 2k_{et}$	+13.075	+3.719	+11.333	+2.807
$u'_t = .9u_t$	+1.585	+0.509	-0.283	-0.074
$L'_t = .5L_t$	+8.010	+2.395	+5.208	+1.265
As percent of baseline				
All always at 1953-IV levels,	-39.90	-9.26	-28.38	-4.86
Changes in 1973-I: $k'_{et} = 2k_{et}$	+14.19	+4.04	+12.36	+3.05
$u'_t = .9u_t$	+1.72	+0.55	-0.31	-0.08
$L'_t = .5L_t$	+8.69	+2.60	+5.68	+1.37
Structures				
Billions of 1972 dollars				
All always at 1953-IV levels, SL Dep.	-11.997	-10.311	-10.030	-8.669
Changes in 1973-I: $k'_{st} = 8.1\%$	+2.754	+3.080	+3.396	+3.164
$u'_t = .9u_t$	+1.107	+1.132	+0.386	+0.248
$L'_t = .5L_t$	+3.335	+3.549	+3.333	+2.923
As percent of baseline				
All always at 1953-IV levels, SL Dep.	-27.53	-23.74	-22.87	-19.76
Changes in 1973-I: $k'_{st} = 8.1\%$	+6.33	+7.09	+7.74	+7.21
$u'_t = .9u_t$	+2.54	+2.61	+0.88	+0.57
$L'_t = .5L_t$	+7.67	+8.17	+7.60	+6.66

The original DRI model equations generate, along with MPS, the largest effects of tax incentives on equipment investment. The doubling of the investment tax credit for equipment beginning in 1973-I results in an increase in equipment spending of $13.1 billion 1972 dollars in 1977-IV, or 14 percent of baseline, according to our simulation. Splitting the pY/c variable again results in a huge decrease in the simulated effect, to $3.7 billion or 4.04 percent of baseline. Simulation of the ρ' equations makes a lesser difference but again reduces the predicted effects, to $2.81 billion in the equation with separate p/c and Y variables or 3.05 percent of baseline. Thus, given the 8.1 percent effective rate of credit in the DRI equipment equations, from a simulated effect of $1.75 of added equipment spending for each dollar of tax revenues lost through the investment tax credit indicated by the original DRI equation, we move to an indicated effect of only $0.38 of added equipment investment for each dollar of revenues lost from the investment tax credit when we worked with our modified ρ' equation with separate p/c and Y.

Similarly contrasting effects are to be found with the acceleration of depreciation and reduction in the corporate tax rate, although in the ρ' equations, the net effect on investment of a corporate tax reduction is slightly negative. The result stems from the greater effect of the lower u in raising the after tax cost of capital when that is made to depend wholly on deductible interest payments. In the original formulation, the adjusted dividend–stock price ratio component was presumably unaffected by changes in the corporate tax rate.

The halving of depreciation lives raised 1977-IV equipment investment by $8 billion 1972 dollars in the original DRI model equation, or 8.69 percent of baseline. The simulation with the p/c and Y split reduced the accelerated depreciation effect to $2.4 billion, or 2.60 percent of baseline. And the split with the ρ' equation lowered that predicted effect still further, to $1.3 billion, 1.37 percent of baseline or less than one-sixth of the effect shown in the original DRI equation.

Modification of the structures equation in the DRI model does not bring similar changes. As suggested earlier in our discussion of those equations, perhaps because structures spending is not that closely related to output over the preceding nine quarters, the coefficients of the pY/c variables in the original DRI structures equation were not high (nor were they statistically significant).

Reestimated equations did not therefore have much scope for reduced estimates, and indeed, the free p/c coefficient was slightly higher. Our structures simulation in fact showed somewhat greater additions to investment resulting from increasing or introducing the investment tax credit. As in equipment, the ρ' specification suggested sharply lesser effects of reducing the corporate tax rate than the original DRI ρ equation.

Michigan

We have done no simulations with the Michigan structures equations because they contain no tax parameters. Taxes indeed have mixed effects in the Michigan equipment equations.

Tax depreciation is defined as a rate rather than, as in the other models, in terms of length of life and method of depreciation, which feed into the present value term, z. In our Michigan depreciation simulations, therefore, we have doubled tax depreciation rates rather than halving lives. The particular form of the rental price of capital variable in the Michigan model, we may also note, is such that the partial derivative of rental price with respect to the rate of corporate taxation is negative unless (as was true according to the rates assumed in the Michigan model before 1962) the rate of tax depreciation plus the rate of price inflation was far less than the assumed rate of economic depreciation of one-sixth.

In all three of the equipment sectors, the Michigan simulations, as reported in Table 1–11, indicated only very small effects of the investment tax credit. In no case did doubling it in 1973 and thereafter raise equipment spending by more than 2.78 percent of baseline.

The corporate tax rate did in fact manifest a "perverse" effect, lowering it to 90 percent of its historical rate from 1973 on actually reduced equipment investment in most instances. Doubling the tax depreciation rate turned out, however, to have a very large effect. This would appear to be a consequence of the very large assumed tax depreciation rates of some 21 percent and 36 percent in recent years.

Our alternate c' equations, splitting relative price effects from the rental price variable, did not indicate consistent differences in simulated results. In some sectors, parameter changes suggested lesser effects on investment and in some cases greater effects.

Table 1-11. Michigan Simulations, Equipment (Production, Agriculture, and Other) and Structures, Change in Investment, 1977–IV.

(1) Tax Parameters	(2)	(3)	(4)	(5) Equations	(6)	(7)	(8)	(9)
	Equipment						Structures	
	EX, c	EX, c'	EA, c	EA, c'	EO, c	EO, c'	S, c	S, c'
Billions of 1972 dollars								
All always at 1953–IV levels, SL dep.	−2.870	−1.142	−0.053	+0.239	−4.501	−6.900	0	0
Changes in 1972–I:								
$k'_{et} = 2k_{et}$	+0.523	+0.218	+0.029	+0.078	+0.839	+1.298	0	0
$u'_t = .9u_t$	−0.363	−0.145	−0.008	+0.022	−0.579	−0.890	0	0
$TD'_t = 2TD_t$	+2.890	+1.150	+0.103	−0.043	+4.570	+7.034	0	0
As percent of baseline								
All always at 1953–IV levels, SL dep.	−15.24	−6.18	−1.01	+5.00	−6.45	−9.84	0	0
Changes in 1973–I:								
$k'_{et} = 2k_{et}$	+2.78	+1.18	+0.55	+1.62	+1.20	+1.85	0	0
$u'_t = .9u_t$	−1.93	−0.79	−0.15	+0.45	−0.83	−1.27	0	0
$TD'_t = 2TD_t$	+15.34	+6.22	+1.95	−0.91	+6.55	+10.03	0	0

71

MPS

The MPS simulations for equipment (Table 1–12) show extreme sensitivity to equation specification. Simulation of the original MPS equation with no constant term and with our estimated σ of 1.03 substituted for the specified σ of unity indicates very large effects of tax parameters on investment. Setting all tax parameters at 1953-IV levels leads to a predicted decline of equipment investment of over $25 billion by the fourth quarter of 1977, or 30.3 percent below baseline. When the equation including a constant term is used for simulation, that reduction is lessened to 23.3 percent. The ρ' equation without a constant term generates a predicted drop of 19.7 percent below baseline, while the ρ' equation with a constant term indicates a drop of only 6.81 percent, less than one-quarter of that suggested by the investment in equipment equation specified in the MPS model.

The other equipment simulations bring similarly contrasting results. Thus, the original ρ equation indicates that doubling the equipment tax credit beginning in 1973-I would cause an increase in equipment investment of $12.7 billion 1972 dollars, 15.12 percent of the baseline. The MPS orders for equipment equation with a constant term, however, generates a simulated reduction of only 10.68 percent of baseline. The ρ' equation, in which the interest rate is substituted for the dividend–stock price ratio, suggests an increase of only 8.28 percent of baseline. And the ρ' equation with a constant term knocks the added equipment investment down to 2.78 percent of baseline, only 18.4 percent of the effects indicated in the originally specified MPS model. Roughly similar, contrasting results are found with changes in the corporate tax rate and in the lives of assets used in depreciation for tax purposes.

The results of structure simulations in Table 1–12 are, as anticipated, not nearly as dramatic. Indeed here, since the introduction of a constant term somewhat raises the low estimates of σ, the simulated results suggest correspondingly somewhat greater effects on investment. Substituting the interest rate for the dividend–stock price ratio in the definition of ρ, however, does generally lower the predicted effects of tax parameters, particularly when the structures equation is estimated, as in the MPS model, without a constant term. In none of the structures equations, it may be noted, does increased investment come close to equaling the loss in tax revenues resulting

Table 1-12. MPS Simulations, Change in Investment, 1977-IV.

(1) Tax Parameters	(2)	(3)	(4)	(5)
		Equations		
	ρ	ρ with Constant Term	ρ'	ρ', with Constant Term
Equipment				
Billions of 1972 dollars				
Always at 1953-IV levels, SL dep.	−25.383	−20.273	−19.365	−6.621
Changes in 1973-I:				
$k'_{et} = 2k_{et}$	+12.656	+9.304	+8.133	+2.707
$u'_t = .9u_t$	+1.605	+1.190	+1.117	+0.372
$L'_t = .5L_t$	+7.790	+5.730	+4.967	+1.658
As percent of baseline				
All always at 1953-IV levels, SL dep.	−30.32	−23.26	−19.73	−6.81
Changes in 1973-I:				
$k'_{et} = 2k_{et}$	+15.12	+10.68	+8.28	+2.78
$u'_t = .9u_t$	+1.92	+1.37	+1.14	+0.38
$L'_t = .5L_t$	+9.30	+6.57	+5.06	+1.71
Structures				
Billions of 1972 dollars				
All always at 1953-IV, SL dep.	−1.449	−1.928	−1.141	−2.145
Changes in 1973-I:				
$k'_{st} = 8.5\%$	+2.420	+3.094	+1.824	+3.171
$u'_t = .9u_t$	+0.957	+1.222	+0.716	+1.240
$L'_t = .5L_t$	+2.452	+3.137	+1.840	+3.197
As percent of baseline				
All always at 1953-IV levels, SL dep.	−3.39	−4.61	−2.46	−4.60
Changes in 1973-I:				
$k'_{st} = 8.5\%$	+5.66	+7.40	+3.93	+6.80
$u'_t = .9u_t$	+2.24	+2.92	+1.54	+2.66
$L'_t = .5L_t$	+5.74	+7.50	+3.96	+6.86

from the tax incentives. This can be seen clearly again in the case of introduction of an investment tax credit of 10 percent beginning in the first quarter of 1973. In that simulation, resultant investment by the fourth quarter of 1977 increases over a range of from 3.93 percent of baseline to 7.4 percent of baseline, thus, given the 8.5 percent effective rate of investment tax credit in the MPS equipment equations, generating from 46 to 87 cents of added investment for each dollar of lost tax revenue. Of course, as in all of these simulations, the results relate only to the investment equations, without feedback from the rest of the model.

Wharton

The Wharton model calculates total aggregate investment expenditure and then divides the estimate between aggregate equipment and structures. Thus, the effects of alterations in tax parameters will tend to have symmetric effects on spending for equipment and structures. An increase of 10 percent in the investment tax credit rate for structures and a doubling of the rate for equipment beginning in 1973-I lead to an approximately 4.91 percent increase in nonresi-

Table 1-13. Wharton Simulations, Equipment and Structures Investment, Change in Investment, 1977-IV.

(1) Tax Parameters	(2)	(3)	(4)	(5)
		Equa	tion	
	Equipment		Structures	
	ρ	ρ'	ρ	ρ'
Billions of 1972 dollars				
Changes in 1973-I:				
$k'_{et} = 2k_{et}; k'_{st} = 10\%$	+5.100	+3.200	+2.400	+1.500
$u'_t = .9u_t$	+0.500	+0.200	+0.300	+0.100
$L'_t = .5L_t$	+2.100	+1.100	+1.000	+0.500
As percent of baseline				
Changes in 1973-I:				
$k'_{et} = 2k_{et}; k'_{st} = 10\%$	+4.88	+2.94	+4.96	+2.98
$u'_t = .9u_t$	+0.48	+0.18	+0.62	+0.20
$L'_t = .5L_t$	+2.01	+1.01	+2.07	+0.99

dential investment in the original Wharton equations and a 2.95 percent increase in our modified set, as reported in Table 1–13. In performing this simulation, we assumed that these increases in investment tax credit rates were such that the relative price between equipment and structures was not affected.[10]

A 10 percent cut in the corporate income tax rate had little effect on either set of estimates, with total investment approximately 0.53 and 0.19 percent higher than the baseline values in the original and modified equations, respectively. This low response is due to the recognition of the tax deductability of interest payments in the Wharton rental price of capital. Under sufficiently high rates of inflation (as exist currently), with interest deductability and a high value of tax depreciation, cuts in the corporate income tax rate can actually increase the rental price of capital.

SUMMARY AND CONCLUSION

Investment equations in the six models under consideration (BEA, Chase, DRI, Michigan, MPS, and Wharton) differ in specification, estimated parameters, and results. The results in the equipment equations have differed sharply, primarily as a result of differences in the implicit or explicit values of σ, the elasticity of investment with respect to the rental price of capital. Where there were high values of σ—whether due to a constraint tying the rental price of capital to output, as in DRI, constrained homogeneity (no constant term) in MPS, or use of the ratio of earnings or of dividends to stock prices as a component of the cost of capital (BEA, Chase, DRI, MPS, and Wharton)—even with a growth in earnings term, the impact of tax parameters on investment was high. Where σ did not have a high value, the impact was low.

The differences across models are striking. As shown in Table 1–14, our simulations of the original equipment investment equations indicate that doubling the equipment tax credit beginning in 1973 generated a range of effects on equipment investment by the fourth quarter of 1977 from a low of $1.4 billion 1972 dollars for Michigan to a high of $13.1 billion for DRI, with MPS not far behind. The BEA simulation indicted a high middle estimate of $9

10. We also assumed that the discrepencies between the National Income and BEA Survey data remained at their historic values.

billion while Chase and Wharton came in fairly low, at $4.3 and $5.1 billion, respectively. The mean figure from the six simulations was $7.6 billion, some 8.3 percent of actual equipment investment in 1977-IV.

Our preferred revised equations—eliminating the dividend–stock price ratio from the cost of capital variable, splitting output and the rental price of capital into separate variables in DRI, and removing the homogeneity constraint in MPS—bring drastic reductions in the effects of tax parameters in the original models. The Chase, DRI, and MPS results of doubling the investment tax credit for equipment are knocked down to the range of $2.7 to $2.8 billion. The BEA estimates remain relatively high, due apparently to the persistently high estimate of σ, 0.65 in our revised equation. All in all, simulations of our revised equations yield a mean increase in equipment investment of $3.5 billion, down to 3.8 percent of actual equipment investment and only 46.3 percent of the mean figure derived from simulation of the original equations.

Investment classified in the models as structures amounted to less than half of that in the equipment category and was generally much less responsive to tax parameters in simulations of the original model equations. There were no tax parameters in the Michigan structures equation; hence, changing tax parameters could have no effect on structures investment there. Over the other models, the range of effects from instituting a 10 percent credit for investment in structures varied considerably less than effects from the analogous doubling of the investment tax credit for equipment. Aside from Michigan, the range of predicted added investment in the original equations extended from $1.4 billion for Chase and BEA, to $2.4 billion for MPS, and a high of $2.8 billion for DRI. The mean for all five models was $1.7 billion, only 4.3 percent of actual structures investment.

In the case of structures investment, however, with the original equations containing explicit values of σ of 0.18629 and 0.36 and implicit values also generally low, as indicated by coefficients of rental price of capital variables, our revised equations offered results that were not substantially different from those of the original model equations. The mean of predicted increases in structures investment derived from our revised equations was identical to that for the original equations, calculated to the first decimal.

Thus, the effects on total business fixed investment of essentially adding ten percentage points of investment credit in both equipment

Table 1-14. Comparison of Simulations, Change in Investment, 1977–IV, Resulting from 1973–I Doubling of Investment Tax Credit for Equipment and Institution of 10 Percent Credit for Structures, Original and Revised Model Specifications, Billions of 1972 Dollars.

(1) Model	(2) Equipment Original	(3) Equipment Revised	(4) Structures Original	(5) Structures Revised	(6) Total Original	(7) Total Revised
BEA ($k_s' = 7.37\%$)	9.032	7.955	1.399	1.132	10.431	9.087
Chase	4.281	2.840	1.361	1.342	5.642	4.182
DRI ($k_s' = 8.1\%$)	13.075	2.807	2.754	3.164	15.829	5.971
Michigan	1.391	1.594	0	0	1.391	1.594
MPS ($k_s' = 8.5\%$)	12.656	2.707	2.420	3.171	15.076	5.878
Wharton	5.100	3.200	2.400	1.500	7.500	4.700
Mean	7.589	3.517	1.722	1.718	9.312	5.235
Actual Investment	91.507	91.507	40.149	40.149	131.656	131.656
Mean difference as percent of actual investment	8.29	3.84	4.29	4.28	7.07	3.98

and structures ranged, with the original model equations, from a low of $1.4 billion in the Michigan model to a high of $15.8 billion in the DRI model, a difference of over 1,000 percent. The mean of the disparate estimates came to $9.3 billion, or 7.07 percent of the actual investment figure of $131.7 billion. Because of our distinctly lower simulated results in equipment, our revised equations yielded, along with a smaller spread, a considerably lower mean of $5.2 billion, or 3.98 percent of total investment. In either set of equations, but of course a fortiori in the revised set, it may be noted that a 10 percent increase in the tax credit brought considerably less than 10 percent in added investment. The mean results from the original model equations suggest that each dollar of federal tax loss would result in about 84 cents of added investment. The revised equations offer a comparable figure of only 47 cents. Both sets of results ignore losses in state and local tax revenues, which in most cases are tied to federal tax calculations.[11]

All this, it must be recalled again, includes only the direct effects of changing tax parameters in the investment equations themselves. Full model simulations can alter the results, depending in each case on the extent and manner of feedback from other equations in the system. Some of that story, again, is to be found in Chirinko and Eisner (1981).

APPENDIX A. RENTAL PRICE AND OPPORTUNITY COST OF CAPITAL, BY MODEL

BEA

$$c_E = q_E(\rho_E - \dot{p}' + .38)(1 - .737379k_E - uz_E)/(1 - u)$$

$$\rho_e = .22i'(1 - .2u) + .001\frac{div}{SP}$$

$$c_s = q_s(\rho_s - \dot{p}' + .16)(1 - k_s - uz_s)/(1 - u) \qquad k_s = 0$$

$$\rho_s = 22i'(1 - .2u) + .4\frac{div}{SP}$$

---

11. In 1979, corporate tax payments to states came to 18.5 percent of corporate tax payments to the U.S. Treasury.

Chase

$$c_E = \frac{q_E(\rho_E + .181)(1 - k - uz_E)}{1 - u} \qquad \rho_E = \left(i + 2\frac{\text{prat}}{\text{SP}}\right)/3$$

$$c_S = \frac{q_s(\rho_s + .095)(1 - uz_s)}{1 - u} \qquad \rho_s = \left(i + \frac{\text{prat}}{\text{SP}}\right)/2$$

DRI

$$c_m = q_m (\rho + \delta_m)(1 - k_m - uz_m(1 - k_m Dk)/(1 - u) \qquad m = E,S$$

$$\rho = i(1 - u)wt + \left(\frac{\text{div}}{\text{SP}} + g\right)(1 - wt)$$

k_m = effective investment tax credit rate $\qquad (k_s = 0)$
u = effective corporate profits tax rate

Michigan

$$c_E = q_E \left\{i - \underline{\dot{\underline{p}}} + \frac{1}{6} - \frac{\left[\frac{k}{6} + \frac{5k}{6}DF + u\left(TD - \frac{1}{6} + \underline{\dot{\underline{p}}}\right)\right]}{1 - u}\right\}$$

$$c_s = q_s(i + .06)$$

MPS

$$c_E = q_E(\rho_E + \delta_E)\frac{(1 - k_E - uz_E)}{1 - u}$$

$$\rho_E = (1 - uv)\left(2\left[\frac{\text{div}}{\text{SP}} - .01\right] + \tilde{\sigma}_Y\right)$$

k_E = effective rate of investment tax credit

$$c_s = q_s(\rho_s + \delta_s)\frac{(1 - k_s - uz_s)}{1 - u} \qquad k_s = 0$$

$$\rho_s = (1 - uv)\ .05 + 2\frac{\text{div}}{\text{SP}}$$

Wharton

$$c_m^j = q_m(\rho + \delta^j)(1 - k_m - u_m z_m^j(1 - k_m Dk) - wt\, u^j i)/(1 - u^j)$$

$m = $ E, S

$j = $ AG,MG,MFD,MFN,COMU,UTIL,TRAN,COMMERCIAL (SIC sectors)

$\rho = wt\,(i - \dot{P}) + (1 - wt)$ div/SP

$k_m = $ effective investment tax credit rate ($k_S = 0$)

$u^j = $ effective corporate profits tax rate for sector j

$wt = .3868$

APPENDIX B. GLOSSARY OF VARIABLES

Variable	Description
ADP	Proportion of new investment depreciated using accelerated depreciation method
c	The user cost or rental price of capital
cd	Consumption expenditures, durables
cnd	Consumption expenditures, nondurables
CRED	Index of credit rationing
DASTRIKE	Dummy variable for auto strikes
DDB	Fraction of depreciation taken according to the double-declining method
DF	Discount factor
div	Average dividends per share
Dk	Dummy variables for the suspension of the investment tax credit
DP	Dummy variables to take account of double ordering during the price controls period (1973.4–1975.1)
DS	Debt service variable defined as the ratio of debt payments to gross cash flow
δ	The rate of economic depreciation
E	Investment expenditures on producers' durable equipment
$(E + S)^a$	Investment expenditures, producers' durable equipment and structures

$(E + S)^1$	Investment anticipations, producers' durable equipment and structures, one quarter ahead
$(E + S)^2$	Investment anticipations, producers' durable equipment and structures, two quarters ahead
g	Expected growth in earnings per share
i	The nominal rate of interest
i'	The expected nominal rate of interest
k	The rate of the investment tax credit
K	Capital stock, producers' durable equipment and structures
KE	Capital stock, producers' durable equipment
KS	Capital stock, producers' structures
L	Tax life of a capital good
NOR	New orders, all manufacturing, constant dollars
ORE	New orders for producers' durables, constant dollars
$OURE$	Unfilled orders for producers' durables, constant dollars
P	Price index
$\dot{P}$	Percentage change in the price index
$\dot{P}'$	Expected percentage change in the price index
$\dot{P}_F$	Percentage change in the price index of gross farm product
$\dot{P}_{NF}$	Percentage change in the price index of private, nonfarm GNP
$prat$	After tax corporate profits
q	The supply price of capital goods
ρ	The opportunity cost of capital
S	Investment expenditure on producers' structures
SL	Fraction of depreciation taken according to the straight line method
SP	Standard and Poor index of 500 stocks
SYD	Fraction of depreciation taken according to the sum of the years digit method
σ	The elasticity of substitution
$\tilde{\sigma}_x$	A measure of the variation in variable x
TD	Rate of tax depreciation
u	The rate of business income taxation
un	The rate of unemployment
UT	The rate of capacity utilization

UTP	The expected rate of capacity utilization
v	The proportion of the opportunity cost of capital that is tax deductible
VNWAR	A dummy variable for the Vietnam War period (1965.1–1966.4)
ω	The proportion of capital gains or losses effectively taxed
w	The wage rate
wt	Percentage of financing due to debt issue
Y	Level of output
Y'	Expected level of output
YC	Level of potential output
$Y\text{mil}$	Level of output, defense and space equipment
z	The original present value of the tax depreciation expected from a dollar of investment

REFERENCES

Bischoff, C.W. 1971. "Business Investment in the 1970s: A Comparison of Models." *Brookings Papers on Economic Activity* 1: 13–63.

Chirinko, R.S., and R. Eisner. 1980a "The Effects of Tax Parameters in the Investment Equations of Macroeconomic Econometric Models." Phase I. Washington, D.C.: U.S. Department of the Treasury, Office of Tax Analysis, February.

———. 1980b. "The Effects of Tax Parameters in the Investment Equations of Macroeconomic Econometric Models." Phase II. Washington, D.C.: U.S. Department of the Treasury, Office of Tax Analysis, May.

———. 1980c. "The Effects of Tax Parameters in the Investment Equations of Macroeconomic Econometric Models." Phase III. Washington, D.C.: U.S. Department of the Treasury, Office of Tax Analysis, August.

———. 1981. "The Effects of Tax Policies on Investment in Macroeconometric Models: Full Model Simulations." OTA Paper 46. Washington, D.C.: U.S. Department of the Treasury, Office of Tax Analysis, January.

Clark, P.K. 1979. "Investment in the 1970s: Theory, Performance and Prediction." *Brookings Papers on Economic Activity* 1: 73–124.

Coen, R.M. 1968. "Effects of Tax Policy on Investment in Manufacturing." *American Economic Review* 58 (May): 200–11.

————. 1969. "Tax Policy and Investment Behavior: Comment." *American Economic Review* 59 (June): 370–79.

Eisner, R. 1969a. "Investment and the Frustrations of Econometricians." *American Economic Review* 59 (May): 50–64.

————. 1969b. "Tax Policy and Investment Behavior: Comment." *American Economic Review* 59 (June): 379–88.

————. 1969c. "Fiscal and Monetary Policy Reconsidered." *American Economic Review* 59 (December): 897–905.

————. 1978. *Factors in Business Investment*. Cambridge, Massachusetts: Ballinger, for the National Bureau of Economic Research.

Eisner, R., and P.J. Lawler. 1975. "Tax Policy and Investment: An Analysis of Survey Responses." *American Economic Review* 65 (March): 206–12.

Eisner, R. and M.I. Nadiri. 1968. "On Investment Behavior and Neoclassical Theory." *Review of Economics and Statistics* 50 (August): 369–82.

————. 1970. "Neoclassical Theory of Investment Behavior: A Comment." *Review of Economics and Statistics* 52 (May): 216–22.

Eisner, R., and R.H. Strotz. 1963. "Determinants of Business Investment." In Commission on Money and Credit, *Impacts of Monetary Policy*, pp. 60–337. Englewood Cliffs, New Jersey: Prentice-Hall.

Fromm, G., ed. 1971. *Tax Incentives and Capital Spending*. Washington, D.C.: Brookings. [Includes papers by R.E. Hall and D.W. Jorgenson, C.W. Bischoff, R.M. Coen, L.R. Klein and P. Taubman, and discussion by F.M. Fisher and A.C. Harberger.]

Green, R.J. 1980. "Investment Determinants and Tax Factors in Major Macroeconometric Models." In G.M. von Furstenberg, *The Government and Capital Formation*, pp. 337–81. Cambridge, Massachusetts: Ballinger.

Hall, R.E., and D.W. Jorgenson. 1967. "Tax Policy and Investment Behavior." *American Economic Review* 57 (June): 391–414.

Hendershott, P.H., and S-C Hu. 1980. "The Relative Impacts of Various Proposals to Stimulate Business Investment." In G.M. von Furstenberg, *The Government and Capital Formation*, pp. 321–36. Cambridge, Massachusetts: Ballinger.

Hirsch, A.A.; S.H. Hymans; and H.T. Shapiro. 1978. "Econometric Review of Alternative Fiscal and Monetary Policies, 1971–75." *Review of Economics and Statistics* 60 (August): 334–45.

Joint Economic Committee. 1978. Economic Stabilization Policies: The Historical Record, 1962–76. [Including "Data Resources, Inc.—Fiscal Policy: The Scoreboard Between 1962 and 1976"; "Wharton Econometric Forecasting Associates, Inc.—A Study in Counter-Cyclical Policy"; and Comments by Arthur M. Okun and Alan Greenspan.]

Jorgenson, D.W. 1963. "Capital Theory and Investment Behavior." *American Economic Review* 53 (May): 247–59.

Kilpatrick, R.W. 1977. Private Memoranda of June 16, June 30, July 15, and August 4, from the Office of Management and Budget, on "Simulations of Investment Tax Incentives in the Chase and Wharton Models," "A Correction to My Previous Memo on Investment Tax Incentives," "The Effect of Tax Changes on the User Cost of Capital in Wharton, Chase, and DRI," and "Investment Tax Incentives and Capacity Utilization in the Chase Model." (Authorized for private use only.)

Klein, L.R., and E. Burmeister, ed. 1976. *Econometric Model Performance, Comparative Simulation Studies of the U.S. Economy.* Philadelphia: University of Pennsylvania Press.

Kopcke, R.W. 1977. "The Behavior of Investment Spending During the Recession and Recovery, 1973–76." *New England Economic Review* (November-December): 5–41.

_____. 1977. "The Outlook for Investment Spending to 1980." *New England Economic Review* (November/December): 42–59.

Lucas, R.E., Jr. 1976. "Econometric Policy Evaluation: A Critique." In Karl Brunner and Allan H. Meltzer, *The Phillips Curve and Labor Markets,* pp. 19–46. Amsterdam: North-Holland.

McClain, D. 1979. "The Recent Tracking Performance of Business Fixed Investment Equations in Four Large-Scale Econometric Models." Private Memorandum of April 16 at Council of Economic Advisers.

McKee, M. 1978. Private Memoranda of December 8, 1978, and December 27, 1978, written at the Council of Economic Advisers, entitled "The Ponies."

_____. 1979. Private Memorandum of January 26, 1979, entitled "Determinants of Investment."

McNees, S.K. 1979. "The Forecasting Record for the 1970s." *New England Economic Review* (September-October): 1–21.

Nerlove, M. 1966. "A Tabular Survey of Macro-Econometric Models." *International Economic Review* 7 (May): 127–75.

Sargent, T.J. 1981. "Interpreting Economic Time Series." *Journal of Political Economy* 89 (April): 213–48.

Taubman, P., and T.J. Wales. 1969. "The Impact of Investment Subsidies in a Neoclassical Theory of Investment Behavior." *Review of Economics and Statistics* 51 (August): 287–97.

2 DEMOGRAPHIC VARIABLES IN DEMAND ANALYSIS AND WELFARE ANALYSIS

Robert A. Pollak
University of Pennsylvania
and
Terence J. Wales
University of British Columbia

INTRODUCTION

Demographic variables such as family size and age composition are major determinants of household consumption patterns. In the first section we describe five general procedures for incorporating demographic variables into complete demand systems—that is, demand systems describing the allocation of expenditure among an exhaustive set of consumption categories. The procedures are general in the sense that they do not assume that the original demand system has a particular functional form, but can be used in conjunction with any complete demand system. Some of the procedures we discuss are new, while others have been proposed or estimated before by ourselves or others. In the second section we use these procedures to incorporate a single demographic variable, the number of children in the family, into a "generalized CES" demand sytem. We present estimates of this system based on British

Pollak's research was supported in part by the National Science Foundation, the U.S. Bureau of Labor Statistics, and the National Institutes of Health. Wales' research was supported in part by the Canada Council. This chapter is a revised and expanded version of material that originally appeared in Pollak and Wales (1979) and (1981). We are grateful to B.K. Atrostic and John Bigelow for useful comments on an earlier draft and to Judith Lachterman for editorial assistance.

household budget data for the period 1966–72 and compare these procedures with each other and with two alternative specifications— a "pooled" specification in which data from different household types are combined under the assumption that demographic variables do not affect household consumption patterns and an "unpooled" specification in which data from different household types are treated separately under the assumption that demographic variables affect all demand system parameters.

In the third section we examine the role of demographic variables in welfare analysis. In demand analysis, equivalence scales permit us to pool data from households of different sizes or, more generally, with different demographic profiles; such scales are usually estimated from the observed data on household consumption patterns. In welfare analysis, equivalence scales purport to answer questions of the form: What expenditure level would make a family with three children as well off as it would be with two children and $12,000? We argue that the equivalence scales required for welfare analysis ("unconditional equivalence scales") are logically distinct from those that arise in demand analysis ("conditional equivalence scales"). Conditional equivalence scales can be estimated from observed differences in the consumption patterns of households with different demographic profiles (e.g., different number of children). The usual practice is to base welfare comparisons on these conditional equivalence scales. This is illegitimate. The expenditure level required to make a three child family as well off as it would be with two children and $12,000 depends on how the family feels about children: Observed differences in the consumption patterns of two and three child families cannot even tell us whether the third child is regarded as a blessing or a curse. Constructing unconditional equivalence scales requires more information than household consumption data contain, even if households regard demographic characteristics as fixed or predetermined. If households regard demographic profiles as decision variables, then unconditional preferences might be inferred from their unconditional choices (e.g., choices of family size and a consumption vector). We conclude by suggesting that the widespread belief that different treatments of various family types (e.g., in tax or family allowance schedules or income maintenance programs) are appropriate need not rest on comparing their welfare levels. The last section is a brief summary.

GENERAL PROCEDURES

This section discusses five general procedures for incorporating demographic variables into classes of demand systems and the related notion of "economies of scale in consumption." We begin with an original class of demand systems, $\{x_i = h^i(P,\mu)\ i = 1,\ldots,n\}$ where p denotes prices, x's quantities, and μ total expenditure.[1] We assume that these original demand systems are "theoretically plausible"—that is, that they can be derived from "well-behaved" preferences—and we denote the corresponding indirect utility function by $\psi(P,\mu)$ (the direct utility function by $U(X)$). Each procedure replaces this original class of demand systems by a related class involving additional parameters and postulates that only these additional parameters depend on the demographic variables. The specification is completed by postulating a functional form relating these newly introduced parameters to the N demographic variables, $(\eta_1,\ldots,\eta_N)$.[2]

The five procedures we consider are demograpic translating; demographic scaling; the "Gorman procedure," a specification that includes both translating and scaling as special cases; the "reverse Gorman procedure," a new procedure that is a mirror image of Gorman's procedure; and a specification we call the "modified Prais-Houthakker procedure." Finally, we discuss "economies of scale in consumption."

---

1. We distinguished between "expenditure" (i.e., total expenditure on the consumption categories included in our analysis) and "income" (i.e., receipts, as reported in our data). Consumption categories can be broad aggregates such as "food," "clothing," etc.

2. The treatment of demographic effects in the context of theoretically plausible demand systems dates from Barten (1964). Recent work in this vein includes Parks and Barten (1973), Lau, Lin and Yotopoulos (1978), Muellbauer (1977), and Pollak and Wales (1978, 1980). In this respect the classic work of Prais and Houthakker (1955) is the culmination of an earlier tradition that analyzed the demand for each good separately and without reference to utility maximization. Prais and Houthakker use expenditure as their independent variable and construct an exhaustive set of consumption categories. But they rely on a single equation rather than a complete system approach, and most of their estimates are based on double log and semi log demand equations that, when summed over all goods, do not satisfy the budget identity see Prais and Houthakker (1955: 83–85) for a discussion of the "adding up" problem. Maximum likelihood estimation of complete demand systems takes full account of the budget constraint in the demand equations and the stochastic structure.

Demographic Translating

Demographic translating replaces the original demand system by

$$h^i(P,\mu) = d_i + h^{-i}(P,\mu - \Sigma p_k d_k) \tag{2.1}$$

where the ds are translation parameter that depends on the demographic variables $d_i = D^i(\eta)$.[3] Translating can sometimes be interpreted as allowing "necessary" or "subsistence" parameters of a demand system to depend on the demographic variables.[4] If the original demand system is theoretically plausible, then the modified system is also, at least when d is close to zero. The modified system satisfies the first-order conditions corresponding to the indirect utility function $\bar\psi(P,\mu) = \bar\psi(P,\mu - \Sigma p_k d_k)$ and the direct utility function $U(X) = \bar U(x_1 - d_1, \ldots, x_n - d_n)$.

When translating is used to introduce demographic characteristics into complete demand systems, there is a close relation between the effects of changes in demographic variables and the effects of changes in total expenditure. The total effect on $p_i h^i$ of a change in η_t is given by

$$\frac{\partial p_i h^i}{\partial \eta_t} = p_i \frac{\partial D^i}{\partial \eta_t} - \frac{\partial p_i h^i}{\partial \mu} \Sigma p_k \frac{\partial D^k}{\partial \eta_t} \tag{2.2}$$

where $\partial p_i h^i / \partial \mu$ is "the marginal budget share" for the ith good. Notice that μ appears in this expression only through the marginal budget share, while prices enter through the marginal budget share (which, in general, depends on all prices and expenditure) and also linearly through the terms $p_i \partial D^i / \partial \eta_t$ and $\Sigma p_k \partial D^k / \partial \eta_t$. The former represents a "specific effect" of the change in η_t on the value of $p_i h^i$, while the latter, after multiplication by the marginal budget share,

3. Σ without indexes or limits of summation means $\Sigma_{k=1}^n$.
4. Demographic translating was first employed by Pollak and Wales (1978). Gorman (1976) describes a more general procedure that includes demographic translating and demographic scaling as special cases.
5. In some cases this interpretation is misleading. There are two distinct problems. First, d can be negative. Second, with some demand systems, regularity conditions require d_i to be greater than x_i, and in these cases, it is more natural to interpret d as "bliss points" than as "necessary quantities." The demand system generated by the addictive quadratic direct utility function provides a familiar example See Samuelson (1947: 93) or Pollak (1971).

represents a "general effect" operating through all of the translation parameters.[6].

A change in η_t causes a reallocation of expenditure among the consumption categories, but since total expenditure remains unchanged, any increases in the consumption of some goods must be balances by decreases in the consumtpion of others. The sign of the effect on $p_i h^i$ of a change in η_t cannot be inferred from the sign of its effect on d_{ij}; changes in the demographic variables affect all of the ds simultaneously, and the specific effect, $p_i \partial D^i/\partial\eta_t$, may be outweighed by the general effect $(\partial p_i h^i/\partial\eta)(\Sigma p_k \partial D^k/\partial\eta_t)$. Furthermore, there is no a priori presumption that an increase in a demographic variable such as family size will increase rather than decrease d_i since changes in the ds, regardless of their direction, imply a reallocation of expenditure among the goods but leave total expenditure unchanged.[7]

Under demographic translating, the effects of changes in different demographic variables are closely related to one another. From equation (2.2) we see that $\partial p_i h^i/\partial\eta_t$ depends linearly on the n derivatives $\partial D^k/\partial\eta_t$. The coefficients of these derivatives are simply p_k times the marginal budget share of good i, and these coefficients are the same regardless of which demographic variable we are considering. Since the term $\Sigma p_k \partial D^k/\partial\eta_t$ is independent of the good whose response we are considering, it is easy to establish a relationship between the effects of a change in a particular demographic variable on different goods, but the resulting equations are not particularly enlightening.

Linear demographic translating

$$D^i(\eta) = \sum_{r=1}^{N} \delta_{ir} \eta_r \qquad (2.3)$$

6. This distinction between "specific" and "general" effects presupposes that demographic effects operate through demographic translating. In the next section we describe an alternative decomposition that presupposes demographic scaling. Neither coincides with the Prais and Houthakker distinction between "specific scales" and "income scales" that we discuss in Section 1D.

7. In contrast, in models of habit formation a change in the past consumption of x_i influences a parameter analogous to d_i but leaves parameters analogous to the other ds unchanged (see Pollak 1970). Hence, the effect of a change in past consumption of a particular good can be inferred because the "general effect" cannot outweigh the "specific effect" unless the marginal budget share is greater than unity.

provides a convenient specification of the function relating the translating parameters to the demographic variables and is the one we estimate.[8] With linear demographic translating, equation (2.2) becomes

$$\frac{\partial p_i b^i}{\partial \eta_t} = p_i \delta_{it} - \frac{\partial p_i b^i}{\partial \mu} \Sigma p_k \delta_{kt} \tag{2.4}$$

Linear demograpic translating adds at most $n \times N$ independent parameters to the original demand system.[9]

Demographic Scaling

Demographic scaling replaces the original demand system by

$$b^i(P,\mu) = m_i b^{-i}(p_1 m_1, \ldots, p_n m_n, \mu) \tag{2.5}$$

where the ms are scaling parameters which depend on the demographic variables—$m_i = M^i(\eta)$.[10] If the original demand system is theoretically plausible, then the modified system is also, at least for ms close to one. The modified system satisfies the first-order conditions corresponding to the indirect utility function $\psi(P,\mu) = \bar{\psi}(p_1 m_1, \ldots, p_n m_n, \mu)$ the direct utility function $U(X) = \bar{U}(x_1/m_1, \cdot_1 \cdot \cdot, x_n/m_n)$.

If the scaling functions are the same for all goods, we can interpret their common value as reflecting the number of "equivalent adults" in the household. If the scaling functions differ from one good to another, then m_i measures the number of equivalent adults on a scale

8. We have not included constant terms in the definition of linear demographic translating (as we unfortunately did in Pollak and Wales 1978 because such constants are better treated as part of the specification of the original demand system than as part of the demographic specification. Regardless of whether constant terms are treated as part of the demographic specification or the original demand system, they should be included whenever demographic translating is used; any demand system that does not include "translation parameters" (i.e., constant terms) can easily be modified to incorporate them. If linear demographic translating is applied to a demand system that does not include translation parameters and if the original system is misspecified (i.e., if the true system includes translation parameters), then a demographic variable that exhibits little variation may appear significant because it acts as a proxy for the omitted constant terms.

9. "At most" because in some demand systems (e.g., the nonhomogeneous fixed coefficient system) not all of the ds are identified.

10. Demographic scaling was first proposed by Barten (1964); see Muellbauer (1977) for a recent discussion of demographic scaling and an attempt to test it.

appropriate to good i. In either case we can view both preferences and demand behavior in terms of demographically scaled prices and quantities. That is, we can interpret the household's preferences as depending not on the number of gallons of milk it consumes, but on gallons per (milk) equivalent adult. Similarly, the relevant price—the price corresponding to x_i/m_i—is not the price per gallon, but the price per gallon per (milk) equivalent adult, $p_i m_i$. The interpretation of the m as commodity-specific "equivalent adults" should not be taken too literally. Indeed, there is not even a presumption that an increase in a demographic variable will increase rather than decrease the m, since changes in the m, regardless of their direction, imply a reallocation of expenditure among the goods but leave its total unchanged.

Under demographic scaling, the effects of changes in demographic variables are closely related to the effects of price changes. The relationship is most clearly visible in elasticity form. Let E_k^i denote the elasticity of demand for the ith good with respect to the kth price and $\hat{M}_t^k$ the elasticity of m_k with respect to η_t. Then it is easy to verify by differentiating equation (2.5) that the elasticity of demand for the ith good with respect to η_t, E_t^i, is given by [11]

$$E_t^i = \hat{M}_t^i + \Sigma \, E_k^i M_t^k \quad [12] \tag{2.6}$$

We can use this formula to decompose the impact on good i of a change in a demographic variable into a "specific" and a "general" effect. [13] The specific effect is the elasticity of m_i with respect to the demographic variable; the general effect is a weighted sum of elasticities of all the ms with respect to the demographic variable, with the price elasticities as weights. This decomposition suggests that the sign of E_t^i, the effect of η_t on h^i, cannot be inferred from the sign of $\hat{M}_t^i$, its effect on m_i, since the general effect may outweigh the specific effect.

With demographic scaling, as with demographic translating, the effects of changes in different demographic variables are closely related. From equation (2.6), E_t^i is a weighted sum of $\hat{M}_t^k$ values, and

11. Somewhat inelegantly, but without loss of clarity, we denote the elasticity of the ith good with respect to the price of goods i, j, and k by E_i^i, E_j^i, and E_k^i and the elasticity with respect to the demographic variables r, s, and t by E_r^i, E_s^i, and E_t^i. We use k as a summation index for goods and r as a summation index for the demographic variables.

12. When appears to be a very simple way to obtain the results of Muellbauer (1974: 105) and Barten (1964: 282).

13. This decomposition presupposes that demographic effects are incorporated by scaling.

the weights, which involve price elasticities, are the same for all demographic variables. It is only through these weights that prices and expenditures enter the demographic elasticities. It is possible to eliminate a cross-price elasticity between the equations for E_t^i and E_r^i, but the resulting expression is not particularly transparent.

Linear demographic scaling, the specification we estimate, is given by

$$M^i(\eta) = 1 + \sum_{r=1}^{N} \epsilon_{ir} \eta_r \qquad (2.7)$$

Linear demographic scaling adds at most $n \times N$ independent parameters to the original demand.[14,15] If the ϵs are independent of i, then the common value of the ms reflects the number of equivalent adults in the households.

With "log linear demographic scaling"

$$M^i(\eta) = \sum_{r=1}^{N} (\eta_r)^{\epsilon_{ir}} \qquad (2.8)$$

the ϵs are the elasticities of the ms with respect to the demographic

14. In certain exceptional cases, not all of the n scaling parameters are identified. The demand system implied by the Cobb-Douglas utility function provides an extreme example in which none of the ms are identified.

15. It might seem natural to include a multiplicative constant in the specification of linear demographic scaling:

$$M^i(\eta) = m_i^* \left[1 + \sum_{r=1}^{N} \epsilon_{ir} \eta_r \right]$$

We have not done so for two reasons. First, such a constant term is better described as part of the specification of the original demand system than as part of the demographic specification. Second, the m^*s are not identified in any class of demand systems that is "closed under unit scaling." (A demand system is closed under unit scaling if, whenever some demand system in the class is exactly consistent with the data in one set of units and the data are rescaled in new units, then there exists another demand system in the class that is exactly consistent with the rescaled data). We believe that only closed classes of demand systems should be used for empirical demand analysis. Any class not closed under unit scaling can easily be generalized to one that is. Virtually all classes of demand systems that have been used in demand analysis are closed under unit scaling; Diewert's "Generalized Cobb-Douglas' appears to be the only exception (see Wales and Woodland 1976; no. 10; and Berndt, Darrough, and Diewert 1977; 11).

variables and equation (2.6) becomes

$$E_t^i = \epsilon_{it} + \Sigma E_k^i \, \epsilon_{kt} \qquad (2.9)$$

Gorman Specification

Gorman (1976) proposes a specification that replaces the original demand system by

$$b^i(P,\mu) = d_i + m_i b^{-i}(p_1 m_1, \ldots, p_n m_n, \mu - \Sigma p_k d_k) \qquad (2.10)$$

where the ds and the ms (and only these parameters) depend on the demographic variables. This demand system is theoretically plausible (at least for ds near zero and ms near one) and is generated by the indirect utility function $\psi(P,\mu = \bar{\psi}(p_1 m_1, \ldots, p_n m_n, \mu - \Sigma p_k d_k)$ (the direct utility function $U(X) = \bar{U}(x_1 - d_1/m_1, \ldots, x_n - d_n/m_n))$. Demographic translating (demographic scaling) corresponds to the special case in which the ms are unity (the ds are zero). Gorman's specification can be obtained from the original demand system by first scaling and then translating.

The "reverse Gorman" specification is obtain by first translating and then scaling. This yields the demand system

$$b^i(P,\mu) = m_i[d_i + b^{-i}(p_1 m_1, \ldots, p_n m_n, \mu - \Sigma p_k m_k d_k)] \qquad (2.11)$$

which satisfies the first-order conditions corresponding to the indirect utility function $\psi(P,\mu) = \bar{\psi}(p_1 m_1, \ldots, p_n m_n, \mu - \Sigma p_k m_k d_k)$ (the direct utility function $U(X) = \bar{U}(x_1/m_1 - d_1, \ldots, x_n/m_n - d_n))$.

If we impose particular forms for $D(\eta)$ and $M(\eta)$, then the Gorman and reverse Gorman procedures are distinct and the reverse Gorman procedure is new.[16] For example, suppose the original demand system is linear in expenditure and we require linear forms for $D(\eta)$ and $M(\eta)$. Then the reverse Gorman specification yields demand functions quadratic in the demographic variables, while the Gorman specification implies demand functions linear in them.

Postulating that the ds and ms are linear functions of the

16. If we do not impose particular forms, these procedures are not distinct. This follows immediately from the observation that when we define new variables d_i by $d_i = d_i m_i$ and new functions $D^i(\eta)$ by $D^i(\eta) = D^i(\eta) M^i(\eta)$, substituting the new variables into the reverse Gorman specification yields the Gorman specification.

demographic variables allows us to test linear translating and linear scaling against more general hypotheses. The specifications we estimate—

$$D^i(\eta) = v \sum_{r=1}^{N} \beta_{ir} \eta_r \qquad (2.12)$$

and

$$M^i(\eta) = 1 + (1 - v) \sum_{r=1}^{N} \beta_{ir} \eta_r \qquad (2.13)$$

requires only one more parameter than either linear translating or linear scaling separately; translating corresponds to $v = 1$, and scaling to $v = 0$.[17]

The Modified Prais-Houthakker Procedure

The "modified Prais-Houthakker procedure" replaces the original demand system by

$$h^i(P,\mu) = s_i h^{-i}(P,\mu/s_o) \qquad (2.14)$$

where the s_is, $i = 1,\ldots,n$, are "specific scales" for commodities that depend on the demographic variables, $s_i = S^i(\eta)$, and s_o is an "income scale" implicitly defined by the budget constraint

$$\Sigma p_k s_k h^{-k}(P,\mu/s_o) = \mu \qquad (2.15)$$

Thus, the income scale is a function of all prices and expenditures as well as the demographic variables—$s_o = S^o(P,\mu,s_1,\ldots,s_n)$.[18]

Prais and Houthakker (1955: 9) proposed a technique for

17. Replacing v by v_i in equations (2.12) and (2.13) yields a more general specification that allows the balance between translating and scaling to differ for different goods. With one demographic variable, allowing the v_is to differ is equivalent to assuming that $D(\eta)$ and $M(\eta)$ are unrestricted linear forms given by equations (2.3) and (2.7).

18. If the left-hand side of equation (2.15) is an increasing function of μ/s_o then it defines s_o uniquely; the absence of inferior goods is sufficient to guarantee this.

incorporating demographic variables into demand equations using a single income scale and a specific scale for each good, but they never reconciled their technique with an overall budget constraint. They use data from a single budget study to estimate the effects of changes in demograpic variables and expenditure (but not prices) on household consumption patterns. Their proposal should be viewed against the background of earlier techniques.[19] Given a body of household budget data, the simplest way to introduce a single demographic variable such as family size is to postulate that per capita consumption of each good is a function of per capita expenditure. This per capita approach treats all types of individuals (e.g., adults and children) as identical and does not allow for systematic differences in their "needs" or "requirements." This defect can be remedied by postulating an "equivalence scale" that converts the household's demographic profile, η, into the corresponding number of "equivalent adults" and makes consumption per "equivalent adult" a function of expenditure per equivalent adult. This implies expenditure equations (with prices suppressed) of the form $p_i x_i / s = \phi^i(\mu/s)$ or $p_i x_i = s \, \phi^i(\mu/s)$, where s is given by $s = S(\eta)$.[20,21] But this specification assumes a single equivalence scale for all goods—the same for food as for housing, for milk as for beer. The Prais-Houthakker proposal avoids this assumption by introducing separate "specific scales" for each good. In particular, it postulates that the expenditure equations can be written as $p_i x_i = s_i \phi^i(\mu/s_0)$.[22]

Muellbauer (1977, 1980) proposes defining the income scale

19. Prais and Houthakker (1955: 126) provide references to this literature and note that their view is "essentially that expressed by Sydenstricker and King" (1921).

20. For example, adult males = 1, adult females = 0.9, children under two = 0.1.

21. In suppressing prices we have followed Prais and Houthakker and the equivalence scale literature; since its focus was on the analysis of data from a single budget study, ignoring prices was relatively harmless. Barten (1964) was the first to emphasize the role of prices in connection with demographic variables, but he was primarily interested in using variations in demographic characteristics instead of variations in prices to identify all of the parameters of a theoretically plausible demand system. Muellbauer (1974) argues that Barten's contention that demographic scaling permits us to dispense with price variation is incorrect; in any event, Barten's use of prices in conjunction with demographic variables in a complete demand system framework is an important development.

22. Prais and Houthakker (1955: 128) assume a linear form for the specific scales. They are less explicit about the way the income scale depends on the demographic variables, but they do assume that it is independent of expenditure, as is clear from their calculation of the income (i.e., expenditure) elasticity (1955: 129). Barten (1964: 283–86) also interprets the Prais-Houthakker techniques as requring the income scale to be independent of expenditure.

implicitly through the budget constraint.[23] If the specific scales are identical for all goods, then equation (2.15) implies that the income scale is also equal to this common value, which we can interpret as the number of "equivalent adults" in the household. Furthermore, with identical specific scales for all goods, the modified Prais-Houthakker procedure is equivalent to scaling with identical scaling functions for all goods.[24]

The modified Prais-Houthakker procedure, unlike the other procedures we have considered, need not yield a theoretically plausible demand system. Indeed, we show that it does so only in very special cases and conjecture that it does so if and only if the original demand system corresponds to an additive direct utility function. Two theorems (whose proofs are given in Appendix A of this chapter) lend credence to this conjecture.

Theorem 1: If the modified Prais-Houthakker procedure is applied to a demand system corresponding to an additive direct utility function

$$\bar{U}(X) = \Sigma u^{-k}(x_k) \tag{2.16}$$

then the resulting demand system is theoretically plausible and corresponds to the additive direct utility function

$$U(X) = \Sigma s_k u^{-k}(x_k/s_k) \tag{2.17}$$

Theorem 2: If the modified Prais-Houthakker procedure is applied to a theoretically plausible demand system linear in expenditure, then the resulting demand system is theoretically plausible only if the original demand system corresponds to an additive direct utility function.[25]

23. Muellbauer puts forward his proposal in the context of demand sytems that rule out substitution in response to relative price changes and argues that this restriction is needed to permit welfare comparisons between households with different demographic profiles. We reject his welfare comparisons even in the no substitution case, for reasons discussed in Section 3. Regardless of one's views on welfare comparisons, the no substitution restriction is unnecessary for analyzing the effects of demographic differences on consumption patterns, so that Muellbauer's proposal can be used to define empirically interesting demand specifications. The name "modified Prais-Houthakker" procedure is ours.

24. Proof: Since the demand functions are homogeneous of degree zero in prices and expenditure, the income scale can be viewed as multiplying all prices instead of dividing expenditure.

25. The proof also assumes that $n \geq 3$, that no good has a zero marginal budget share, and that the utility and demand functions are differentiable enough to support the calculus arguments employed in Pollak (1976). If $n = 2$, then the mathematical integrability conditions are automatically satisfied.

We illustrate the modified Prais-Houthakker procedure using an original demand system linear in expenditure, since in this case we can solve the budget identity to obtain an explicit expression for the income scale and a closed form expression for the demand equations. Gorman (1961) established that any theoretically plausible demand system linear in expenditure can be written in the form

$$h^i(P,\mu) = f_i - \frac{g_i}{g}f + \frac{g_i}{g}\mu = f_i + \gamma^i(\mu - f) \tag{2.18}$$

where $\gamma^i = g_i/g$ and $f(P)$ and $g(P)$ are functions homogeneous of degree one. Using the modified Prais-Houthakker procedure, we write the demand functions as

$$h^i(P,\mu) = s_i f_i + s_i \gamma^i\left(\frac{\mu}{s_0} - f\right) \tag{2.19}$$

where s_0 is defined by

$$\Sigma p_k s_k f_k + \Sigma p_k s_k \gamma^k \left(\frac{\mu}{s_0} - f\right) = \mu \tag{2.20}$$

To find the implied demand functions, we solve equation (2.20) for $\mu/s_0 - f$ and substitute into equation (2.19) to obtain

$$h^i(P,\mu) = s_i f_i + \frac{s_i \gamma^i}{\Sigma p_k s_k \gamma^k}(\mu - \Sigma p_k s_k f_k) \tag{2.21}$$

We can solve equation (2.20) explicitly for the income scale

$$S(P,\mu,s_1,\ldots,s_n) = \frac{\mu \Sigma p_k s_k \gamma^k}{\mu - \Sigma p_k s_k f_k + f \Sigma p_k s_k \gamma^k} \tag{2.22}$$

which clearly depends on prices and expenditures as well as on the specific scales.[26]

With the modified Prais-Houthakker procedure, the effects of changes in the demographic variables are closely related to the effects of changes in expenditure. The relationship can be stated most clearly in elasticity form, where E_0^i and $\hat{S}_0^0$ denote the expenditure elasticities of h^i and S^0, and $\hat{S}_t^i$ and $\hat{S}_t^0$, the elasticities of S^i and S^0 with respect to the demographic variable η_t. Taking the logarithmic

26. If the original demand system exhibits expenditures proportionality $h^i(P,\mu) = \gamma^i(P)\mu$, then the income scale is independent of expenditures.

derivatives of equation (2.14) with respect to μ and η_t, it is easy to verify that

$$E^i_t = S^i_t - \frac{E^i_o S^o_t}{1 - S^o_o} \qquad (2.23)$$

Using this formula, we can decompose the effect of a change in a demographic variable into a "specific effect" and a "general effect."[27] The specific effect is the elasticity of s_i with respect to the demographic variable; the general effect is the product of the elasticity of s_o and h^i. This decomposition implies that the sign of E^i_t cannot be inferred from a knowledge of $\hat{S}^i_t$ alone, since the general effect need not operate in the same direction as the specific effect and may outweigh it.[28] It is tempting to associate the decomposition with the Prais-Houthakker distinction (1955: 129) between "specific scales" and "income scales," but because the modified Prais-Houthakker procedure is not identical to the Prais-Houthakker technique, the association is rather loose.

The "linear modified Prais-Houthakker procedure"

$$S^i(\eta) = 1 + \sum_{r=1}^{N} \sigma_{ir}\eta_r \qquad (2.24)$$

provides a convenient specification of the function relating the specific scale parameters to the demographic variables and is the one we estimate.[29] It adds at most $n \times N$ independent parameters to the original demand system.[30] If the σs are independent of i, then the

27. This decomposition presupposes that demographic effects operate as specified by the modified Prais-Houthakker procedure.

28. There are some obvious cases in which inferences are possible. For example, if the income elasticity is zero, then $E^i_t = S^i_t$. If the signs of S^i_t, S^o_t, S^o_o, and E^i_o are known, then we can determine the sign of E^i_t in those cases in which the specific effect and the general effect work in the same direction.

29. As with translating and scaling, we have not included constant terms in our specification of the linear modified Prais-Houthakker procedure because we prefer to treat such constants as part of the original demand system.

30. For example, if the original demand system corresponds to a Cobb-Douglas utility function, $h^i(P,\mu) = (a_i/\Sigma a_k) \cdot (\mu/p_i)$, then the modified Prais-Houthakker procedure yields $h^i(P, \mu) = (a_i s_i/\Sigma a_k s_k) \cdot (\mu/p_i)$. The as in the original system are not all identified—only $n-1$ of them are independent identifiable parameters—and similarly, with this demand system the linear modified Prais-Houthakker procedure involves only $N \times (n-1)$ independent parameters. The situation is similar for other demand systems exhibiting expenditure proportionality and corresponding to additive direct utility functions—the CES and the Leontief or homogeneous fixed coefficient system.

scales are the same for all goods, and the modified Prais-Houthakker procedure is equivalent to scaling. In the "log linear modified Prais-Houthakker procedure"

$$S^i(\eta) = \prod_{r=1}^{N} (\eta_r)^{\sigma_{ir}} \qquad (2.25)$$

the σs are the elasticities of the ss with respect to demographic variables, and equation (2.23) becomes

$$E^i_t = \sigma_{it} - \frac{E^i_o S^o_t}{1 - \hat{S}^o_o} \qquad (2.26)$$

Economies of Scale in Consumption

"Economies of scale in consumption" is the rubric of empirical demand analysis under which investigators explore alternative functional forms relating demographic variables to parameters of demand systems.[31] In this section we discuss a quadratic generalization of the linear specification thus far considered.

Demographic translating places no restrictions on the form of the functions $\{\#D^i(h)\$\}$, but in equation (2.3) we emphasized linear demographic translating. One straightforward and tractable generali-

31. A different notion of "economies of scale in consumption" involves welfare comparisons between households with different demographic profiles; that notion is defined in terms of the effect of an increase in family size on the expenditure required to attain a particular standard of living. Although Prais and Houthakker (1955: 10) use welfare considerations to motivate their discussion of economies of scale in consumption, that discussion serves as a springboard for introducing more general functional forms relating the demographic variables to the specific and income scales.

There are two notions of economies of scale in consumption that do not involve demographic effects at all. The first presupposes a household production model (Becker 1964; Michael and Becker 1973; Pollak and Wachter 1975) in which the household uses inputs of "market goods" and time to produce "basic commodities" that are the arguments of its utility function. Economies of scale in consumption are then defined in terms of the returns to scale properties of the household's technology. The second notion assumes that the prices paid for the market goods are functions of the amounts purchased and defines economies of scale in consumption as the availability of "quantity discounts" to bulk purchases. Both notions are discussed in David (1962: 10–19). These two notions of economies of scale in consumption are easily confused because economies of scale in the household technology may imply that the shadow prices of commodities fall as their consumption increases.

zation of the linear demographic translating is the quadratic specification,

$$D^i(b) = \sum_{r=1}^{N} w_{ir} b_r + \sum_{r=1}^{N} r_{ir} b_r^2 \tag{2.27}$$

The quadratic specification does not require all demographic characteristics to have the same "economies of scale" implications, but this generality is achieved at the cost of introducing $n \times N$ more parameters than in the linear specification.

With demographic scaling we considered both the linear and the log linear specifications. Log linear demographic scaling, equation (2.8), already permits economies of scale in consumption; we can restrict it and impose constant returns to scale by requiring the coefficients in equation (2.8) to satisfy

$$\sum_{r=1}^{N} \epsilon_{ir} = 1, \quad i = 1, \ldots, n$$

One simple generalization of linear demographic scaling, equation (2.7), is the quadratic specification

$$M^i(\eta) = 1 + \sum_{r=1}^{N} \epsilon_{ir} \eta_r + \sum_{r=1}^{N} \theta_{ir} \eta_r^2 \tag{2.28}$$

involving $n \times N$ additional parameters. These scaling specifications apply equally to the modified Prais-Houthakker procedure. In the following section we discuss estimates of demograpic scaling and the modified Prais-Houthakker procedure based on this quadratic specification.

EMPIRICAL COMPARISONS

This section estimates and compares the five general procedures described in the first section, using each of them to incorporate a single demographic variable, the number of children in the household, into the "generalized CES" demand system. An unambiguous ranking of procedures is not possible, but the modified Prais-

Houthakker procedure and scaling make the strongest showings, and translating makes the weakest. All five procedures imply similar marginal budget share and elasticity estimates.

Our estimates are based on British household budget data for the seven years 1966–72.[32] The data are from the Family Expenditure Survey (FES) series, an annual publication that reports income, expenditure patterns, and some demographic characteristics for a sample of British households. We consider only households consisting of one man, one woman, and at least one child. Although the FES reports purchases of consumer durables, we exclude them from our analysis and focus on the allocation among a set of nondurable consumption categories of total expenditure on those categories. To simplify the computations, we analyze only three categories— "food," "clothing," and "miscellaneous."[33] The FES cross-classifies households by income and number of children, and for each cell reports mean expenditure on each category.[34] Our basic data consist of 108 cells, which we treat as if they were consumption patterns of households rather than cell means.[35] Since the generalized CES demand system is linear in expenditure, aggregation over households is relatively harmless.

32. These seven years are the longest interval over which "children" were reported and defined consistently. Before 1966 the data do not include the number of children. After 1972, persons were classified as children if they were eighteen or under, while in earlier years they were so classified if they were sixteen or under. The only additional demographic information available concerns the ages of children, and this is available on a consistent basis only for the five years 1968–72.

33. Our "food" category does not include alcoholic drink. Our "clothing" is officially "clothing and footwear." Our "miscellaneous" is the sum of two categories from the survey— "other goods" and "services." The principal subcategories of "other goods" are—"Leather, travel and sport goods; jewelry; fancy goods, etc."; "books, magazines, and periodicals"; "toys and stationery goods, etc."; and "matches, soap, cleaning materials, etc." The principal subcategories of "services" are "radio and television, licenses and rentals"; "educational and training expenses"; and "subscriptions and donations; hotel and holiday expenses; miscellaneous other services." The survey reports seven major expenditure categories that we omitted entirely—"housing," "fuel, light, and power," "alcoholic drink," "tobacco," "durable household goods," "transport and vehicles," and "miscellaneous." Our three categories of food, clothing, and miscellaneous account for approximately 50 percent of total consumption expenditures in each year.

Current expenditures on these categories were obtained directly from the surveys, and the corresponding price indexes from Central Statistical Office (1975: 400, Table XV).

34. For six of the seven years we consider, the FES reports income and expenditure patterns for three relevant household types—one-child households, two-child households, and three- or more child households; for the last it reports the average number of children in each income class. For one year (1972) it reports data on four relevant household types, reporting separately on three-child households and four- or more child households.

35. Appendix B of this chapter describes the composition of these 108 cells.

The generalized CES demand equations (in share form) are given by

$$w_i = \frac{p_i b_i}{\mu} + \frac{a_i^c p_i^{1-c}}{\Sigma a_k^c p_k^{1-c}} [1 - (\Sigma p_k b_k)/\mu], \qquad \Sigma a_k = 1 \qquad (2.29)$$

where μ is total expenditure on the included categories, and w_i the share of total expenditure devoted to the ith category, and a, b, and c are parameters to be estimated.[36] The parameter c is the elasticity of substitution between "supernumerary quantities," $(x_i - b_i)$. With three goods, the generalized CES contains six independent parameters.

We obtain a stochastic specification for this demand system by adding a disturbance term to the share form of each demand equation. We denote the 3×1 vector of disturbances corresponding to the τth cell by $e_\tau = (e_{\tau 1}, e_{\tau 2}, e_{\tau 3})$ and assume that $E(e_\tau) = 0$, , $E(e_\tau e_\tau')$ = Ω for all τ and that the e_τ are independently normally distributed. Since the dependent variables are shares and the nonstochastic terms in the equations sum to one for each cell, the covariance matrix is singular. Hence maximum likelihood estimates of the system can be obtained by minimizing the determinant of the sample error covariance matrix with respect to the parameters after dropping any equation.

We begin by examining two threshold questions—(1) are demographic variables significant determinants of consumption patterns, and (2) if so, do demographic variables affect some but not all of the demand system parameters, as implied by the five procedures for incorporating demographic variables? Table 2–1 presents the summary statistics necessary to answer these questions. It reports log likelihood values and some other statistics for seven specifications— the five procedures described in section one for which demand equations are given in Appendix C and parameter estimates in Appendix D; the "pooled" specification, that combines data from different family types and estimates a single demand system,

---

36. The generalized CES was first proposed in Christensen (1967) and Pollak (1967), subsequently published as Pollak (1971). The indirect utility function is given by $\psi(P, \eta) = [\eta - f(P)]/g$, where $f(P) = \Sigma p_k b_k$ and $g(P) = [\Sigma a_k^c p_k^{1-c}]^{1/1-c}$. The generalized CES was first estimated by Wales (1971) and subsequently by Gamaletsos (1973). Deaton (1976) estimates the generalized CES as well as a related nonadditive generalization of the linear expenditure system. The generalized CES is a special case of a $(3n-1)$ parameter functional form proposed by Johansen (1969) and of the S-branch utility tree of Brown and Heien (1972).

Table 2-1. Summary Statistics.

	Translating	Scaling	Gorman	Reverse Gorman	Modified Prais-Houthakker	Unpooled	Pooled
Log likelihood	861.6262	863.4707	864.4165	864.5088	864.5157	870.5274	772.212
v	1	0	1.35	1.32	n/a	n/a	n/a
c	2.57	2.31	2.66	2.63	2.58	(1.66, 4.00, 2.09)[3]	2.88
Number of estimated parameters	9	9	10	10	9	18	6
Chi-square[4]	17.80	14.11	12.22	12.04	12.02	n/a	196.63

Notes:

n/a = not applicable.

[a]For translating and scaling, the value of v is set to 1 and 0, respectively.

[b]Corresponds to families with one child, two children, and 3 or more children.

[c]Calculated as minus twice the difference between 870.5274 and the log likelihood value in the column.

103

implicitly assuming that consumption patterns are independent of demographic variables; and the "unpooled" specification, which estimates three separate demand systems, one for each family type, implicitly assuming that demographic variables affect all demand system parameters.[37]

The answers to both threshold questions are affirmative: (1) Family size significantly affects consumption patterns. Comparing the pooled results with those obtained using each of the five procedures, we find a very significant decrease in the value of the likelihood function in each case. (2) Demographic variables affect some but not all demand system parameters. Comparing each of the five procedures with the unpooled specification, the decrease in the likelihood function is significant at the 5 percent level only for demographic translating.[38] Because these results confirm the validity of incorporating demographic variables into the generalized CES by means of the five procedures described in the first section, we do not report marginal budget shares or price elasticities for the pooled or the unpooled specifications.

All five procedures yield estimated parameters that correspond to "well-behaved" preferences in all or virtually all of the 108 price-expenditure-demographic situations represented in our data.[39] Further, all yield similar values of c, the elasticity of substitution between supernumerary quantities: Estimates range from 2.31 to 2.66.[40,41]

37. In the "unpooled specification," the family types are households with one child, two children, and three or more children. Since data are available on households with exactly three children in one year only (1972), these data are used together with those for households with four or more children in 1972 to form the family type consisting of three or more children.

38. The decrease is not significant for demographic translating at the 1 percent level.

39. For translating, scaling, and the Gorman procedures, the Slutsky matrix was negative semidefinite in all situations; in the reverse Gorman and modified Prais-Houthakker procedures, in 107 of 108 situations.

40. As Table 2–1 shows, the unpooled estimates exhibit a wider range.

41. For all five procedures, the generalized CES is significantly superior to the linear expenditure system (LES) at the 5 percent level. The generalized CES reduces to the LES when $c = 1$, and we have tested whether our estimated value of c differs significantly from one. With the LES, the modified Prais-Houthakker procedure yields a likelihood value of 862.5833, while the other four procedures imply identical estimating equations and yield a likelihood value of 859.6875. It is easy to verify that scaling and translating are equivalent for the LES. Their equivalence to the Gorman procedures is less obvious but follows from the observation that v is not identified when $c = 1$. To see this, consider equation (2.40) in Appendix C: When $c = 1$, the marginal budget shares are constant and the α's and v enter only in terms of the form $[1 + (1-v) \alpha_i \eta] b_i + v \alpha_i \eta$. Rewriting these as $b_i + \alpha_i [v + b_i(1-v)] \eta$ and denoting $\alpha_i [v + b_i(1-v)]$ by π_i, it is clear that estimates of b_i and π_i, but not of v, can be obtained: All values of v yield the same likelihood values, since as v changes, the α_i can adjust to give the same estimates of π_i.

The modified Prais-Houthakker procedure makes a very strong showing against the other four procedures on the basis of the value of the likelihood function: The nine-parameter modified Prais-Houthakker procedure yields a value of the likelihood function that is not only greater than that of the other two nine-parameter procedures (translating and scaling), but one that is also greater than that of the two ten-parameter procedures (Gorman and reverse Gorman).[42] However, no formal classical tests are possible because none of the other four procedures are nested in the modified Prais-Houthakker procedure, nor is it nested in any of them.[43]

Scaling compares favorably with the remaining three procedures. It has a higher likelihood value than translating, which is also a nine-parameter procedure. It is not rejected at the 5 percent level against the unpooled specification nor against either the Gorman or reverse Gorman procedures.[44,45]

The reverse Gorman procedure is superior to the Gorman on the basis of the values of their likelihood functions. Since both procedures involve ten parameters, this provides a plausible basis for comparison, although no formal classical tests are possible.[46]

42. We also estimated the special case of the modified Prais-Houthakker procedure in which the specific scales are the same for all goods and the even more restrictive special case in which the common value is such that children receive the same weight as adults. Since our basic units of observation are households with two adults and at least one child, this implies a coefficient of 0.5, so that a household with four children (i.e., six persons) spending 400 shillings per week purchases twice as much of every good as a household with one child (i.e., three persons) spending 200 shillings per week. The likelihood values for these models are 860.5457 and 814.2324, respectively; at the 5 percent level, these restrictions are rejected against the unpooled specification.

43. Although new techniques have recently been proposed for testing nonnested hypotheses (e.g., Pesaran and Deaton 1978; Davidson and MacKinnon 1981), their application is beyond the scope of this chapter.

44. The two special cases of the modified Prais-Houthakker procedure described in note 42 are also special cases of scaling.

45. Muellbauer (1977) rejects scaling against the unpooled specification as a method for incorporating household size into demand analysis. In addition to using a different functional form, Muellbauer uses data for a somewhat different period (1968–73), includes households with no children, and uses ten consumption categories, some of which include consumer durables.

46. Both the Gorman and reverse Gorman procedures yielded estimates of v outside the range [0,1]. This does not violate regularity conditions, nor does it imply predicted responses to changes in the demographic variables very different from those implied by the other procedures. The likelihood functions corresponding to the Gorman and reverse Gorman procedures each had two maxima, a local maximum corresponding to a value of v below 0 and a global maximum corresponding to a value greater than 1. The values corresponding to the global maxima are given in Table 2–1. The estimated value of v at the local maximum for the Gorman (reverse Gorman) procedure is −0.60 (−0.13), and the corresponding value of the likelihood function is 864.3657 (864.1946).

Translating is the weakest of the five procedures. It has a lower likelihood value than the modified Prais-Houthakker procedure and scaling, which also have nine-parameters, and it is rejected at the 5 percent (but not at the 1 percent) level against the Gorman and reverse Gorman procedures.[47]

Table 2–2 presents marginal budget shares and own price elasticities implied by our estimates of each of the five procedures for households with one, two, and three children. Price elasticities are evaluated at 1970 prices (all equal to 100) and an expenditure level of 300 shillings per week, which is close to the median expenditure for households in 1970, marginal budget shares are also evaluated at 1970 prices, but in the generalized CES they are independent of expenditure levels.

The marginal budget share estimates implied by the five procedures are strikingly similar. In the generalized CES, translating necessarily yields marginal budget shares that are independent of the number of children, so the marginal budget shares for translating could not exhibit the same pattern of variation with family size as the other four procedures. However, the marginal budget share estimates for translating are essentially identical to those implied by the other four procedures for two-child households. The four procedures permitting marginal budget shares to vary with family size all show that the marginal budget share for food increases with family size, that for clothing is almost constant, while that for miscellaneous decreases. However, the magnitudes of these changes are small.

A comparison of estimated own price elasticities also suggests that the differences between procedures are small, especially for households with two children. For one-child households the largest difference between procedures occurs for clothing, but this difference is only 0.21; for three-child families the largest difference, also for clothing, is 0.14. We have calculated both own and cross-price elasticities corresponding to expenditure levels of 200, 300 and 400 shillings per week at 1970 prices, although we report only own price elasticities at 300 shillings per week. Estimated cross-price elas-

---

47. It might be argued that our maintained hypothesis that the demand system is generalized CES prejudices our evaluation of translating, since translating, when applied to any demand system linear in expenditure, does not allow the marginal budget shares to vary with the demographic variables. However, Pollak and Wales (1980) found translating inferior to scaling when both procedures were applied to the "quadratic expenditure system" and to the "generalized translog," both of which are nonlinear in expenditure.

Table 2-2. Marginal Budget Shares and Own Price Elasticity by Family Size, for Different Procedures Used to Incorporate Family Size.

Number of Children	Consumption Category								
	Food			Clothing			Miscellaneous		
	1	2	3	1	2	3	1	2	3
MARGINAL BUDGET SHARES									
Translating	0.29	0.29	0.29	0.23	0.23	0.23	0.48	0.48	0.48
Scaling	0.27	0.29	0.30	0.23	0.23	0.23	0.50	0.48	0.47
Gorman	0.27	0.29	0.31	0.23	0.22	0.23	0.50	0.49	0.47
Reverse Gorman	0.27	0.29	0.30	0.23	0.22	0.23	0.50	0.49	0.47
Modified Prais-Houthakker	0.27	0.29	0.31	0.22	0.22	0.23	0.51	0.49	0.46
OWN PRICE ELASTICITIES									
Translating	-0.78	-0.75	-0.72	-1.43	-1.49	-1.56	-1.41	-1.51	-1.65
Scaling	-0.81	-0.76	-0.71	-1.64	-1.55	-1.44	-1.57	-1.56	-1.54
Gorman	-0.73	-0.75	-0.76	-1.43	-1.50	-1.58	-1.42	-1.52	-1.66
Reverse Gorman	-0.73	-0.74	-0.76	-1.44	-1.50	-1.57	-1.42	-1.52	-1.65
Modified Prais-Houthakker	-0.78	-0.75	-0.72	-1.56	-1.51	-1.46	-1.53	-1.53	-1.53

Note:
Price elasticities are evaluated at 1970 prices (all equal to 100) and expenditure level of 300 S. per week; marginal budget shares are also evaluated at 1970 prices, but are independent of expenditure.

ticities are very similar for all five procedures, and the size of these differences decreases with expenditure—the largest difference between comparable elasticities at 300 shillings per week is only 0.15.

To test for quadratic economies of scale in consumption in the two most promising specifications, scaling and the modified Prais-Houthakker procedure, we estimated the quadratic specification and tested whether it was significantly superior to the corresponding linear specification. In each case, restricting the three additional parameters to zero did not significantly decrease the likelihood value, even at the 25 percent level.[48] Thus, our data show no evidence of quadratic economies of scale in consumption.

WELFARE COMPARISONS AND EQUIVALENCE SCALES

Conditional Equivalence Scales

In demand analysis, the "objects of choice" are consumption vectors, X, and preferences over them depend on a predetermined vector of demographic variables, η; we call such a preference ordering "conditional." We denote the conditional preference ordering by $R(\eta)$ and interpret the statement "$X^a R(\bar{\eta}) X^b$" to mean that the family finds X^a at least as good as X^b when its demographic profile is given by $\bar{\eta}$.[49] If each family takes it demographic profile as fixed when choosing its consumption pattern, demand analysis need never ask how it would choose between alternatives that differ with respect to the demographic variables; hence, conditional preferences are an appropriate foundation for demand analysis.

Earlier in the chapter we discussed a number of alternative ways of

48. The Chi-square statistics are 2.44 for scaling and 0.76 for the modified Prais-Houthakker procedure.

49. By "family preferences" we mean the preferences of the adults in the family; preferences of children are ignored. For a family containing one adult, this notion of family preferences is unambiguous, but for a family containing two adults, there is an aggregation problem unless the adults' preferences happen to coincide. We ignore this and assume that the notion of "family preferences" is well defined. Basing welfare comparisons on family preferences means that we can only compare demographic profiles whose adult compositions are identical; thus, we cannot compare the welfare of a family consisting of one adult and two children with that of a family of two adults and two children.

incorporating demographic variables into demand analysis by allowing some of the parameters of a demand system to be functions of
demographic variables. These functions, which we call "conditional
equivalence scales," are usually estimated along with the parameters
of the demand system by combining data from households with
different demographic profiles. The alternatives to this procedure
are (1) to analyze separately data from households with distinct
demographic profiles or (2) to combine data from households with
different demographic profiles using conditional equivalence scales
estimated from other data or specified a priori. The assumptions that
demand functions are independent of demographic variables, or that
per capita consumption of each good is a function of per capita total
expenditure are examples of a priori specifications of conditional
equivalence scales.

The familiar linear expenditure system (LES) provides a convenient example. Without demographic effects, the LES is given by

$$x_i = b^i(P,\mu) = b_i - \frac{a_i}{P_i} \sum_{k=1}^{n} p_k b_k + \frac{a_i}{P_i}\mu \qquad \Sigma a_k = 1 \qquad (2.30)$$

where the as and the bs are parameters to be estimated. These
demand functions are generated by the direct utility function

$$U(X) = \prod_{k=1}^{n} (x_k - b_k)^{a_k} \qquad \Sigma a_k = 1, \ x_i - b_i > 0 \qquad (2.31)$$

In the case of the LES, linear demographic translating and linear
demographic scaling are equivalent, implying that the as are independent of the demographic variables and that demographic effects
operate linearly through the bs. That is,

$$b_i = b_i^* + \sum_{r=1}^{N} \beta_{ir}\eta_r \qquad (2.32)$$

where $(\eta_1,\ldots,\eta_N)$ is a vector of demographic variables and the b^*s
and the βs are parameters to be estimated.

Unconditional Equivalence Scales

In contrast to demand analysis, welfare analysis must compare the well-being of a family in alternative situations that differ with respect to its demographic profile as well as its consumption pattern. For example, we might ask whether a family with given tastes would prefer to have two children and $12,000 or three children and $13,000 at a particular set of goods prices. The traditional approach to welfare comparisons ignores the fact that such comparisons cannot be based on conditional preferences but require a conceptual framework in which preferences are defined over family size as well as goods. In general, welfare analysis requires us to define the objects of choice to include not only the consumption vector but also the demographic variables that, from the standpoint of conditional preferences, are predetermined. We call an ordering over such an augmented set of alternatives an "unconditional preference ordering," and denote it by R: The statement "$(X^a, \eta^a) \, R \, (X^b, \eta^b)$" means that the family finds (X^a, η^a) at least as good as (X^b, η^b). The additional information contained in the unconditional preference ordering is irrelevant for demand analysis; but for welfare comparisons it is indispensible.

Unconditional equivalence scales are index numbers that reflect the ratio of the expenditures required to attain a particular indifference curve under alternative demographic profiles.[50] Corresponding to the unconditional preference ordering, R, we define the "unconditional expenditure function," $E[P, \eta, (P^0, \mu^0, \eta^0)]$, whose value is the minimum expenditure required to reach the indifference curve attained in the price-expenditure-demographic situation (P^0, μ^0, η^0),

---

50. This corresponds to Muellbauer's definition of equivalence scales as "budget deflators which are used to calculate the relative amounts of money two different types of households require in order to reach the same standard of living" (1977: 460). Muellbauer uses what we have called conditional equivalence scales to make welfare comparisons, and his paper provides numerous references to other studies that do so. We contend that such an approach is not valid because unconditional equivalence scales rather than conditional equivalence scales are required for welfare comparisons. Our objection to the use of conditional equivalence scales in welfare analysis does not depend on whether families can or do regulate their fertility.

Deaton and Muellbauer (1980: 208) endorse welfare comparisons based on equivalence scales estimated from observed differences in the consumption patterns of households with different demographic profiles. They dismiss our argument that such scales have no welfare significance, saying "this seems to us to be too negative a position." Deaton (1980: section 7c) recognizes the validity of our objections.

when the household faces prices P with the demographic profile η. The "unconditional equivalence scale," $I[(P^a,\eta^a), (P^b,\eta^b) (P^o,\mu^o,\eta^o)]$, is defined by

$$I[(P^a,\eta^a), (P^b,\eta^b), (P^o,\mu^o,\eta^o)] = \frac{E[P^a,\eta^a,(P^o,\mu^o,\eta^o)]}{E[(P^b,\eta^b,(P^o,\mu^o,\eta^o)]} \qquad (2.33)$$

If we let the base indifference curve correspond to the "reference situation" (P^b,μ^b,η^b), then the denominator is μ^b and the index is equal to $E[P^a,\eta^a,(P^b,\mu^b,\eta^b)]/\mu^b$. In our example, the index shows the percentage expenditure adjustment that would enable a family with three children to attain the same indifference curve it would attain with two children and \$12,000.[51]

We illustrate this with an unconditional preference ordering that is consistent with the LES conditional demand functions. Consider the direct utility function

$$W(X,\eta) = \prod_{k=1}^{n} (x_k - b_k^* - \beta_k\eta)^{a_k} + \Lambda(\eta) \qquad \Sigma a_k = 1, x_i - b_i^* - \beta_i\eta > 0 \qquad (2.34)$$

where η is the number of children in the family; in some very informal sense the function $\Lambda(\eta)$ represents the "direct" contribution of children to family utility. Substituting the conditional demand functions (given by equations (2.30) and (2.32) with one demographic variable) into this direct utility function yields a "mixed" indirect utility function whose arguments are P, μ, and η:

$$V(P,\mu,\eta) = (\mu - \Sigma p_k b_k^* - \eta\Sigma p_k\beta_k) \Pi(p_k)^{-a_k}(a_k)^{a_k} + \Lambda(\eta) \qquad (2.35)$$

Solving for μ yields the unconditional expenditure function:

$$E(P,\mu,\eta,V_o) = \Sigma p_k b_k^* + \eta\Sigma p_k\beta_k + [V_o - \Lambda(\eta)] \Pi(p_k)^{a_k}(a_k)^{-a_k} \qquad (2.36)$$

where o is the value of the utility function given in equation (2.34) evaluated at any point on the base indifference curve. To find the

51. The conventional cost of living index holds the demographic profile fixed and compares the expenditure required to attain a particular indifference curve under alternative price regimes. Such an index can be interpreted as a "subindex" of the unconditional equivalence scale, which is itself the "complete index." Pollak (1975) develops the theory of subindexes of the cost of living index. In this chapter we are concerned with complete indexes, or at least with indexes complete enough to include the demographic variables. Subindexes (i.e., conventional cost of living indexes) can be constructed separately for each family type, but such indexes do not permit comparisons of families of different types.

unconditional equivalence scale evaluated at the base indifference curve corresponding to (P^b, μ^b, η^b), we divide the unconditional expenditure function evaluated at $V_o = V(P^b, \mu^b, b^b)$ by μ^b. This yields

$$I[(P^a, \eta^a), (P^b, \eta^b), (P^b, \mu^b \eta^b)] = \{\Sigma p_k^a b_k^* + \eta \Sigma p_k^a \beta_k + [(\mu^b - \Sigma p_b^b b_k^* - \eta^b \Sigma p_k^b \beta_k)$$

$$\Pi(p_k^b)^{-a_k}(a_k)^{a_k} + \Lambda(\eta^b) - \Lambda(\eta^a)] \; \Pi(p_k^a)^{a_k}(a_k)^{-a_k} \; /\mu^b{}^{52} \qquad (2.37)$$

Identification of Unconditional Equivalence Scales

Since the unconditional equivalence scale corresponding to $W(X, \eta)$ depends on the function $\Lambda(\eta)$, we must estimate this function. But if we interpret our data in terms of conditional choices (i.e., choices in which the number of children is taken to be fixed or predetermined) the function $\Lambda(\eta)$ is not identified.[53] All functions $\Lambda(\eta)$ imply the same conditional demand functions for goods, so information about how a family would reallocate its expenditure among consumption categories as the number of children varies is not sufficient to identify $\Lambda(\eta)$.

There are two ways in which we might identify the function $\Lambda(\eta)$. If we confine ourselves to data that represent conditional choices, then we can only identify $\Lambda(\eta)$ by assumption—for example, by assuming that $\Lambda(\eta)$ is a constant or a particular quadratic expression such as $\Lambda(\eta) = -\eta^2 + 4\eta$. Alternatively, if we free ourselves from exclusive reliance on conditional choices, we might bring to bear additional information that will enable us to identify $\Lambda(\eta)$.

52. The unconditional preference ordering corresponding to the direct utility function $W(X, \eta) = \Sigma a_k^* \log(x_k - b_k - \beta_k \eta) + \Lambda(\eta)$ is not the same as that corresponding to $W(X, \eta)$, and hence these two unconditional preferences orderings yield distinct unconditional equivalence scales. However, both imply the same LES conditional demand functions and, hence, the same conditional equivalence scales.

53. Whether a particular demographic variable should be treated as predetermined or as an object of choice is not automatically resolved by the fact that the variable in question is controlled or chosen by the family and hence could legitimately be treated as an object of choice. For purposes of demand analysis, it is useful to treat family size as predetermined and to work with conditional demand functions. When we treat such choices as unconditional, estimation of (unconditional) preferences requires us to reconstruct the feasible set from which the choice was made. But estimation of unconditional preferences is a secondary issue for us. We are primarily concerned with drawing the distinction between conditional and unconditional preferences and arguing that the latter are required for welfare comparisons.

Identification by assumption is poorly regarded, and those who adopt this approach seldom describe it this way. Nevertheless, it is the only way to bridge the gap between conditional choices and unconditional equivalence scales, the only way to go from observed differences in household consumption patterns to welfare conclusions.

In addition to our general objection to identification by assumption, we object to the specific assumption that is usually made about the function $\Lambda(\eta)$—namely, that it is a constant.[54] This assumption has grossly implausible implications for unconditional preferences and unconditional choices involving family size. In particular, consider a "perfect contraceptive society"—one in which there are no economic costs or preference drawbacks associated with fertility regulation. If $\Lambda(\eta)$ is a constant and $\Sigma\ p_k\beta_k$ is positive, then the family will have no children; if $\Lambda(\eta)$ is a constant and $\Sigma\ p_k\beta_k$ is negative, the family will have as many children as it can. This follows immediately from the fact that when $\Lambda(\eta)$ is a constant, the utility function (2.37) depends linearly on η.

Another illustration of the counterintuitive results that may occur when we make the transition from household consumption patterns to welfare conclusions by assuming that $\Lambda(\eta)$ is a constant is provided by the LES estimated by Pollak and Wales (1978) using U.K. household budget data. The estimated conditional demand functions exhibit reasonable price and expenditure elasticities and reasonable consumption responses to changes in family size. The estimated βs, however, are all negative, so $\Sigma\ p_k\beta_k < 0$. Hence, when $\Lambda(\eta)$ is assumed to be constant, the unconditional expenditure function decreases with η, and the corresponding unconditional equivalence scale implies that large families need less money than small families to attain any fixed indifference curve.

If unconditional preferences cannot be recovered from conditional demand functions, how can they be discovered? For some demographic variables, information about unconditional preferences is revealed by observable choice behavior. For example, in advanced industrial societies where deliberate choice of completed family size is the rule rather than the exception, an argument can be made for treating the observed consumption–family size configurations as observable unconditional choices, using them to infer unconditional

54. All constants, including zero, have identical implications for both conditional and unconditional preferences and choices.

preferences, and using these preferences to make welfare comparisons.[55] Thus, in a perfect contraceptive society, if a family chooses to have three children and $12,000 when it could have had two children and $12,000, then a revealed preference argument implies that the family prefers the alternative it chose.[56] Other demographic variables (e.g., race) are not susceptible to deliberate control, while still others (e.g., the sex of a family's first child) may be moving from the uncontrollable to the controllable category. Unconditional preferences for demographic variables might also be obtained by analyzing responses to direct questions about preferences or hypothetical choices, although economists have traditionally been suspicious of this approach.[57]

Welfare Comparisons with Taste Differences

Taste differences—that is, differences in families' unconditional preferences—substantially complicate welfare comparisons.[58] There are two approaches. The first is to select a particular unconditional preference ordering as the appropriate base for welfare comparisons

55. Muellbauer (1977) puts forward several telling objections to the simplest version of the revealed preference approach. First, families do not regulate completed family size with perfect accuracy. Second, the decision problem is a multiperiod one, and the argument in the text is formulated in terms of a one-period planning or decision model. Third, all uncertainties (e.g., those associated with income, employment, and health) have been ignored. These considerations suggest that the simple revealed preference argument should be applied with caution. We have no desire to defend the simple revealed preference approach, nor is it our intention to propose a technique for discovering unconditional preferences. We do, however, insist that unconditional preferences are required for welfare analysis. Furthermore, as noted above, our objection to the use of conditional equivalence scales in welfare analysis holds regardless of whether families can regulate their fertility.

56. Multiple births create special problems that we ignore. We interpret the $12,000 as total expenditure on goods and ignore both the labor-leisure choice and the dependence of taxes on demographic variables.

We should be more explicit about the feasible set from which this unconditional choice was made. We assume that the family can choose any integer number of children it wants, between zero and fifteen. The direct medical costs associated with the birth of a child (to the extent that they are not covered by insurance) are reflected in the family's expenditure on medical care. Similarly, the extra food, clothing, and space "requirements" associated with an extra child are reflected in the conditional preference ordering. Of course, the family must meet these extra "needs" by reallocating its fixed total expenditure among these consumption categories.

57. For an example of an equivalence scale constructed from responses to a questionnaire asking individuals what income level corresponds to such verbal evaluations as "good," "sufficient," "bad," etc., see Kapteyn and van Praag (1976).

58. One adult and two adult families presumably have different unconditional preferences.

and to proceed as before. The selection is trivial if a particular preference ordering is obviously appropriate, as when all families have identical unconditional preferences. It is especially troublesome when systematic differences in preferences are associated with systematic differences in the demographic variables, as is the case with family size or other demographic variables over which families exercise partial or complete control. For some demographic variables, it may be plausible to assume that families with different demographic profiles have the same unconditional preferences or, more precisely, that the distribution of unconditional preferences is independent of the distribution of demographic characteristics. But for demographic variables over which families exercise some deliberate control, this independence assumption is clearly unwarranted.

Suppose, for example, that some families have a strong desire for children, while others have a weak desire for children. Then the expenditure required to make a family with three children as well off as it would be with two children and $12,000 depends on which unconditional preference ordering it has. Hence, the unconditional equivalence scale depends on which of the two unconditional preference orderings we select as the base: But neither selection compares the welfare levels of families with different tastes. Instead, they compare two situations—three children, $13,000 versus two children, $12,000—on the basis of a particular preference ordering—whichever one is selected as the appropriate base for the comparison.[59]

The second approach to welfare comparisons requires interpersonal (interfamily) comparisons of happiness or satisfaction. Technically, we need a mapping that associates with each indifference curve from one unconditional indifference map a corresponding curve on the other, so that the corresponding curves represent the same levels of happiness or satisfaction. Only if such a correspondence exists can we compare the welfare of families with different tastes in alternative situations—for example, strong desire for children, three children, $13,000 versus weak desire for children, two children, $12,000.

59. Similarly, the cost of living index does not compare the welfare of families with different tastes. It uses a particular base preference ordering to compare alternative price regimes (e.g., Japanese versus U.S.) or, more generally, alternative sets of constraints. But if U.S. tastes differ from Japanese tastes, the cost of living index does not tell us how much a Japanese family would require to make it as well off as an American family with $12,000.

CONCLUSION

This chapter has described, estimated, and compared five procedures for incorporating demographic variables into complete demand systems. Some of the procedures are new, while others have been discussed or estimated before; all of them can be used in conjunction with any complete demand system. Our comparisons are based on a generalized CES demand system into which we incorporated a single demographic variable, the number of children in the household, estimated from British household budget data for the seven years 1966–72. We also estimated the pooled specification in which demographic variables have no effect on consumption patterns and the unpooled specification in which they affect all demand system parameters.

We rejected the pooled specification against each of the five procedures, indicating that the number of children does affect consumption patterns. Of the five procedures, only demographic translating could be rejected against unpooled specification, indicating that the other four procedures are reasonably consistent with the data. These four procedures imply similar responses to changes in prices, total expenditure, and the number of children. Although no formal ranking of these procedures is possible, statistical tests can be applied to pairs of procedures that are nested, and the likelihood value provides a plausible basis for comparing procedures with the same number of independent parameters. Using these criteria, translating made the weakest showing, the two Gorman procedures were dominated by scaling, and the modified Prais-Houthakker was best of all.

The implications of our analysis of welfare comparisons and equivalence scales should be stated explicitly: First, even if all families have identical unconditional preferences, conditional equivalence scales estimated from observed differences in the consumption patterns of families with different demographic profiles cannot be used to make welfare comparisons. For example, we cannot use such data to determine the amount needed to make families with three children as well off as those with two children and $12,000. Unconditional equivalence scales are required to make welfare comparisons. Second, if tastes vary systematically with demographic characteristics, then the construction of unconditional equivalence scales requires the selection of an appropriate base unconditional preference ordering, theory offers little guidance in making this selection, but there is no selection that permits us to compare the welfare of a family with a strong desire for children with that of one with a weak desire for children. Such comparisons require interpersonal or interfamily comparisons of welfare levels. The question of whether such comparisons are meaningful and, if so, how they can be made, is beyond the scope of this chapter.

Our analysis suggests that it is very difficult to make welfare comparisons between families with different demographic profiles. But are comparisons of this sort the principal basis of the widespread belief that it is appropriate to treat different family types differently in income tax or family allowance schedules or in income maintenance programs? We think not. For example, differences in treatment might be justified in terms of effects on the children's present or future welfare, the effects on the children's future productivity, or the effect on the family's fertility.[60] Our analysis implies that differences in treatment cannot easily be justified by an appeal to equity or fairness if this is interpreted in terms of "family preferences" (i.e., the welfare of the adult members of the family). But the arguments one would advance to justify providing children in large families with consumption levels that society somehow establishes to be "socially adequate" are very different from those one would advance for making the adults in large and small families equally well off. The problem of defining socially adequate consumption levels is a difficult one that has received virtually no attention from economists, in part because of the profession's unfortunate preoccupation with welfare comparisons and equivalence scales.[61]

In summary, the use of equivalence scales estimated from observed differences in consumption patterns to make welfare comparisons between families with different demographic profiles reflects a failure to distinguish between conditional and unconditional equivalence scales. Conditional equivalence scales reflect only conditional preferences, and they do not permit welfare comparisons between families of different types. If all families have identical unconditional preferences, unconditional equivalence scales are

60. The relevance of these considerations and of welfare comparisons will vary from one policy question to another.

61. There is no reason to think that conditional equivalence scales have any role to play in the determination of socially adequate consumption levels.

required to make welfare comparisons, and a fortiori, they cannot be inferred from observed differences in consumption patterns. If families have different unconditional preferences, welfare comparisons require interfamily comparisons of their welfare levels, not merely their unconditional preferences. Finally, although welfare comparisons are interesting and important, many policy questions involving the treatment of different family types do not require such comparisons.

APPENDIX A

Proof of Theorem 1

It suffices to show that the implied demand functions correspond to the utility function $U(X)$. To show this, we observe that the original demand functions are solutions to the first order conditions.

$$u^{i'}(x_i) = -\lambda p_i$$

$$\Sigma p_k x_k = \mu$$

The modified demand functions are defined in terms of the original demand functions by

$$b^i(P,\mu) = s_i b^{-i}(P,\mu/s_o)$$

where s_o is implicitly defined by

$$\Sigma p_k s_k b^{-k}(P,\mu/s_o) = \mu$$

We must show that these modified demand functions satisfy the first-order conditions corresponding to the utility function $U(X)$—namely,

$$u^{i'}(x_i s_i) = -\lambda p_i$$

$$\Sigma p_k x_k = \mu$$

That is, we must show that the modified demand functions satisfy

$$u^{i'}[b^i(P,\mu)/s_i] = -\lambda p_i$$

$$\Sigma p_k b^k(P,\mu) = \mu$$

or, equivalently,

$$u^{i'}[b^{-i}(P,\mu/s_o)] = -\lambda p_i$$

$$(*) \quad \Sigma p_k s_k b^{-k}(P,\mu/s_o) = \mu$$

The original demand functions $\{b^i(P,\mu/s_o)\}$ maximize the utility function $\bar{U}(X)$ subject to the budget constraint $\Sigma p_k x_k = \mu/s_o$, so they satisfy the first-order conditions

$$u^{i'}[b^{-i}(P,\mu/s_o)] = -\lambda p_i$$

$$\Sigma p_k b^{-k}(P,\mu/s_o) = \mu$$

where s_o is defined implicitly by

$$\Sigma p_k s_k b^{-k}(P,\mu/s_o) = \mu$$

But this means that the condition (*) is satisfied. QED.

Proof of Theorem 2

The proof depends on establishing that the conditions for the existence of theoretically plausible demographic demand functions are identical with those for the existence of theoretically plausible long-run demand functions in a linear habit formation model. This permits us to make immediate use of a theorem from Pollak (1976: 284) characterizing this class of functions.

If the original demand system is theoretically plausible and linear in expenditure, then the modified Prais-Houthakker procedures yields demand functions of the form given in equation (2.16). We write equation (2.16) as

$$(**) \quad h^i(P,\mu) = B^i(P) - \Gamma^i(P)\Sigma p_k B^k(P) + \Gamma^i(P)\mu$$

where $B^i(P)$ and $\Gamma^i(P)$ are defined by

$$B^i(P) = \frac{f_i(P)}{1 - \beta_i}, \quad \Gamma^i(P) = \frac{\gamma^i(P)/(1 - \beta_i)}{\Sigma p_k \gamma^k(P)/(1 - \beta_k)}$$

and β_i by $\beta_i = 1 - 1/s_i$, hence $s_i = 1/(1-\beta_i)$.

Except for the absence of the $b*$s in the expressions for the βs, (**) is precisely the form of the long-run demand functions given in Pollak

Appendix B. The 108 Cells Used as Basic Data Points in the Estimation of all Equations are Obtained as Follows:

Year	Number of Children in Household	Number of Income Levels	Total Number of Cells
1966	1, 2, 3 or more	4	12
1967	1, 2, 3 or more	5	15
1968	1, 2, 3 or more	5	15
1969	1, 2	5	10
	3 or more	4	4
1970	1, 3 or more	4	8
	2	6	6
1971	1, 2, 3 or more	6	18
1972	1, 2	6	12
	3	5	5
	4 or more	3	3
			108

Note: All households consist of one man, one woman, and at least one child.

(1976: eq. 3.7). Since variations in the b^*s play no role in the proof of the theorem (Pollak 1976: 284), it follows that our demographic demand functions are theoretically plausible if and only if the original demand system satisifies the conditions established in Pollak (1976) and these conditions are equivalent to the requirement that the original demand system correspond to an additive direct utility function. QED.

APPENDIX C

Introducing the number of children in the household (η) into the "generalized CES" demand system given in equation (2.29) using the five methods discussed in the text gives the following equations:[62]

62. All summations are over k from 1 to 3.

Translating

$$w_i = \frac{P_i}{\mu}(b_i + \alpha_i\eta) + \frac{a_i^c p_i^{1-c}}{\Sigma a_k^c p_k^{1-c}}\left[1 - \frac{\Sigma p_k(b_k + \alpha_k\eta)}{\mu}\right] \qquad (2.38)$$

Scaling

$$w_i = \frac{P_i}{\mu}(1 + \alpha_i\eta)b_i + \frac{a_i^c[(1 + \alpha_i\eta)p_i]^{1-c}}{\Sigma a_k^c[(1 + \alpha_k\eta)p_k]^{1-c}}\left[1 - \frac{\Sigma p_k(1 + \alpha_k\eta)b_k}{\mu}\right] \qquad (2.39)$$

Gorman

$$w_i = \frac{P_i}{\mu}[(1 + [1 - \nu]\alpha_i\eta)b_i + \nu\alpha_i\eta] + \frac{a_i^c[(1 + [1 - \nu]\alpha_i\eta)p_i]^{1-c}}{\Sigma a_k^c[(1 + [1 - \nu]\alpha_k\eta)p_k]^{1-c}} \cdot$$
$$\left[1 - \frac{\Sigma p_k[(1 + [1 - \nu]\alpha_k\eta)b_k + \nu\alpha_k\eta]}{\mu}\right] \qquad (2.40)$$

Reverse Gorman

$$w_i = \frac{P_i}{\mu}[1 + (1 - \nu)\alpha_i\eta](b_i + \nu\alpha_i\eta) + \frac{a_i^c[(1 + [1 - \nu]\alpha_i\eta)p_i]^{1-c}}{\Sigma a_k^c[(1 + [1 - \nu]\alpha_k\eta)p_k]^{1-c}}$$
$$\left[1 - \frac{\Sigma p_k[1 + [1 - \nu]\alpha_k\eta](b + \nu\alpha_k\eta)}{\mu}\right] \qquad (2.41)$$

Modified Prais-Houthakker

$$w_i = \frac{P_i}{\mu}b_i(1 + \alpha_i\eta) + \frac{a_i^c(1 + \alpha_i\eta)p_i^{1-c}}{\Sigma a_k^c(1 + \alpha_k\eta)p_k^{1-c}}\left[1 - \frac{\Sigma p_k b_k(1 + \alpha_k\eta)}{\mu}\right] \qquad (2.42)$$

Note that all summations are over k from 1 to 3.

Appendix D: Parameter Estimates for Equations (2.38) through (2.42).

Parameter	Equation (2.38)		Equation (2.39)		Equation (2.40)		Equation (2.41)		Equation (2.42)	
a_1	.320	(.006)	.296	(.017)	.307	(.010)	.306	(0.11)	.291	(.016)
a_2	.290	(.015)	.290	(.014)	.293	(.013)	.294	(.012)	.291	(.016)
b_1	1.003	(.148)	.877	(.077)	1.065	(.119)	1.043	(.115)	.974	(.116)
b_2	.227	(.113)	.085	(.076)	.240	(1.00)	.233	(.090)	.167	(.096)
b_3	.395	(.260)	.049	(.152)	.391	(.223)	.375	(.206)	.190	(.243)
c	2.570	(.800)	2.305	(.710)	2.66	(.727)	2.629	(.759)	2.579	(.841)
α_t	.108	(.056)	.161	(.035)	.084	(.049)	.104	(.046)	.125	(.027)
α_2	-.022	(.042)	.263	(.076)	-.020	(.030)	-.019	(.019)	.034	(.050)
α_3	-.100	(.098)	.308	(.075)	-.073	(.065)	-.067	(.035)	-.021	(.049)
ν	—		1.346	(.243)	1.323	(.215)	—		—	
Log likelihood	861.6262		863.4707		864.465		864.5088		864.5157	

Notes: Numbers in parentheses are asymptotic standard errors. All prices are equal to 100 in 1971. The subscripts 1, 2, and 3 refer to food, clothing, and miscellaneous, respectively.

122

REFERENCES

Barten, A.P. 1964. "Family Composition, Prices and Expenditure Patterns." In *Econometric Analysis for National Economic Planning: 16th Symposium of the Colston Society,* ed. by P. Hart, G. Mills, and J.K. Whitaker. London: Butterworth.

Becker, G.S. 1965. "A Theory of the Allocation of Time." *Economic Journal* 75: 493–517.

Berndt, E.R.; M.N. Darrough; and W.E. Diewert. 1977. "Flexible Functional Forms and Expenditure Distributions: An Application to Canadian Consumer Demand Functions." *International Economic Review* 18: 651–75.

Brown, M., and D. Heien. 1972. "The S-Branch Utility Tree: A Generalization of the Linear Expenditure System." *Econometrica* 40: 737–47.

Central Statistical Office. 1975. *National Income and Expenditure, 1964–1974.* London: Her Majesty's Stationery Office.

Christensen, L.R. 1967. "Saving and the Rate of Return." Ph.D. dissertation, University of California, Berkeley.

David, M.H. 1962. *Family Composition and Consumption.* Amsterdam: North-Holland.

Davidson, R., and J.G. MacKinnon. 1981. "Several Tests for Model Specification in the Presence of Alternative Hypotheses." *Econometrica* 49: 781–93.

Deaton, A. 1976. "A Simple Nonadditive Model of Demand." In *Private and Enlarged Consumption: Essays in Methodology and Empirical Analysis,* ed. by L. Solari and J.N. Du Pasquier. Amsterdam: North-Holland.

———. 1980. "Demand Analysis." In *Handbook of Econometrics,* edited by Z. Griliches and M. Intrilligator.

Deaton, A., and J. Muellbauer. 1980. *Economics and Consumer Behavior.* Cambridge: Cambridge University Press.

Department of Employment and Productivity. Various years. *Family Expenditure Survey.* London: Her Majesty's Stationery Office.

Gamalestos, T. 1973. "Further Analysis of Cross-Country Comparison of Consumer Expenditure Patterns." *European Economic Review* 4: 1–20.

Gorman, W.M. 1961. "On a Class of Preference Fields." *Metroeconomica* 13: 53–56.

———. 1976. "Tricks with Utility Functions." In *Essays in Economic Analysis: Proceedings of the 1975 AUTE Conference, Sheffeld,* ed. by M.J. Artis and A.R. Nobay. Cambridge University Press.

Johansen, L. 1969. "On the Relationships Between Some Systems of Demand Functions." *Liiketaloudellinen Aikakauskirja* 1: 30–41.

Kapteyn, A., and B. van Praag. 1976. "A New Approach to the Construction of Family Equivalence Scales." *European Economic Review* 7: 313–35.

Lau, L.J.; W.L. Lin; and P.A. Yotopoulos. 1978. "The Linear Logarithmic Expenditure System: An Application to Consumption-Leisure Choice." *Econometrica* 46: 843–68.

Michael, R.T., and G.S. Becker. 1973. "On the New Theory of Consumer Behavior." *Swedish Journal of Economics* 75: 378–96.

Muellbauer, J. 1974. "Household Composition, Engel Curves and Welfare Comparisons Between Households." *European Economic Review* 5: 103–22.

―――. 1977. "Testing the Barten Model of Household Composition Effects and the Cost of Children." *Economic Journal* 87: 460–87.

―――. 1980. "The Estimation of the Prais-Houthakker Model of Equivalence Scales." *Econometrica* 48: 153–76.

Parks, R.W., and A.P. Barten. 1973. "A Cross-Country Comparison of the Effects of Prices, Income and Population Composition on Consumption Patterns." *Economic Journal* 83: 834–52.

Pesaran, M.H., and A.S. Deaton. 1978. "Testing Non-nested Nonlinear Regression Models." *Econometrica* 46: 677–94.

Pollak, R.A. 1967. "Additive Utility Functions and Linear Engel Curves." University of Pennsylvania Discussion Paper 53.

―――. 1970. "Habit Formation and Dynamic Demand Functions." *Journal of Political Economy* 78: 745–63.

―――. 1971. "Additive Utility Functions and Linear Engel Curves." *Review of Economic Studies* 38: 401–14.

―――. 1975. "Subindexes in the Cost of Living Index." *International Economic Review* 16: 135–50.

―――. 1976. "Habit Formation and Long-Run Utility Functions." *Journal of Economic Theory* 13: 272–97.

Pollak, R.A., and M.L. Wachter. 1975. "The Relevance of the Household Production Functions and Its Implications for the Allocation of Time." *Journal of Political Economy* 83: 255–77.

Pollak, R.A., and T.J. Wales. 1978. "Estimation of Complete Demand Systems from Household Budget Data: The Linear and Quadratic Expenditure Systems." *American Economic Review* 68: 348–59.

―――. 1979. "Welfare Comparisons and Equivalence Scales." *American Economic Review, Papers and Proceedings* 69: 216–21.

―――. 1980. "Comparison of the Quadratic Expenditure System and Translog Demand Systems with Alternative Specifications of Demographic Effects." *Econometrica* 78: 595–612.

―――. 1981. "Demographic Variables in Demand Analysis." *Econometrica*.

Prais, S.J., and H.S. Houthakker. 1955. *The Analysis of Family Budgets.* Cambridge: Cambridge University Press.

Samuelson, P.A. 1947. *Foundations of Economic Analysis.* Cambridge, Massachusetts: Harvard University Press.

Sydenstricker, E., and W.I. King. 1921. "The Measurement of Relative Economic Status of Families." *Quarterly Publication of the American Statistical Association* 17: 842–57.

Wales, T.J. 1971. "A Generalized Linear Expenditure Model of the Demand for Non-Durable Goods in Canada." *Canadian Journal of Economics* 4: 471–84.

Wales, T.J., and A.D. Woodland. 1976. "Estimation of Household Utility Functions and Labor Supply Response." *International Economic Review* 17: 397–410.

PART
II

3 SOME NEW PERSPECTIVES ON TESTS OF CAPM AND OTHER CAPITAL ASSET PRICING MODELS AND ISSUES OF MARKET EFFICIENCY

John Lintner
Harvard University

INTRODUCTION

The primary purpose of this chapter is to provide some apparently new perspectives on recent tests of CAPM and related but more general models of the formation of capital asset prices. Since it is well known that all the standard tests of market efficiency are necessarily tests of the joint hypothesis of the validity of some assumed pricing model and of market efficiency, our analysis has a direct bearing on these broader issues as well.

A common characteristic of all the well-known tests of CAPM and other pricing models is their reliance on classical econometrics to determine whether a given sample of data is consistent with the assumed model at some (arbitrarily chosen or traditional) "confidence" level. In contrast, at least in a broad but fundamental sense, the approach in most of this chapter will be explicitly Bayesian. I will take the position that the reported (classical statistical) results of some particular test of a particular model must be interpreted in the light of other often equally solid empirical results—frequently (but not always) involving tests of a different model that is inherently relevant to the assessment of the "significance" of the given test. At other points, I will argue that the rigorous implications of "external" observations of market structure or the characteristics of information

129

flows or of other well-confirmed characteristics of market behavior are similarly essential to drawing the proper conclusions from the summary statistics reported on particular tests of given pricing models. In somewhat more formal terms, I use such evidence (external to the given statistical sample or study) to inform my "prior," and my "posterior" conclusion must be an appropriate mixture of the given sample evidence with this prior information.

The present chapter will have accomplished its underlying objective if it succeeds in illustrating the potential power of this approach and nudges the profession toward further research along the lines being suggested and urged here. To provide a common frame of reference, much of the following analysis will focus primarily on tests of what has come to be known as the capital asset pricing model (CAPM)—in either its original version, assuming the existence of (and unlimited borrowing or lending in) a riskless asset, or the so-called "two-parameter" version in which (following Black 1972) the minimum variance zero-beta portfolio takes the place of the riskless asset assumed in the earlier version.

Both formulations of CAPM are of course essentially single period, cross-sectional equilibrium models of asset prices that rest on explicit assumptions that investors are risk-averse maximizers of the utility of their end of period wealth, that capital markets are perfect with no transactions costs or taxes or restrictions on short sales of any asset, and that all information is immediately and costlessly available to all investors, who consequently derive the same (and correct) assessments of the distribution of the future value of any asset or portfolio—the so-called "homogeneous expectations" assumption. These ex ante models, however, can only be tested with ex post data for holding period returns on individual securities or portfolios. Empirical tests consequently require specification of the stochastic process assumed to be generating the observed period-to-period returns. On grounds of market efficiency, the standard assumption has been that the returns follow a stationary stochastic process with independently and identically distributed increments in discrete time or a stationary diffusion (Weiner) process in continuous time.

The union of this assumed return-generating process with either version of the given time equilibrium CAPM rigorously implies four critical and testable propositions: The risk premium in the equilibrium market return must be (1) positive and (2) proportional to its beta (covariance) risk with the common "market" portfolio and (3) strictly linear in its beta and (4) independent of its total (or "residual") risk.[1] Taken together, these properties imply that when the stochastic risk premium in the return of any security (or portfolio) is regressed on the security's beta, the estimated value of the coefficient on the first power of the beta should equal the expected value of the risk premium on the market portfolio over the period of estimation, and that the value of the constant term and the coefficients on any higher powers of beta or any other "extraneous" term should not differ significantly from zero.

Numerous studies by different authors using different data over different time periods and even using different specifications of the "market" portfolio have failed to reject any of the first three testable propositions listed above. But the results of the available direct tests of proposition (4) have been much less uniform and conclusive. Miller and Scholes (1972) have shown that the strong association between individual risk premium and total or residual risk shown in the early studies of Lintner (1965b) and Douglas (1969) could in part be explained by careful allowance for error in variables phenomena and that the remaining association could be explained on the grounds that this variable was proxying for a latent "skewness preference." The well-known work of Black, Jensen, and Scholes (1972) included no tests of the residual variance proposition. They were primarily concerned with the choice between the two versions of CAPM; in implementing their tests on grouped data, they simply assumed that the unobserved residuals of each of their portfolios were equal (p. 114).

More recently, Fama (1976) and Fama and MacBeth (1973) used extensive monthly data "to avoid almost all the problems discussed by Miller and Scholes" (Fama and MacBeth 1973: 613) and conclude that they "cannot reject the hypothesis of the two-parameter (CAPM) model that no measure of risk in addition to portfolio (Beta) risk systematically affects average returns" (ibid: 633). This conclusion was strongly supported by regressions run over the full thirty-three year period 1935–68 as a whole, and the coefficient on an added residual variance term was not significant in any of the five

1. Fama and MacBeth (1973) combined our points (2) and (4) into the single testable proposition that "β_i is a complete measure of the risk of security i in efficient portfolio m; no other measure of the risk of i appears" (610). I separate (2) and (4) here in order to accomodate later consideration of "multi-factor" and the Ross APT models.

or ten year intervals tested within the overall period. However, the "significance of the lack of significance" of the coefficient on an added residual variance term is somewhat muted by noting that the unquestionably relevant beta term was "significant" in only one of the three ten-year intervals tested and only "significant and positive" in two of the six five-year intervals, even when residual variance was not included, and in only one of the six when it was included.[2]

Friend and Westerfield (1979) have recently pointed out that the Fama-MacBeth tests may have failed to detect a geniune effect of residual variances on returns because of their reliance on an equally weighted index of stocks rather than the value-weighted market portfolio implied by theory and also because when they formed groups of stocks to minimize measurement error, they grouped only on the prior period betas without also cross-classifying observations within beta groups in terms of residual variance. Friend and Westerfield, cross-grouping quarterly data in the latter manner for the period 1952–78 and using value-weighted market indexes, find that residual variances are statistically significant in three of the five sixty-month intervals tested, while β was statisticaly significant and positive in only two of the intervals.[3] This leads them to conclude that "the beta coefficient may be no more significant and may be less significant than residual or total variance (or standard deviation) in explaining returns on risky assets" (Friend and Westerfield 1979: 30).

While this conclusion seems rather overstated,[4] this and other

2. See Panels A and C in Fama and MacBeth (1973: Table 3). We should perhaps also observe that Table 5 in their text goes on to analyze the extent to which variations in the fitted values of parameters obtained in various five-and ten-year subperiods within the overall thirty-five-year period covered are due to variations in the "true" values between periods and how much to estimation error. In this context, they report (p. 629) that "table 5 |shows| that there are variables in addition to $\hat{\beta}_p$ that systematically affect period-to-period returns. Some of these variables are apparently related to $\hat{\beta}_p^2$ and $\bar{S}_p$ ($\bar{\varepsilon}_i$). But the latter are almost surely proxies, since there is no economic rationale for their presence in our stochastic return model." No question is raised regarding the validity of this position with respect to the squared beta term, but the possibility that there are valid economic rationales for the inclusion of a residual variance term is specifically addressed later in the text.

3. Compare the results of the Fama-MacBeth tests of the significance of β over five-year periods noted above.

4. Quite apart from various technical problems in the Friend and Westerfield (1979) study that need not concern us here, at least from my Bayesian point of view, this conclusion is overdrawn. I have a strong prior—as I am sure all other serious students of this question do—that the beta on the market is "significant," even though I do not necessarily believe that it is either stable or fully forecastable nor that it is necessarily the only relevant explanatory variable in a positive, scientific sense (see below).

related work at least suggests the need for further analysis and investigation before finally ruling out the possibility that an "augmented CAPM," which includes a residual variance term along with the standard beta coefficient, provides a more satisfactory model for the scientific explanation of observed uncertain security returns than the now standard "beta only" CAPM.

If, as appears to be the case, classical statistical tests have not fully resolved the "residual variance" question in the context of the basic CAPM model itself,[5] it seems appropriate to bring other evidence to bear. There is in fact a substantial amount of other work and knowledge that has a direct bearing on this issue. In particular, subsequent sections will examine the implications for the residual variance question of the results of direct tests of the CAPM and of the Modigliani-Miller (MM) invariance propositions and the fact that corporations do have reasonably stable relative capital structures; the validity of the options pricing model (OPM) an the proven nonstationarity of variances and expected risk premiums on "the market"; and the existence of short selling and other prima facie evidence of diverse information sets, assessments, and portfolios even in otherwise perfect markets. Finally, I develop further implications of diverse assessments and costly information for related issues that arise in certain other well-known asset-pricing models as well as their implications for broader questions of market efficiency and the Roll's critique of any tests of the two-factor model.

IMPLICATIONS OF DIRECT TESTS OF MM-INVARIANCE PROPOSITONS AND THE OBSERVED STABILITY OF RELATIVE CAPITAL STRUCTURES AMONG CORPORATIONS

The capital asset pricing model has provided one of the important building blocks in the development of the theory of corporation finance. The resulting contributions to our understanding have essentially taken the form of developing the implications of CAPM, assuming its validity, for the costs of equity and debt capital, for capital budgeting decisions on a net present value criterion, and so

---

5. Many other studies have also found significant coefficients on a standard deviation or residual variance term. See, for instance, Friend, Westerfield, and Granito (1978) and Levy (1978).

on. But our initial concerns in this chapter are with tests of the scientific validity of CAPM itself and, later, with the associated hypotheses of market efficiency. In the context of such tests, the first illustration of our Bayesian approach is to argue that well-known evidence on the stability of relative capital structures provides independent information that must also be taken into account, along with the test statistics on direct estimates of the model on various samples of stock price data, in reaching conclusions on the scientific validity of these embedded hypotheses.

If CAPM is valid, the risk of any security is exhaustively measured by its beta β_i with the efficient market portfolio m. Both ex ante and ex post, conditional on the expected risk premium on the market portfolio $(\bar{R}_m - R_*)$ where R_* represents either the risk-free rate or the expected return on the orthogonal minimum-variance "z-factor," the expected holding period return $\bar{R}_i$ and the expected risk premium $(\bar{R}_i - R_*)$ on any security i must be given by the equation

$$\bar{R}_i - R_* = \beta_i(\bar{R}_m - R_*) \tag{3.1}$$

with no significant intercept or any other "extraneous element" entering into the equation. In particular, the opportunity cost of any firm's unlevered equity $\bar{R}_{iu}$ will be given by this equation using the systematic risk β_{iu} of the returns on the firm's assets. Moreover, since CAPM necessarily implies the Modigliani-Miller theorems,[6] the market-value-weighted average of the systematic risk β_{iv} on the company's levered equity together with that on its debt must identically equal the risk on its composite assets, β_{iu}. As is well known (see, for instance, Hamada 1969; Rubenstein 1973; or Braeley and Myers 1981), this directly implies that the cost of levered equity capital $\bar{R}_{iv}$ will be given by

$$
\begin{aligned}
\bar{R}_{iv} &= R_* + \beta_{iv}[\bar{R}_m - R_*] \\
&= \bar{R}_{iu} + (1 - \tau)[\bar{R}_{iu} - \bar{R}_{ib}](B_i/S_i) \\
&= R_* + \beta_{iu}[\bar{R}_m - R_*] + (1 - \tau)[\bar{R}_{iu} - \bar{R}_{ib}](B_i/S_i) \tag{3.2}
\end{aligned}
$$

6. CAPM requires the separation property and identical assessments which imply identical composition of risk asset portfolios which in turn imply equal proportional holdings of all the (risky) debt issues of any company *and* of its outstanding equity—which is equivalent to holding its unlevered equity. Stiglitz (1969 and 1973) and others have of course demonstrated that the MM theorems hold under more general conditions than those required for CAPM. All I need here is that the validity of CAPM is *sufficient* for the validity of the MM-theorems, and that violations of the latter necessarily imply violations of the CAPM.

where τ represents the next tax advantage of corporate debt,[7] $\bar{R}_{ib}$ is the required return on outstanding debt with a market value of B_i, and S_i is the market value of the levered equity itself. In this model, an equation similar to the first line of equation (3.2) expresses the cost of debt capital $\bar{R}_{id}$ as a linear function of the systematic risks β_{id} of the returns to debtholders. The weighted average cost of capital (for unregulated firms [8]) under suitably stationary conditions declines linearly as a function of its leverage ratio $(0_i = B_i/(B_i + S_i))$ according to:

$$\rho_i = (1 - \theta_i)\bar{R}_{iv} + (1 - \tau)\theta_i\bar{R}_{id} = \bar{R}_{iu}(1 - \tau\theta_i) \tag{3.3}$$

Correspondingly, the value of the levered firm $V_{id} = B_i + S_i$ will be equal to its unlevered value V_{iu} plus the present value of the net tax shield provided by its debt ($PVTS_i$):

$$V_{id} = V_{iu} + PVTS_i \tag{3.4}$$

Although these familiar linear relations (3.3) and (3.4) were originally derived by (and are generally associated with) Modigliani and Miller, they are also directly implied by CAPM itself. Violations of the MM-propositions are necessarily contradictions of CAPM relations. The rational (maximizing) behavior imputed to investors in deriving CAPM clearly also implies maximizing behavior on the part of corporate managers. The predictions of this model with respect to the debt-equity financing decisions of corporations are quite clear— and are also well-known by all students of Corporation Finance (as distinguished perhaps from students of capital markets per se) to be widely at variance with the observed facts.

Within the CAPM–MM model of equations (3.3) and (3.4), there are only two relevant cases: The net tax advantage of corporate

7. Modigliani and Miller (1963) initially ignored personal taxes (or implicitly assumed they were neutral). Under strong perfect market assumptions, more recent work (Miller 1977; Haley and Schall 1979: 390–404, 435–40) concluded that the net tax advantage of debt to the corporation vanishes when personal tax rates "span" the corporate rate. But still more recent work by deAngelo and Masulus (1980a, 1980b) demonstrates a positive tax advantage under efficient but incomplete markets, making $\tau > 0$ (and $PVTS > 0$), even though the net rate τ is substantially smaller than the corporate rate standing alone. In what follows I will simply abstract from any problems that arise from the nonconstancy of τ (and nonlinearities in $PVTS$). These, where present, are not germane to the main thrust of my argument here.

8. Since regulatory commissions, in effect, reduce the earnings before interest and taxes (EBIT) allowable in the absence of debt by the full tax savings on debt interest, the relevant weighted average cost of capital for regulated firms uses pre-corporate-tax debt cost. The implications are developed in Lintner (1981).

dept (τ) is either zero or positive. If it is zero, the model implies that all capital structures will provide equal firm value and have equal cost. But Litzenberger and Sosin (1977) have provided a remarkably "clean" test of this proposition using data on so-called "dual purpose" funds that have demonstrated strong effects on firm value as proportions of debt and equity capital were varied. The conditions of the model were well-satisfied because the market values of the fund's assets (NAV) and of its income ("debt") and capital ("equity") shares are regularly quoted in active trading and because a unit of an income and a capital share and its NAV are always in an identical risk class. Moreover, tax shields are precisely zero because payments to income ("debt") shares are nondeductible and bankruptcy costs are irrelevant. Litzenberger and Sosin attribute the observed strong firm value effects of shifting capital structures to the incompleteness of markets and institutional restrictions on short selling. But these are facts of life in the world CAPM-MM attempt to model. These results of direct tests require the introduction of additional terms to reduce (and hopefully eliminate) the persistent bias in the "pure" equations (see also the confirming evidence from Sosin 1978 and from Masulis 1980, cited in Litzenberger 1981).

In addition to such direct positive evidence, we also observe that maximizing behavior under CAPM-MM with $\tau = 0$ would imply that the ratios of debt to equity (or total) capital would be randomly distributed across firms at any and all points in time and also that the fraction of debt used to finance each (major) new investment project should (or may as well) be drawn randomly from a rectangular zero-one distribution. But far from being random across firms in this way, balance sheet data (either in book value or market value terms) establish the existence of clear patterns in the *relative* use of either long or total debt liabilities as a source of financing for firms in different industries, and work in progress is showing the patterns to be rather remarkably stable over time. Moreover, the direct observation of business practice in deciding the fraction of debt to use in the financing of major new investment projects (and to allow for in their selection) uniformly finds that firms in fact make these decisions to some greater or lesser (but always nonzero) degree in terms of the total (or "residual") as well as the systematic risk of the project. These observations are in keeping with the theoretical and practical "advice" in leading finance textbooks as well (see, for instance, Braeley and Myers 1981; Haley and Schall 1979; Weston and Brigham 1981; and Van Horne 1980).[9]

The alternative relevant assumption in equations (3.3) and (3.4) is that the net tax advantage of debt is positive, but $\tau > 0$ implies that all firms at all points in time should be issuing all debt securities they can sell and borrowing all the funds they can get—that is, they should continuously maximize their utilization of whatever "debt capacity" they may have. I am confident that everyone who has made substantial observations at first hand and seriously analyzed the behavior and decisions of lenders and investment bankers will agree that the available supplies and terms of debt are in fact an inverse function of the unsystematic as well as the systematic risks of the borrowing firm. But I do not need this condition for the conclusions being drawn.[10] Suppose, on the contrary, that there were in fact an infinitely elastic supply of debt capital available to each firm (as is implied by equation (3.3) and (3.4)). Even in this unrealistically favorable context, the uniform (qualitative) conclusion of extra– or post– CAPM-MM theory is that corporations can and should maximize the value of the firm by relying on debt financing to an optimal degree that necessarily falls short of the debt capacity of the firm once the confirmed and observable incompleteness and imperfections of the capital markets that are inconsistent with the CAPM–MM model are recognized (see Scott 1976; Kim 1978; Chen and Kim 1979; Myers 1977; Litzenberger 1981; Haley and Schall 1979: 14, 15; Copeland and Weston 1979: 12; Braeley and Myers 1981: 17, 18).

The standard general statement of these augmented models in the theoretical literature and in the more theoretically oriented textbook on corporation finance is to rewrite equation (3.4) as

$$V_{id} = V_{iu} + PVTS_i - PVFD_i \tag{3.5}$$

9. The "advice" in these textbooks can be summarized as requiring that each (major) investment project (1) be analyzed with an imputation of that degree of debt that will maximize its contribution (ΔV_{id}) to the value of the firm and (2) be undertaken only if its $NPV = \Delta V_{id} \geq 0$, when equation (5) rather than (3.4) is used in evaluating ΔV_{id}. The optimal level of debt financing to be use and allowed for in evaluating any project is thus a function of the contribution such debt would make to the $PVFD$ term is that equation—and thereby a function of nonsystematic risk, as discussed later in the text.

10. If accepted, this "supply condition" does however reinforce these conclusions and reduce the otherwise optimal level of debt financing.

where the first and second derivatives of the present value of financial distress (*PVFD*) with respect to the relative degree of debt financing are both positive. The graph of V_{id} is of course an inverted parabola, with the optimal level of debt determined by the point at which the marginal tax shield no longer exceeds the increasing "distress costs" when both are measured in terms of present values.

The *PVFD* term itself is the summation of several elements emphasized by different authors, including the increases in agency and monitoring costs with increasing debt (Jensen and Meckling 1976); the loss of "financial flexibility" (Donaldson 1962, 1969); the loss of sales due to weakened assurance of delivery (Lintner 1962; Robicheck and Myers 1965); increasing inability to undertake otherwise profitable future investment opportunities (Robichek and Myers 1965; Myers 1977); and increasing probablities of costly violations of restrictive indenture provisions and of incurring dead-weight bankruptcy costs (Scott 1976; Lintner 1977; Kim 1978). Some of these negative effects involve dead-weight costs paid to third parties, while others act to lower the whole probability distribution (and specifically the expected values) of future elements in the income streams available to shareholders and bondholders together as debt is increased. All these components of the *PVFD* term are increasing functions of the total (or "residual") risks of the firm's cash flows, as well as of its systematic β_{iu} risks and the level of its debt obligations. In addition, since many of these separate effects become progressively (rather than just proportionately) larger, *PVFD* increases at an increasing rate as more debt is used to finance any given set of real assets.

These properties of *PVFD* in equation (3.5) require that we rewrite our CAPM- MM based equations (3.2) and (3.3). In general, bond yields are increased to cover the expected value of all these added costs and risks to bondholders and are thus an increasing function of β_{iu}, $\sigma_{i \cdot m}$, and θ_i. But the net burden of this added compensation to bondholders falls on the equity holders, and even though bondholders are compensated for bearing their part of these added risks, the bulk of these risks of financial distress and loss of financial flexibility will continue to fall on the residual equityholders. Since these added risks and contingent costs to shareholders will increase at least in proportion to the firm's basic systematic and "residual" risk and more than in proportion to any increase in leverage, we must add a term such as $f(\beta_{iu}, \sigma_{i \cdot m}^2, \theta_i)$ with f_1, f_2, f_3, f_{22},

$f_{32}, f_{33} > 0$ to the expression for $\bar{R}_{iv}$ in equation (3.2). The cost of equity capital thus becomes

$$\bar{R}_{iv} = \bar{R}_{iu} + (1 - \tau)\theta_i[\bar{R}_{iu} - \bar{R}_{ib}] + f(\beta_{iu}, \sigma^2_{i.m}, \theta_i)$$

$$= R_* + \beta_{iv}[\bar{R}_m - R_*] + f(\beta_{iu}, \sigma^2_{i.m}, \theta_i) \qquad (3.6)$$

Similarly, using equation (3.6) in the definition of the weighted averaged cost of capital, we have

$$\rho_i = (1 - \theta_i)\bar{R}_{iv} + (1 - \tau)\bar{R}_{ib} = \bar{R}_{iu}(1 - \tau\,\theta_i) + g(\beta_{iu}, \sigma^2_{i.m}, \theta_i) \qquad (3.7)$$

where the partial derivatives on the last term are also positive. It will be observed that in contrast to the simple CAPM (or Modigliani-Miller) version of equation (3.3), the "after tax interest" weighted average cost of capital ρ_i in equation (3.7) does have a well-defined minimum, with leverage far short of the maximum debt the firm could issue.

But our concern is with the implications for tests of the CAPM itself. The inference should be clear. The cost of equity capital to the firm is the expected rate of return to the investing shareholder. If all firms estimated the cost of their equity capital in terms of the CAPM equation (3.2), independent of nonsystematic risk, maximizing behavior would require either maximal (or purely random) use of debt according to the derived equations (3.3) and (3.4). But this is contrary to fact.

All the known theories explaining the regularities in observed capital structure behavior rely on the essential relevance of the firm's nonsystematic (as well as its systematic) risks in the (incomplete and somewhat imperfect) capital markets within which the firm's financing is done. The more general equations (3.5) and (3.7) incorporating these nonsystematic risks imply interior solutions much more consistent with the facts of observed corporate behavior, and these equations in turn require the "extra term" in equation (3.6) for the cost of equity capital.

The fact that the costs of debt and equity capital in terms of which corporate financing decisions are made require the use of augmented CAPM equations based on (residual) variances as well as betas of course does not by itself necessarily prove that the unaugmented standard CAPM equation is wrong. For instance, it might be argued that corporation managements persistently base their financing decisions on significantly biased assessments of the returns really required by the market. But this explanation would seem to violate the assumptions of the informational efficiency of security markets to an unreasonable and improbable degree.[11] Alternatively, the discrepancies might be explained in terms of non-value-maximizing behavior. This explanation, however, would wreck havoc for all our theorems regarding the primary functions of efficient securities markets for the efficient allocations of real resources in the broader economy. Moreover, most of us would be especially reluctant to believe that this is a serious problem with respect to the *financing* of whatever investments firms may choose to make and whatever assets they may choose to hold. Lower average financing costs that maximize the value of whatever the firm decides to do are a "plus" whatever the broader context of its other decisionmaking may be.

If we thus rule out other explanations of the persistent discrepancies noted earlier, we are left with the conclusion that corporate financing policy seems to be acting quite consistently in terms of market financing costs, which do vary to at least some significant degree with unsystematic as well as systematic risk. My conclusion is that this "indirect" evidence belongs in our Bayesian prior as we assess the "significance" of the "sample" results of standard tests of the CAPM equation (3.2) in forming our posterior judgments on the issue of whether residual variances "really belong" in the equation for stock returns.

IMPLICATIONS OF THE VALIDITY OF THE OPTIONS PRICING MODEL

The original derivations of the capital asset pricing model were concerned directly with establishing the conditionally optimal mixture of risky assets in investors' portfolios and the resulting equilibrium sets of market prices and expected rates of return. Primary attention was given to equity prices (returns), and empirical

11. Quite apart from the well-known evidence supporting the informational efficiency of capital markets in general, we observe that these corporation financing decisions are heavily influenced if not fully determined by financial officers who are involved with and dealing in the financial markets for their companies on a regular basis. Nor does the well-established profitability of "insider trading" on personal account cast doubt on the position taken here. This profitable trading merely shows that the market is not fully efficient on Fama's "Strong Form" definition, but does not establish any persistent bias, since insiders at times are net buyers and at other times net sellers.

testing has applied the resulting well-known CAPM equation directly to stock prices and holding period returns. But everyone seems to agree that the option pricing model (OPM), initially developed by Fischer Black and Myron Scholes (1973) and almost concurrently generalized by Robert Merton (1973), represents one of the most important contributions to finance since the earlier development of the capital asset pricing model (CAPM). And the suggestion by Black and Scholes in the same paper that the equilibrium solution to the option pricing problem can be used to value other complex contingent claims—and specifically the equity of a levered firm—has been regarded as "one of the most important observations in the field of finance in the last ten years" (Smith 1976: 5). Extensive empirical tests with daily data have strongly supported the twin hypotheses of the validity of the option pricing model and the efficiency of the options market (see, for instance, Black and Scholes 1972; Galai 1977, 1978; and the additional references cited in the latter). It is consequently appropriate to examine the implications of OPM pricing of equities for the standard tests of returns on common stocks based on the CAPM equation.

For this purpose, following Galai and Masulis (1976),[12] we assume that the equilibrium market value of the firm (i.e., its stocks and bonds combined) at all given times is such that the rate of return on its assets exactly satisfies the standard CAPM relation

$$\bar{r}_i = r_f + \beta_i(\bar{r}_m - r_f) \qquad (3.8)$$

where all variables have the usual definitions, though the rs are now specified as instantaneous rates of return.[13] If we now assume that this i^{th} firm has only a single issue of pure discount bonds outstanding, which prohibits any cash returns to equity until after the bonds mature T time periods later, the current market value of the company's common stock will be determined by the standard OPM formula (which need not be reproduced here) wherein the stock is valued as a call on the uncertain market value of the entire company (or all its assets) T periods hence.

12. See Galai and Masulis (1976: 54–55) and Copeland and Weston (1979: p. 408) for the detailed assumptions necessary for OPM and CAPM validly to be applicable simultaneously in the market. As lawyers would say, these assumptions are specifically "incorporated by reference."

13. Merton (1971; 1973) originally derived this continous time version of CAPM assuming a stationary Weiner process in returns with only one source of stochastic variation, and he established the necessity of these conditions.

It is well known that within OPM, the value of the stock S is not a simple direct function of the firm's expected rate of return $\bar{r}_i$ (as given by equation (3.8)) nor of its systematic risk β_V. However, S does vary essentially and directly with (1) the value V of the firm and (2) the variance σ^2 of the firm's rate of return, (3) the level of the riskless rate of return r_f (assumed constant), and (4) the maturity T of the bonds, but (5) inversely with their face value C. Moreover, the systematic risk of the equity is the product of the firm's systematic risk and the elasticity of the equity value (i.e., $\beta_S = \eta_S \beta_V$), since the stochastic rate of return on the equity bears this same proportional relation to the stochastic returns on the firm's assets (i.e., $\tilde{r}_S = \eta_S \tilde{r}_V$; see Galai and Masulis 1976: 58). Both this elasticity η_S, and consequently the systematic risk of the stock β_S, are direct functions of the same five primary arguments (V, σ^2, r_f, T, and C) as the stock price itself, though the signs of the partial derivations are of course reversed.

Merton's derivation and theoretical validation of the "clean," continuous time CAPM (equation (3.8)) required the assumption of a strictly stationary Weiner diffusion process in a single stochastic factor generating the random components of the returns in question. Taking these returns to apply to the values V placed on the firm (and its assets) implies that the firm's systematic risk β_V is constant. However, the underlying premise of the model is that the value of the firm V and the rates of return provided by holding the firm (or its assets) $\tilde{r}_v$ follow a pure stationary "white noise" diffusion process, and the stochastic variations in these returns means that the systematic risk of the equity β_S will almost surely be *nonstationary even when* the systematic risk of the firm β_V is strictly constant. Moreover, as Galai and Masulis observe (1976: 59, n. 18), β_V itself can be stationary only when the firm's asset structure consists entirely of physical assets, riskless debt, and unlevered equities, but excludes all other financial assets. Most firms do in fact issue risk-bearing debt and hold other financial assets. Quite obviously, the resulting nonstationarity and stochastic variation in the firm's own systematic risk will seriously compound the nonstationary variation in the systematic risk of the equity.

These inferences are of course well known to the profession, but their implications for direct tests of the CAPM do not seem to have been fully developed or brought to bear on the interpretation of the statistical results of such tests. Doing so is my second illustration and application of the essentially Bayesian approach suggested at the outset. My reading of the empirical literature leads me to conclude that results of tests of the OPM have been more uniformly favorable and led to a stronger degree of verification of this model for the pricing of options than have the tests of the CAPM (in either the r_f or the r_z version) applied directly to stock returns. Stipulating the scientific validity of the OPM for options and accepting the empirical relevance of the Black-Scholes characterization of the option type nature of equity returns, several clear implications immediately follow.

First, to the extent that equity returns do have the characteristics of options, the variance rate (at least of the firm's returns, if not of the equity returns themselves) "really belongs" in a properly specified equation for equity returns—as a "proxy for itself" and not (merely) as a proxy for other truly relevant but excluded variables. It is of course quite true that equation (3.8) holds at each given time for the required return $\hat{r}_S$ on the equity of the firm, given the equity beta β_S relevant to that given instant, just as it holds for the required returns on the entire assets of the firm $\hat{r}_v$ given its β_V (assumed constant). But the equity beta β_S relevant to each instant is itself determined by the variance rate and the other primary elements in the OPM.[14] In this model, the instantaneous equity beta β_S is an intermediate and derived stochastic variable, as distinct from the *primary* role of the variance and other basic elements in the OPM.

Second, if equity securities have the essential characteristics of options, they in effect provide a "call" on the assets of the firm. Whenever ex post variance turns out to be greater (or smaller) than the ex ante variance, the ex post return on the "option" (i.e., the common stock) will include an unanticipated positive (or negative) component. Moreover, if stocks are ranked on variances, the odds are strong that most of the high- (or low) ranked stocks will be those whose ex post variance exceeds (or falls short of) their ex ante variance. Since these stocks will also show higher (or lower) returns, any regression with ex post data will show a clearly positive coefficient on the variance term. Moreover, at least from a Bayesian

---

14. Since these other primary elements included V, the instantaneous equity beta β_S is in part determined by the concurrent instantaneous realization of the underlying stochastic process generating the returns on the firm's assets.

point of view, such a result cannot be dismissed as a confusion between ex ante and ex post magnitudes. It is surely far more reasonable to believe that the ex post discrepancies between ex post and ex ante variances are a direct, increasing function of ex ante variances than to rest on the contrary presumption. With this "prior," the conclusion again follows that the variance (at least of the firm's return stream) "really belongs."

Third, the returns on common stocks constitute an inherently nonstationary stochastic process even when the returns on the firm's assets are strictly stationary. Consequently, standard OLS regressions are misspecified in essential ways. The resulting biases directly impair the power of the usual classical tests of the scientific validity and adequacy of the CAPM.

As one particular case in point, it is well known that the use of estimates of β_S, obtained from regressions that implicitly assume constancy over the period of fit when in fact the "true" value varied over time, will introduce biases in the regression coefficient on β_S in the next stage and mechanically produce a positive coefficient on σ_s^2 or $\sigma^2_{i.m}$ in the standard test of CAPM. As Galai and Masulis (1976) have noted, Hamada (1972) and Rosenberg (1974) have made considerable progress in using information on the firm's asset and capital structures in improving the estimates of the forecastable variations in β_S over time, which substantially reduces this source of bias.[15] But we observe (from our first point above) that variance per se is one of the fundamental determinants of stochastic stock returns. After the time series of β_S for any firm has been estimated as well as possible, any remaining positive coefficient on the variance term can safely be attributed entirely to bias only if the researcher has a "spike prior" ($Pr = 1$) on the proposition that his estimates of β_S fully (and accurately) incorporate the true effects of variance. But there is more to the story.

The existence of a "white noise" component in the stochastic process generating the returns of each firm rigorously implies that, along with stock prices and returns, the systematic risks and the

15. While Galai and Masulis call for more information specifically bearing on changes in firm's asset and capital structures (as Rosenberg and others have since done), in principle, other information such as changes in relevant product markets may also be useful. It should be noted that Galai and Masulis also make several valuable observations regarding the implications of treating common stocks as options for tests of the efficiency of the capital market. Without duplicating their discussion, issues of market efficiency are considered later in this chapter.

variances of the returns on levered equity (and risky debt) are *also* in general nonstationary. But this in turn implies that all estimates of β_S will necessarily be made subject to measurement error, which in itself is sufficient to produce a positive coefficient on variance when the latter is included as an "added term" in the test equation. However, in the ideal circumstances hypothesized, this attribute of the β_S estimates will be entirely due to (and a direct function of) the variance of the process generating the firm's returns, and we once again should conclude that the latter variances properly "belong" in the test equation.

The analysis to this point has been built on Merton's (1971, 1973a) single factor, continuous time derivation of the CAPM equation (3.8), assuming that the firm's returns are generated by a stationary Weiner diffusion process, which implies that the covariance σ_{vm}, the market return variance σ_m^2, the systematic risk of the firm β_V, and the market risk premium $(\bar{r}_m - \bar{r}_f)$ are constant over time. We have been concerned with the implications of the fact that, via the OPM, even in this special case the returns on the levered equity will depend directly on the variance and be nonstationary. But extensive work on direct estimates of variance rates themselves, and notably analysis of the variance rates implied by observed option premium data, clearly establishes that variance rates vary substantially and in very imperfectly forecastable ways over time (see Rosenberg 1974; Black 1976). Moreover, these fluctuations in variance rates in turn imply wide changes over time in expected returns and risk premiums on "the market."

This inference follows directly from the fact that risk-averse investors dominate the market for risk assets, and Merton (1980) has used the OPM itself to provide empirical estimates of the resulting fluctuations in market risk premiums. But standard tests of CAPM have almost uniformly taken the market risk premium and variance to be constant over the period of fit. We need merely observe that if there are "measurement error" problems due to the imperfect ex ante forecastability of $(\bar{r}_m - \bar{r}_*)$, as well as in β_S, even more severe problems are created for the standard tests of CAPM (since these terms multiply each other). To my knowledge these problems have not been seriously addressed, but since the degree of "measurement error" in both terms is monotone, increasing in the variance rate and its rate of change, the latter are essential variables in the proper form of the equation to explain and predict returns.

IMPLICATIONS OF THE EXISTENCE OF SHORT SELLING, COSTLY INFORMATION, AND OTHER EVIDENCE OF DIVERSE ASSESSMENTS, INFORMATION SETS, AND PORTFOLIOS EVEN IN OTHERWISE PERFECT MARKETS

It is well known that CAPM among other things rests on an assumption that all relevant information is immediately and cost-lessly available to all investors who consequently select their portfolios of risky assets on the basis of the same and correct assessment of the multivariate distribution of the available uncertain returns and future prices. This assumption of identical expectations and assessments implies that (1) all investors will include all marketable risky assets and securities in their portfolios and that (2) the proportionate composition of risk portfolios will be identical for all investors. The latter in turn implies that (3) all risk assets are held in positive quantities in all portfolios—namely, that there will be no "short positions" in any security. All three implications are clearly violated by substantial evidence, and I am suggesting that such evidence must also be properly taken into account in assessing the direct statistical results obtained when CAPM is tested with any given set of market returns and prices.

Outstanding short positions in major listed stocks are published in the financial press each month. Each monthly list is long, and many of the short positions in each list represent substantial fractions of the total outstanding supplies of the respective stocks. This phenomenon has persisted over a long period of time and also continues to characterize the data in recent years even after firms involved in merger negotiations and those with listed options are deleted from the list. The prevalence of short positions not explainable by merger arbitrage and option hedging is in itself conclusive evidence of diverse assessments of returns and/or risks across securities among investors and of differences in investors' portfolios.

Detailed reports of the purchases and sales of corporate "insiders" are prepared by the SEC at monthly intervals. The extent of such activity is further prima facie evidence of diverse information sets, assessments, and portfolios among investors. The fact that such insider trading on average has provided substantial and significantly positive risk-adjusted returns is simply further evidence that their information sets and assessments are not only different but better than the relevant weighted average of others in the market.[16]

There has been increasing recognition in recent years that the information used in assessing security returns is itself an economic good, valuable to have but costly to acquire. Relevant information is not immediately, costlessly, and uniformly distributed among investors. In general, different investors will start with different information sets and assessments at any given time. Their positions relative to flows of new information will also differ, as will the costs (and delays) involved in acquiring new information. After their respective outlays on information acquisition have been optimized, information sets and assessments will still vary widely among investors, as will their composition of their resulting portfolios even in otherwise perfect markets.[17]

We should also observe that the human capital (and other nonmarketable assets) of different investors will in general have a different vector of correlations (or covariance) with the set of securities being traded in the market. The composition of the optimal portfolios of marketable securities will consequently differ across investors even if their assessments with respect to these securities were identical, as shown in Mayers (1972, 1973). In the more realistic case where the latter assessments are also diverse, human capital and related considerations simply serve to compound the resulting disparity in the observed composition of investors' portfolios.

Moreover, Lintner (1969: 375–80) has shown that investors' portfolios will differ even when all investors act on identical assessments of (real) returns if there is no riskless asset (for instance, because uncertain inflation makes the return on the nominally riskless asset also uncertain). The reason is that the marginal shadow value of wealth, which takes the place of the riskless return in the

16. The classic study is Jaffe (1974). The specific finding that outsiders could use knowledge of such trading after a delay of thirty to forty-five days to make significantly positive risk-adjusted excess returns strictly pertains to the efficiency of the market, discussed below. But it follows a fortiori from the Jaffe result that the insiders must have done very much better still—and the latter inference supports the statement in the text.

17. This general result is all we need for this section of the chapter. Lintner (1969) and Gonedes (1976) have derived the weighted averages that determine security market equilibria when investors act on diverse assessments but markets are otherwise perfect. Further implications of diverse information sets and assessments are discussed below.

determination of each investor's optimal portfolio, is itself a direct function of each investor's risk aversion coefficient and wealth. The latter differ across investors even if their assessments of expected returns and covariance matrixes are identical. Once again, if we more realistically allow for dispersion in the latter assessments of expected returns and/or risks, there will be still more diversity in investors' portfolios even in otherwise perfect markets.[18]

In addition to this indirect evidence of heterogeneous portfolios and assessments provided by the existence of short selling, insider trading, human capital, and so on, there is of course direct survey evidence that establishes a rather remarkable degree of diversity among the portfolios of risk assets actually held by investors (see, for instance, Lewellan, Lease, and Schlarbaum 1974; Blume, Crockett, and Friend 1974; Blume and Friend 1975).

The established facts that portfolios and assessments are actually quite diverse have fundamental implications for the security market line (SML) used in tests of the Capital Asset Pricing Model (CAPM). Williams (1977) has used a simplified but tractable continuous time model to establish that heterogeneous assessments and portfolios

---

18. Although I confine the discussion in the text to evidence indicating diverse assessments and portfolios when markets for securities (and information) are perfect, certain real world imperfections reinforce the conclusions. For instance, there are limitations on the amounts that can be borrowed, and the borrowing rate is almost always higher than the lending rate (and often increases with the degree of portfolio "leverage"). Even when investors' assessments are identical, these circumstances will induce investors with different wealth and risk aversion to hold different portfolios (see Lintner 1965a: 36–37, n. III, IV, V; Blume and Friend 1973). However, the major reason for the wide diversity in the composition of observed portfolios (and the large number of portfolios that contain only limited subsets of securities) is almost surely the fact that most investors have information on only limited numbers of securities. While this circumstance is fully compatible with a Pareto-optimal and purely competitive general equilibrium in the security markets, given the investor's information sets (Lintner 1969: 390–99), the resulting greater diversity in portfolios due to this lack of relevant information compounds the conclusions being drawn.

Many other real world market imperfections commonly cited are probably less important than those mentioned just above in the context of this chapter. Restrictions on short selling only moderately reduce the observed diversity in portfolios due to differing assessments, as does the increased cost of short positions due to the common failure to pay interest on escrowed proceeds and the additional margin investment required on short sales (cf. Lintner 1971). Similarly, transactions costs will be large relative to expected risk premiums for many investors, which means that observed portfolios will not be in continuous frictionless equilibrium, as assumed in theory. But even large transactions costs and infrequent restructuring of portfolios will increase the importance (and coefficient) of the residual variance term in the security market line (SML) for individual stocks only if the dispersion among individual investors' portfolios is greater with inhibited trading than it would have been in frictionless markets—and there is to my knowledge no evidence that this is the case.

necessarily[19] imply that "residual risks appear jointly with beta in the regression equation for each security" (1977: 121), and although the security market line continues to be linear in beta, "beta no longer remains a complete measure of risk" (ibid.).[20] His model is simplified by assuming that each investor faces an identical investment opportunity set and that each knows that the actual returns are being generated by a strictly stationary stochastic Wiener process. However, in contrast to Merton (1973a), Williams introduces heterogeneous beliefs by assuming that at least some investors do not have accurate foreknowledge of the true parameters of the process and consequently must use the available information to estimate the means, variances, and covariances of returns on risky assets. While he shows that with this simple specification of uncertainty the latter can be quite accurately estimated from observed returns, the estimates of means obtainable from such returns will always be subject to error. The heterogeneity of beliefs in Williams' model is thus effectively confined to differences among investors in their respective assessments of the vector of expected returns across securities at any given time, and even this diversity is limited by the assumption that all investors know that the underlying process is stationary.

Even with this limited degree of heterogeneity of assessments, Williams is able to demonstrate that each security's residual risk "really belongs" along with its beta in the SML regression equation for its market return. More realistic models would allow for potentially very significant additional sources of diversity in assessments and portfolios. For instance, many if not most investors are probably not really sure that the underlying stochastic process is actually stable,[21] and they will probably differ in their assessments of

19. Williams notes one special circumstance in which the stated conclusions do not hold—specifically, "if *by chance* the market as a whole behaves indistinguishably from any group of investors with identical, correct probability beliefs" (1977: 234, emphasis added). The same coincidental exception is summarized on page 235: "As long as investors in the aggregate demand securities in the same relative proportions as investors with correct probability beliefs, the standard SML applies of course, such a result typically holds only by accident."

20. Both quotations are from page 221, and the latter statement is also found on page 223. The linearity of the SML in beta is shown on page 237. Note also: "With heterogeneous beliefs beta fails as a complete measure of risk. *For all finite time, both* beta and diversifiable or residual risk affect the market's assessment of required average returns on securities" (p. 234, emphasis added.)

21. As Williams observes: "persistence over time of heterogeneous beliefs requires nonstationary pricing processes more general [than the one used]" (1977: 238). Note also the direct evidence of nonstationarity cited at the end of the preceding section.

the form and parameter values characterizing the instability, as well as in their assessments of the covariance matrix relevant to each given time. Although these more general models have not yet been developed because of their complexity, it seems safe to believe that rigorous examination of these additional sources of diverse assessments will substantially reinforce the significance of the residual variance term Williams established in the simpler continuous time models he investigated. Moreover, from the work of Lintner (1969) and Levy (1978) based on single period mean variance models, the relative importance of the residual variance in the SML equation for different individual stocks at any time will vary inversely both with the weighted average degree of diversification of the particular portfolios within which each appears (the weights depending on both wealth and risk aversion) and with how widely it is held in the market.

It must be emphasized that the residual variance appears along with the beta in the SML for each security in Williams' analysis precisely because of the heterogeneous beliefs of different investors, based on the incomplete information available to them at any given time regarding the true parameter(s) of the underlying stochastic process. At each point, each investor adjusts his or her portfolio to reflect the difference between the true average return on securities and his or her current assessment of the unknown average return, and it is also adjusted to hedge against the correlation between the returns on risky assets and the unanticipated changes he will make in his assessment of the unknown true average returns as more information accumulates (Williams 1977: 220–21 and passim). We have seen that incomplete (and costly) information, heterogeneous assessments, and diverse portfolios are facts of life in the real world. These facts necessarily imply a positive coefficient on the residual variance term. Any particular empirical estimate of the size of this coefficient will of course be subject to error and possible bias, but any finding of a positive coefficient per se cannot be dismissed as necessarily spurious or as entirely due to bias.

It has frequently been observed that if significantly positive residual variance terms truly exist in the market, then large institutional investors could form portfolios with large residual risks that would beat the market averages on the bias of portfolio risk and return (see, for instance, Sharpe 1978: 919). This phenomenon doubtless provides an important explanation for the fact that the computed coefficients on residual variance terms for the large and actively traded securities that dominate most large institutional portfolios are as small as they are (and for the fact that, while positive, they are very often "statistically insignificant"). But there are clearly very real limits on the extent to which this phenomenon can be generalized. Even for the best informed institutional investors, information is costly and incomplete, and they are very conscious of the risk that others in the market may already know something important that they do not know and the risk that upcoming new information will change their current assessments— and these considerations are sufficient to insure some remaining positive coefficients. Moreover, the costs and the uncertainty and diversity of assessments are almost surely relatively greater for the smaller, less actively traded securities in the market, which analytically increases the expected size of their residual variance coefficients even after all profitable ex ante portfolio adjustments have been made.

FURTHER IMPLICATIONS OF DIVERSE ASSESSMENTS AND COSTLY INFORMATION FOR OTHER SECURITY-PRICING MODELS AND TESTS OF MARKET EFFICIENCY

To this point in the chapter, we have been concerned with the implications of diverse assessments and investors' portfolios for the presence of a residual variance term in the SML for individual securities in the basic CAPM. In this section, we briefly consider these issues in the context of other security-pricing models that have been advanced more recently and then turn to their broader implications for more general issues of market efficiency and for Roll's critique of tests of asset pricing theory.

There have been two important and rather different generalizations of the CAPM. Rosenberg and McKibben (1973) and (1974) have analyzed various "extramarket" components of return by introducing a set of "descriptor variables" to predict the intertemporal changes in the parameters of the model. The descriptor variables are firm-specific measures based on accounting records and market data (such as turnover, dividend yields, and book-market ratios). The results have been encouraging. It was found that forecast errors on market rates of return were substantially reduced when vectors of description variables were used to adjust estimates of both current betas and current residual variances. In the context of this chapter, it should be noted that forecast errors were also substantially reduced when the estimated residual variance, as well as the estimated beta, were included in the SMLs.

The other important generalization of the CAPM is Merton's (1973a) generalization of the continuous time version of equation (3.8) to allow for multiple sources of uncertainty in addition to end of period uncertainty over returns per se. In his 1977 paper, Merton particularly emphasized the investors' concern with uncertainties over labor income, the menu of possible consumption goods available in the future and their relative prices, and shifts in the future investment opportunity set—that is, future rates of return on capital. On the assumption that each source of uncertainty follows its own known and strictly stationary Weiner process, optimization leads to the formation of a different mutual fund of securities for each source of uncertainty, and the equilibrium expected return on the ith securities satisfies a "multiple beta" version of CAPM:

$$\bar{r}_i - r_f = \sum_{k=1}^{m} \beta_{ik} [\bar{r}_k - r_f] \tag{3.9}$$

where $\bar{r}_k$ is the expected return on the kth mutual fund, β_{ik} is the instantaneous beta between the randon return on the ith security and that of the kth mutual fund, and m is the number of funds.

Within this model, regressions utilizing only the first fund on the right (the "market portfolio") are sure to produce significant coefficients on residual variances, but only as proxies for the omitted terms or funds. However, there is more to be said. While interest rate uncertainties can be hedged reasonably well by portfolios of longer maturity bonds, the other uncertainties cannot be hedged as well in practice. Moreover, suppose that the proper multiple beta specification of equation (3.9) is used and the coefficients of the underlying stochastic processes are known to be stable; but also that investors' knowledge of these true coefficients is uncertain because they must be estimated from available data. As an immediate generalization of Williams' (1977) results, this uncertainty regarding the true parameters of the underlying stochastic processes introduces residual variances (along with the vector of betas) as an essential term in the SML measuring the markets' assessment of the required average return on each security at every given time. Note again that this is not a case where the residual variance is serving as a proxy for some other variable that should have been included in the regression.

The Arbitrage Pricing Theory (APT) recently advanced by Ross (1976, 1977) takes a somewhat different approach. Rather than attempting to generalize the CAPM, Ross simply assumes an unknown but linear and strictly stationary stochastic process in which returns are generated by a limited number of factors, each represented by a set of "factor loadings" on the raw data. This theory has the advantage of requiring no utility assumptions beyond monotonicity and concavity, and no particular portfolio plays a central role (as does the "market portfolio" in the CAPM). Indeed, after requiring the absence of riskless arbitrage profits, Roll and Ross observe that

> *any* well-diversified portfolio could serve the same function and that, in general, *k* well-diversified portfolios could be found that approximate the *k* factors *better* than any single market index. . . . In the CAPM, it is crucial to both the theory and the testing that all of the universe of available assets be included in the measured market portfolio. By contrast, the APT yields a statement of relative pricing on subsets of the universe of assets. As a consequence, the APT can, in principle, be tested by examining only subsets of the set of all returns. (1980: 1080, emphasis in original)

However—just as with CAPM!—the ex ante APT[22] is converted

22. Although the underlying theory of the APT makes less stringent requirements on the homogeneity of investors' ex ante assessments than CAPM, "sufficient homogeneity" is required (see Ross 1976, 1977: 207, n. 9 and 27). If there is "too much" difference in assessments, the requirement that all opportunities for riskless arbitrage profits be eliminated will fail to determine market prices and returns. To see this, suppose that the market consists of two sets of investors A and B that differ substantially in their assessments. Suppose further that there is a provisional set of prices and returns in the market that, *given* the assessments of the A investors over the k factors they think relevant, strictly satisfies the basic pricing relation of the APT:

$$E_i = \lambda_o + \lambda_1 b_{i1} + \ldots + \lambda_k b_{ik} \qquad \text{for all } i \qquad (3.10)$$

(This is equation (2) in Ross and Roll 1980, derived earlier in Ross 1976, 1977.) Evaluated in terms of their assessments, these prices and returns provide no opportunities for arbitrage profits for A investors. But the same set of prices and returns, evaluated in terms of the significantly different assessments of the B investors, will seem to them to provide opportunities for possibly very substantial arbitrage profits. B investors will have a risk-adjusted profit incentive to continue to readjust their portfolios until the resulting market prices and returns satisfy equation (3.10) in terms of their parameter assessments—but the new set of market prices and returns will lead to portfolio adjustments by A investors, which in turn will lead to further portfolio adjustments by B investors, and so on in an infinite regress unless (and until) sufficient "learning" (homogenization) has occurred.

into a theory testable with ex post data by making the "fundamental intertemporal rationality assumption" that "all individuals agree on both the factor coefficients, b_{ij}, and the expected returns, E_i," on each ith security, where b_{ij} is the 'beta' of that security on the jth factor" (ibid: 1082). On the basis of the evidence on short selling, profitable insider trading, and highly diverse investor portfolios cited in the previous section, this assumption of homogeneous assessments must be seen as seriously contrary to fact in the context of the APT, just as it was in the context of the CAPM.

Proponents of APT will of course dismiss the relevance of the counterfactual character of this assumption on the positivist grounds that "[t]he theory should be tested by its conclusions, not by its assumptions.... The theory says nothing about how close the assumption must fit. Rejection is justified only if the conclusions are inconsistent with the observed data" (Roll and Ross 1980: 1083). Roll and Ross, in an unusually careful and sophisticated study of ten years (1962–72) of the daily returns on 1,260 individual stocks arranged in forty-two groups of thirty stocks each, report results that provide substantial support for the APT. In particular, likelihood ratio tests provide strong support for at least three and perhaps four factors being "priced out" in security returns. The results of other but substantially weaker tests are consistent with the same factors generating returns in each group; and after using an ingenious device to eliminate spurious skewness effects, they find that individual standard deviations add essentially no explanatory power to the factor loadings.

Two observations are nevertheless in order. The authors very naturally let the data determine the loading weights involved in the specification of each factor, but in making their tests, they used the entire ten years of daily returns on all their stocks to estimate the "true" specification of each of the factors. The lack of significance for standard deviations as an added variable in their tests depends heavily on the implicit assumption involved in this procedure that the factor specifications were known and were used by investors in forming their portfolios from the first day of the ten years and stable throughout. If, after the manner of Williams' (1977) analysis, the implicit assumption was merely that the factor specifications were stationary but had to be estimated from the available data, investors' uncertainties at each given time regarding the true factor specifications and their progressive hedging against the correlation between returns on risky securities and unanticipated changes in currently held expectations of true factor specifications would almost surely reintroduce standard deviations as a significant element in security returns. From a Bayesian point of view, the latter test would be preferable and more relevant.

My second observation is that even if the tests of APT reported to date are accepted at full face value, other predictions of the theory are clearly contradicted by the evidence. To cite one example, the APT, no less than the pure CAPM, predicts that no identifiable group of investors can follow a distinctive strategy that yields persistent excess returns. But the evidence cited earlier clearly establishes that "insiders" do in fact realize substantial and continuing excess profits on average on their investments. While a generalized version of CAPM has been developed that very naturally incorporates the different information sets and assessments required to explain these phenomena,[23] it is far from clear that the APT can be similarly generalized to yield predictions consistent with profitable insider trading. The essence of the APT as it has been developed is the elimination of all possibilities of risk-adjusted gain from further shifts in portfolio proportions, and rather fundamental problems will be raised by the introduction of diverse information sets into this model (see note 22).

We now turn to the much broader implications of diverse information sets and costly information for the more general issue of market efficiency. Grossman (1976) has shown that even though an informationally efficient price system will aggregate diverse information perfectly, in doing so the price system would eliminate the private incentive for collecting the information in the first place. If market prices revealed all information at no cost, no one could gain by gathering information—but if no one gathered any information there would be none for the market to reveal. Grossman and Stiglitz (1976) have also pointed up the resulting paradox: Market prices are important conveyors of information only when information is costly, but costless information is a necessary (and not just a sufficient) condition for the market price of securities to fully reflect all available information. Informationally efficient markets—the

23. See Lintner (1969) for the derivation of the purely competitive equilibrium of market prices when each investor holds his or her most preferred portfolio conditional on the investor's own (in general, unique) assessments of the distribution of security returns. See also Gonedes (1976) for a somewhat more specialized model.

"strong form" of the efficient markets hypothesis—are impossible when information is costly. Moreover, the market never fully adjusts to new information because prices are simultaneously serving to clear markets as well as to convey information.[24] More recently Grossman and Stiglitz (1980) have shown that there is an "equilibrium degree of disequilibrium" where the optimal degree of informational inefficiency of the market is a function of the quality and costs of information and the risk aversion of investors.

This basic inconsistency between costly information and any presumption that security markets are fully efficient informationally has a direct bearing on some of the central issues raised by Roll (1977) in his properly famous critique of tests of asset pricing (CAPM) theory. The pure CAPM was of course derived on the explicit assumption of homogeneous assessments and (consequently) portfolios, and given this assumption, CAPM not only implies that the market portfolio is efficient (for every investor), it also follows immediately that the expected return (or risk premium) on each asset will be a positive function of its beta on this market portfolio and no other variables (such as residual risk) if and only if this market portfolio is efficient (for every investor). This is the fundamental "mathematical equivalence between the individual return/'beta' linearity relation and the market portfolio's mean variance efficiency" (Roll 1977: 129) on which Roll bases his analysis. But this "mathematical equivalence" is a property of any optimal individual portfolio. From the earliest derivations, however, it was recognized that each investor's optimal portfolio is a function of his assessments and that the covariance of each security's return (and hence its "beta") with the return on this optimized portfolio depended explicitly on the proportions of all securities held within this portfolio.[25] With the undisputed fact that information is costly, the Grossman-Stiglitz "equilibrium degree of disequilibrium" requires

---

24. To establish this conclusion, the authors analyze a rational expectations model with costly information of a market subject to a series of shocks generated by a stationary stochastic process. In related work, Figlewski (1978) notes that the market weighs traders' information not by its quality but by "dollar votes" and examines the wealth redistribution produced by the differential forecasting ability incident to diverse information. Although he shows that the markets are more efficient the more risk averse the traders and the more homogeneous their information, he again finds that markets never fully adjust.

25. This covariance between the return on the ith asset and the return on the kth portfolio is of course just the expression $\Sigma_{j=1}^{n} h_j \, \sigma_{ij}$ in Lintner (1965a), where the h_j represents the fraction of the jth stock in the kth optimizing portfolio.

that individual investors' information sets and assessments will cross-sectionally differ. With different assessments, the optimal fraction h_i of each investor's portfolio invested in the ith asset will also differ, and consequently, the ith stock's "beta" computed within each kth investor's optimizing portfolio (given his assessments) will vary from investor to investor.[26] But when these β_{ik} differ among the investors in the market, it follows that in general $\beta_{ik} \neq \beta_{im}$ computed with the market portfolio, since the latter is just a weighted average of the vector of β_{ik} values over investors in the market.

In a world with costly information, the SMLs computed with the "market" β_{im} will of course include a positive residual variance term, as shown above. This variable will not appear as a proxy for skewness or some other omitted or extraneous variable, but rather as a direct consequence of the diversity of assessments (or information) and portfolios among the investors in the market, each of whom holds the mean-variance-efficient portfolio that optimizes his position in terms of his own assessments.

In this world, where information is costly and not uniformly and freely available to all, a Pareto-optimal allocation of securities among investors is nevertheless achieved, given their information sets and assessments. Just as the welfare analysis of consumers' markets is judged in terms of the preferences of individual consumers, this seems to be a reasonable standard to use in judging the efficiency of the allocation of securities among investors in the securities market.

REFERENCES

Black, Fischer. 1972. "Capital Market Equilibrium with Restricted Borrowing." *Journal of Business* 5 (July): 444–55.

———. 1976. "Studies of Stock Price Volatility Changes." In *Proceedings* of the 1976 meeting of the American Statistical Association, Business and Economic Statistics Section, Washington, D.C., pp. 177–81.

Black, Fischer, and Myron Scholes. 1972. "The Valuation of Option Contracts and a Test of Market Efficiency." *Journal of Finance* 27, no. 2 (May): 399–418.

26. More formally, if k represents the optimizing portfolio of an individual investor and m represents the "market" portfolio, the representative β_{ik} computed from different investors' portfolios will each equal β_{im} if and only if all the β_{ik} have the same value—namely, if all portfolios and assessments are identical.

———. 1973. "The Pricing of Options and Corporate Liabilities." *Journal of Political Economy,* 81, no. 3, pp. 637–59.

Black, Fischer; Michael C. Jensen; and Myron Scholes. 1972. "The Capital Asset Pricing Model: Some Empirical Tests." In *Studies in the Theory of Capital Markets,* Michael C. Jensen, ed., pp. 79–121. New York: Praeger.

Blume, Marshall, and Irwin Friend. 1973. "A New Look at the Capital Asset Pricing Model." *Journal of Finance* 28, no. 1 (March): 19–33.

———. 1975. "The Asset Structure of Individual Portfolios and Some Implications for Utility Functions." *Journal of Finance* 30, no. 2 (May): 585–603.

Blume, Marshall; Jean Crockett; and Irwin Friend. "Stockownership in the United States: Characteristics and Trends." *Survey of Current Business* 54 (November): 16–40.

Braeley, Richard, and Stewart C. Myers. 1981. *Principles of Corporate Finance.* New York: McGraw Hill.

Copeland, Thomas E., and J. Fred Weston. 1979. *Financial Theory and Corporate Policy.* Reading, Mass.: Addison-Wesley.

DeAngelo, Harry, and Ronald W. Masulis. 1980a. "Optimal Capital Structure under Corporate and Personal Taxation." *Journal of Financial Economics* 8, no. 1 (March): 3–30.

———. 1980b. "Leverage and Dividend Irrelevancy Under Corporate and Personal Taxation." *Journal of Finance* 35 (May): 453–64.

Chen, Andrew H., and E. Han Kim. 1979. "Theories of Corporate Debt Policy: A Synthesis." *Journal of Finance* 34 (May): 371–84.

Donaldson, Gordon. 1962. "New Framework for Corporate Debt Policy." *Harvard Business Review* 40 (March-April): 117–31.

———. 1969. "Strategy for Financial Emergencies." *Harvard Business Review* 49 (November-December): 67–79.

Douglas, George W. 1969. "Risk in the Equity Markets: An Empirical Appraisal of Economic Efficiency." *Yale Economic Essays* 9, no. 1 (Spring): 3–45.

Fama, Eugene F. 1976. *Foundations of Finance.* New York: Basic Books.

Fama, Eugene F., and James D. MacBeth. 1973. "Risk, Return and Equilibrium: Empirical Tests." *Journal of Political Economy* 81, no. 3 (May): 607–36.

Figlewski, Stephen. 1978. "Market 'Efficiency' in a Market with Heterogeneous Information." *Journal of Political Economy* 86, no. 4 (August): 581–97.

Friend, Irwin, and Randolph Westerfield. 1979. "Risk and Capital Asset Pricing." University of Pennsylvania, Rodney White Center, Working Paper No. 5–79.

Friend, Irwin; Randolph Westerfield; and Michael Granito. 1978. "New Evidence on the Capital Asset Pricing Model." *Journal of Finance* 33, no. 2 (June): 903–16.

Galai, Dan. 1977. "Tests of Market Efficiency of the Chicago Board Options Exchange." *Journal of Business,* 50, no. 1, pp. 167–97.

———. 1978. "Empirical Tests of Boundary Conditions for CBOE Options." *Journal of Financial Economics* 6, nos. 2/3 (June-September): 187–212.

Galai, Dan, and Ronald W. Masulis. 1976. "The Option Pricing Model and the Risk Factor of Stock." *Journal of Financial Economics* 3, nos. 1/2 (January-March): 53–82.

Gonedes, Nicholes J. 1976. "Capital Market Equilibrium for a Class of Heterogeneous Expectations in a Two-Parameter World." *Journal of Finance* 31, no. 1 (March): 1–15.

Grossman, Sanford. 1976. "On the Efficiency of Competitive Stock Markets Where Traders Have Diverse Information." *Journal of Finance* 31, no. 2 (May): 573–85.

Grossman, Sanford J., and Joseph E. Stiglitz. 1976. "Information and Competitive Price Systems." *American Economic Review* 66, no. 2 (May): 246–53.

———. 1980. "On the Impossibility of Informationally Efficient Markets." *American Economic Review* 70, no. 3 (June): 393–408.

Haley, Charles W., and Lawrence D. Schall. 1979. *The Theory of Financial Decisions.* 2nd ed. New York: McGraw-Hill.

Hamada, Robert S. 1969. "Portfolio Analysis, Market Equilibrium and Corporation Finance." *Journal of Finance* 24, no. 1 (March): 13–31.

———. 1972. "The Effect of the Firm's Capital Structure on the Systematic Risk of Common Stock." *Journal of Finance* 27, no. 2 (May): 435–52.

Jaffe, Jeffrey F. 1974. "Special Information and Insider Trading." *Journal of Business* 47 (July): 410–28.

Jensen, Michael C., and William H. Meckling. 1976. "Theory of the Firm: Managerial Behavior, Agency Costs and Ownership Structure." *Journal of Financial Economics* 3, no. 4 (October): 305–60.

Kim, E. Han. 1978. "A Mean-Variance Theory of Optimal Capital Structure and Corporate Debt Capacity." *Journal of Finance* 33, no. 1 (March): 45–64.

Levy, Haim. 1978. "Equilibrium in an Imperfect Market: A Constraint on the Number of Securities with Portfolio." *American Economic Review* 68, no. 4 (September): 643–58.

Lewellan, Wilbur G.; Gary C. Schlarbaum; and Ronald C. Lease. 1974. "The Individual Investor: Attributes and Attitudes." *Journal of Finance* 29, no. 2 (May): 413–33.

Lintner, John. 1962. "Dividends, Earnings, Leverage, Stock Prices and Supply of Capital to Corporations." *The Review of Economics and Statistics* 44, no. 3 (August): 243–69.

_____. 1965a. "The Valuation of Risk Assets and the Selection of Risky Investments in Stock Portfolios and Capital Budgets." *Review of Economics and Statistics* 47 (February): 13–37.

_____. 1965b. "Security Prices, Risk, and Maximal Gains from Diversification." *Journal of Finance* 20, 4 (December): 587–615.

_____. 1969. "The Aggregation of Investor's Diverse Judgements and Preferences in Purely Competitive Securities Markets." *Journal of Financial and Quantitative Analysis* 10 (December): 347–400.

_____. 1971. "The Effects of Short Selling, Margin Requirements and Rising Costs of Debt in Purely Competitive Securities Markets." *Journal of Financial and Quantitative Analysis* 6, no. 5 (December): 1173–96.

_____. 1977. "Bankruptcy Risk, Market Segmentation and Optimal Capital Structure." In Irwin Friend and James Ricksler, eds., *Risks and Returns,* vol. II, pp. 1–128. Cambridge, Massachusetts: Ballinger.

_____. 1981. "Allowable Rates of Return on Public Utility Equities: The Theory of Optimal Rate-of-Return Regulation of Utilities and the Double Leverage Controversy." Harvard Business School Working Paper No. 81–82.

Litzenberger, Robert H. 1981. "Debt, Taxes and Incompleteness: A Survey." *Journal of Finance* (May).

Litzenberger, Robert H., and Howard B. Sosin. 1977. "The Theory of Recapitalization and the Evidence of Dual Purpose Funds." *Journal of Finance* 32, no. 5 (December): 1433–56.

Masulis, Ronald W. 1980. "The Effects of Capital Structure Change on Security Prices: A Study of Exchange Offers." *Journal of Financial Economics* 8, no. 2 (June).

Mayers, David. 1972. "Non-marketable Assets and Capital Market Equilibrium Under Uncertainty." In *Studies in the Theory of Capital Markets,* Michael C. Jensen, ed., pp. 223–48. New York: Praeger.

_____. 1973. "Non-marketable Assets and the Determination of Capital Asset Prices in the Absence of a Riskless Asset." *Journal of Business* 46 (April): 258–67.

Merton, Robert C. 1971. "Optimum Consumption and Portfolio Rules in a Continuous-Time Model." *Journal of Economic Theory* 3, no. 4 (December): 373–413.

_____. 1973a. "An Intertemporal Capital Asset Pricing Model." *Econometrica* 41, no. 4 (September): 867–87.

_____. 1973b. "Theory of Rational Option Pricing." *Bell Journal of Economics and Management Science* 4, no. 1 (Spring): 141–83.

_____. 1977. "A Re-examination of the Capital Asset Pricing Model." In

Risk and Return, Irwin Friend and James L. Bicksler, eds., vol. I, pp. 141–60. Cambridge, Massachusetts: Ballinger.

———. 1980. "On Estimating the Expected Return on the Market: An Exploratory Investigation." *Journal of Financial Economics* 8, no. 4 (December): 323–62.

Miller, Merton H. 1977. "Debt and Taxes." *Journal of Finance* 30, no. 2 (May): 261–76.

Miller, Merton H., and Myron Scholes. 1972. "Rates of Return in Relation to Risk: A Re-examination of Some Recent Findings." In *Studies in the Theory of Capital Markets,* Michael C. Jensen, ed., pp. 47–78. New York: Praeger.

Mogliani, Franco, and Merton H. Miller. 1963. "Corporate Income Taxes and the Cost of Capital: A Correction." *American Economic Review* 53, no. 3 (June): 433–43.

Myers, Stewart. 1977. "Determinants of Corporate Borrowing Capacity." *Journal of Financial Economics* 4, no. 1 (November): 147–76.

Robichek, Alexander A., and Stewart C. Myers. 1965. *Optimal Financing Decisions.* Englewood Cliffs, N.J.: Prentice-Hall.

Roll, Richard. 1977. "A Critique of the Asset Pricing Theory's Tests; Part I: On the Past and Potential Testability of the Theory." *Journal of Financial Economics* 4, no. 2 (March): 129–76.

Roll, Richard A., and Stephen A. Ross. 1980. "An Empirical Investigation of the Arbitrage Pricing Theory." *Journal of Finance* 35, no. 5 (December): 1073–1103.

Rosenberg, Barr. 1974. "Extra-Market Components of Covariance in Security Returns." *Journal of Financial and Quantitative Analysis* 9, nos. 1/2 (March): 263–74.

Rosenberg, Barr, and Walt McKibben. 1973. "The Prediction of Systematic and Specific Risk in Common Stocks." *Journal of Financial and Quantitative Analysis* 8, nos. 1/2 (March): 317–33.

Ross, Stephen A. 1976. "The Arbitrage Theory of Capital Asset Pricing." *Journal of Economic Theory* 13, no. 3 (December): 341–60.

———. 1977. "Risk, Return and Arbitrage." In *Risk and Return,* Irwin Friend and James L. Bicksler, eds., pp. 189–218. Cambridge, Massachusetts: Ballinger.

Rubenstein, Mark E. 1973. "A Mean-Variance Synthesis of Corporate Financial Theory." *Journal of Finance* 28, no. 1 (March): 167–81.

Scott, James. "A Theory of Optimal Capital Structure." *Bell Journal of Economics* 7, no. 1 (Spring): 33–54.

Sharpe, William. 1978. "Discussion of New Evidence on the Capital Asset Pricing Model." *Journal of Finance* 33, no. 3 (June): 917–20.

Smith, Clifford W., Jr. 1976. "Option Pricing: A Review." *Journal of Financial Economics* 3, nos. 1/2 (January-March): 3–52.

Sosin, Howard B. 1978. "Neutral Recapitalizations: Predictions and Tests Concerning Valuation and Welfare." *Journal of Finance* 33, no. 4 (September): 1228–34.

Stiglitz, Joseph E. 1974. "On the Irrelevance of Corporate Financial Policy." *American Economic Review* 54, no. 5 (December): 851–66.

_____. 1979. "A Re-examination of the Modigliani-Miller Theorem." *American Economic Review* 69, no. 5 (December): 784–93.

Van Horne, James C. 1980. *Financial Management and Policy.* 5th ed. Englewood Cliffs, N.J.: Prentice-Hall.

Weston, J. Fred, and Eugene F. Brigham. 1981. *Managerial Finance.* 7th ed. Hinsdale, Ill.: Dryden Press.

Williams, Joseph T. 1977. "Capital Asset Prices with Heterogeneous Beliefs." *Journal of Financial Economics* 5, no. 2 (November): 219–40.

4 A FRAMEWORK FOR THE ANALYSIS OF FINANCIAL DISORDER*

Jack Guttentag and Richard Herring
University of Pennsylvania

This is an exploratory essay on the problem of financial disorder. Our analytic framework is constructed from ideas drawn from two disparate areas of research. From the literature on credit rationing, we develop a model of the microeconomics of lending decisions in the presence of default risk and moral hazard. This model enables us to relate risk premiums to subjective expectations of default and to the borrower's capital and to establish the conditions under which borrowers will be rationed. From the literature on natural disasters, which focuses on the issue of how people deal with low probability events that carry high potential losses, we draw our hypotheses regarding the way in which lenders formulate expectations of default. Once the model is assembled, we consider what determines vulnerability to a financal crisis, why vulnerability may increase over time, how a crisis scenario develops, and the role and limitations of a central bank in stemming a financial crisis.

Our chapter is divided into seven sections. The first section develops the notion of a "credit shock" and distinguishes project-specific credit shocks from disastrous credit shocks that affect all projects. The second section presents an analysis of lending decisions in a setting that includes credit shocks and moral hazard. The

*For comments on an earlier draft of this paper, we would like to thank (without implicating) E. Herman, J. Siegel and J. Tobin.

163

determination of risk premiums is analyzed, and lender-imposed capital requirements are explained as a response to moral hazard. In the third section, the model of lender behavior is used to classify borrowers in terms of their capital positions. Section four uses the classification of borrowers by capital position to develop a taxonomy of macroeconomic financial conditions in terms of extent of vulnerability to crisis. In the fifth section the determination of subjective shock probabilities is analyzed. The sixth section explains why economies become increasingly vulnerable to a financial crisis during an expansion, emphasizing the divergence between perceived and actual financial conditions. In addition, it considers the issue of whether financial crises are inevitable. The concluding section reexamines the role of the central bank in dealing with different types of crisis scenarios.

SHOCKS AND THE CAPACITY TO WITHSTAND SHOCKS

A "shock" is defined as an event that causes loss to creditors. Shocks come in varying sizes and have different causes. We distinguish three types of shock. A "credit shock" arises from borrower failure to repay loans. An "interest rate shock" arises from a change in market rates at a time when the duration of the creditor's assets differs from that of his liabilities. A "liquidity shock" arises from an increase in the severity of credit rationing at a time when the creditor's liquidity position (ability to meet cash needs) is low. For the most part, in this chapter we will focus on credit shocks, ignoring the liability side of creditor balance sheets.

In our model creditors make loans,[1] L, at some contract rate of interest, i, with the promised return $L(1 + i)$ that we denote as Z.[2] Borrowers undertake real investment projects that have a stochastic total return, R. (For the moment we assume that the borrower cannot change the riskiness of the project once the lender has made a commitment to lend.) If the borrower's investment returns are not sufficient to repay the loan—that is, if $R < Z$,—the creditor may claim the entire proceeds of the investment project plus as much of

1. All loans are assumed to be a fixed amount, L, perhaps determined by a technologically fixed project size.

2. For easy reference, the chapter appendix contains a glossary of symbols used in the text.

the borrower's capital, K, as necessary to fill the gap between the loan repayment due and the investment returns.[3] If the borrower's total capital is less than the shortfall of investment returns, the creditor suffers a loss on the loan. Thus, a loss arises if $R - Z + K < 0$.

We assume that nature draws investment returns from a cumulative distribution, $F(R,w)$, where w is an index of project-specific risk, and the cumulative distribution is defined over a range extending from zero to some maximum return, R_M. A "credit shock" is defined as a draw from this distribution that causes loss to the lender. The probability of a shock is:

$$Pr(R < Z - K) = F(Z - K,w) \qquad (4.1)$$

And the probability of a shock of magnitude x (where $Z - K \geqslant x > 0$) is:

$$Pr(R < Z - K - x) = F(Z - K - x,w) \qquad (4.2)$$

The schedules in Figure 4–1 show the probability of a shock corresponding to any given value of R on the assumption that the amount promised, Z, exceeds that value of R plus the borrower's capital, K. For example, assuming distribution A and R equal to $(Z - K)$, the probability of a shock is $p(s)$, and the probability of a shock greater than or equal to $\underline{x}$ is $p(\underline{x})$.

The probability of a shock can rise for three reasons:

1. The contractual amount due, Z, rises;
2. The borrower's capital, K, falls;
3. The distribution governing investment returns shifts upward.

We shall pay particular attention to a special case of an unfavorable shift in the distribution of investment returns. Under some conditions, it will be assumed that nature may draw from a disastrous distribution. For simplicity, we assume that this distribution is degenerate with all returns zero. This assumption is made for analytic convenience, not because we wish to model doomsday.

---

3. For convenience, we have assumed that the borrower's capital is pledged as collateral for the loan. In effect, the creditor lends the borrower the full amount of the investment and holds the borrower's capital as collateral rather than permitting the borrower to invest his capital in the project and making a corresponding reduction in the loan size. This assumption enables us to highlight the dual role of capital in countering moral hazard and in providing a buffer between the lender and unfavorable investment outcomes.

Figure 4–1.   Probability of a Shock.

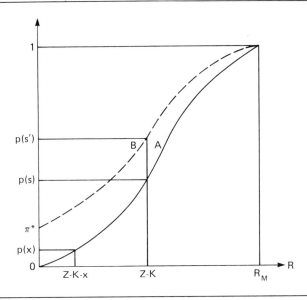

Indeed, it makes little sense to collect risk premiums against a contingency in which "we are all dead." Rather, our concern is with shocks that have less than catastrophic direct consequences on real economic activity, but that, if not adequately anticipated by lenders, have devastating financial consequences that substantially exacerbate the impact of the shock on real economic activity. Examples would include a tenfold increase in the price of oil, a 10 percent decline in U.S. GNP, or a 10 percent drop in the volume of world trade.

The subjective probability that nature will draw from the disastrous distribution is π, where $0 \leq \pi \leq 1$. Thus, where $\pi > 0$, the probability of a shock $p(s')$ is:

$$Pr(R < Z - K) = (1 - \pi)F(Z - K, w) + \pi \qquad (4.3)$$

This is illustrated by the dashed curve, B, in Figure 4–1.

In the case where $\pi = 0$, shocks can be viewed as project specific and thus potentially diversifiable. When $\pi > 0$, shocks can project specific or worldwide, depending on whether Nature draws from the $F(R, w)$ distribution or the disastrous distribution. Ex post, small shocks can be viewed with certainty as having been drawn from the

$F(R,w)$ distribution while large shocks associated with zero investment returns in all projects are almost certain to have been drawn
from the disastrous distribution.

The creditor's capacity to withstand a shock is determined by his
capital, K_c. The larger his capital, the larger the shock he can sustain.
The probability that a creditor will become insolvent is:

$$Pr(R < Z - K - K_c) \qquad (4.4)$$

Figure 4–2 shows the probability of lender insolvency, given the
shock probabilities shown in Figure 4–1, curve B. Note that if $K +
K_c > Z$, the probability of the creditor becoming insolvent is zero. A
rightward movement along the horizontal axis—reflecting either a
rise in the amount promised Z, a decline in the borrower's capital, K,
or a decline in the lender's capital, K_c—is associated with an increase
in the probability of lender insolvency. The probablity of insolvency
may also rise because of an adverse shift in the distribution of project
specific investment returns or an increase in π. Given $R = Z - K -
K_c$ in Figure 4–2, the shift from $\pi^* F(R_M, w)$ to $\pi' F(R'_M, w')$
increases the probability of insolvency.

Figure 4–2. Probability of Lender Insolvency.

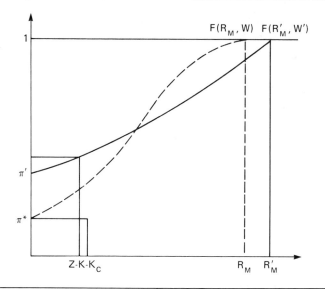

LENDING DECISIONS IN RESPONSE TO
DEFAULT RISK AND MORAL HAZARD

In this section we identify the factors that determine the lender's expected return from a loan and the factors that determine the borrower's expected return from the project financed by the loan. This comparison reveals that, under some circumstances, the borrower may be in a position to make himself better off at the expense of the lender. In order to forestall this, the lender is likely to ration credit and/or impose minimum capital constraints on the borrower. The borrower's capital position thus plays a crucial role in our model.

The Creditor's Expected Return

The expected return to the creditor on a loan with contract rate r to a borrower with capital position, K is:

$$r_c = \frac{\pi K}{L} + \frac{(1-\pi)}{L} \int_0^{Z-K} (K+R)f(R,w)dR + (1-\pi)\frac{Z}{L}\int_{Z-K}^{R_M} f(R,w)dR \quad (4.5)$$

The first term is the expected return if nature draws from the disastrous distribution. Since the investment return is zero, the creditor receives only the borrower's capital. The second and third terms describe the creditor's expected rate of return if nature draws from the regular distribution. The second term is the expected rate of return in the event of a default in which the borrower's capital fails to cover the gap between the investment returns and the contractual repayment due. The third term is the expected rate of return if the borrower does not default. After integrating the second and third term in equation (4.5), this expression can be simplified to yield

$$r_c = \frac{\pi K}{L} + (1-\pi)r - \frac{(1-\pi)}{L} \int_0^{Z-K} F(R,w)dR \quad (4.6)$$

The minimum rate of return to the creditor is determined by the borrower's capital position, while the maximum (which is the promised return) is determined by the loan contract as graphed in Figure 4–3. The lowest return (when the investment return is zero) is K/L, while the promised return is obtained when the investment

Figure 4–3. Actual Rate of Return to Lender.

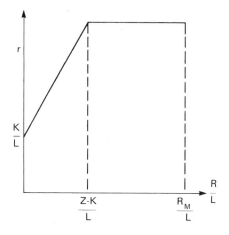

rate is $Z - K/L$, the default point, or higher. Any decline in investment returns below the default point will lower the creditor's return.

The Borrower's Expected Return

The expected return to the borrower with capital position K and contract rate r is:

$$r_b = \frac{-\pi K}{L} - (1 - \pi) \frac{K}{L} \int_0^{Z-K} f(R,w)dR + \frac{(1 - \pi)}{L} \int_{Z-K}^{R_M} (R - Z)f(R,w)dR \qquad (4.7)$$

The first term indicates that the borrower will lose his capital if nature draws from the disastrous distribution. The second and third terms describe the borrower's expected return if nature draws from the regular distribution. The second term is the expected value of the loss if the borrower's capital position falls short of the gap between the contractual repayment due and the investment returns. The third term is the expected value of the gain when the borrower is not forced to default. By integrating the second and third terms, equation (4.7) can be rewritten as:

$$r_b = \frac{-\pi K}{L} - (1 - \pi)r + \frac{(1 - \pi)R_M}{L} - \frac{(1 - \pi)}{L} \int_{Z-K}^{R_M} F(R,w)dR \qquad (4.8)$$

As shown in Figure 4–4, the actual return to the borrower is $-K/L$ when the investment return is below the default point and thereafter rises with the investment return.

Moral Hazard[4]

It is clear that to a degree the interests of the creditor and the borrower are in conflict. The borrower will prefer investments that offer the opportunity to earn very high returns even if such investments also have an increased probability of yielding very low returns. Any incremental returns above the default point accrue entirely to him, while his loss is the same no matter how far investment returns fall below that point. In contrast, returns above the default point are a matter of indifference to the creditor, but if investment returns fall below the default point, the creditor's return will depend on how far below that point they fall. Because increases in the riskiness of the investment affect the creditor and borrower differently, the creditor must be aware of the possibility of moral hazard—the possibility that the borrower after obtaining the loan may act in such a way as to increase both the probability of high returns and the probability of default.[5]

The lender may not be able to control the riskiness of the investment undertaken by the borrower, either because the risk characteristics cannot be sufficiently specified in the loan agreement or because the loan agreement cannot be effectively monitored or because the convenants restricting the borrower's behavior cannot be enforced. In any such case the creditor must assume that the

4. More or less simultaneously Keeton (1979) and Stiglitz and Weiss (1980) have developed models in which moral hazard is the crucial feature that leads to equilibrium credit rationing. This analysis draws heavily on both sources.

5. In this chapter we emphasize the potential for moral hazard in the borrower's selection of investment projects. By assuming that the borrower's capital is the equivalent of pledged collateral, we have assumed away another aspect of moral hazard that may be important in some cases. If the creditor were lending on the basis of the borrower's expected future cash flows, not only would he have to make certain that the borrower does not alter the selection of investment projects after the loan has been made, but he also would have to make certain that the borrower uses the cash flows to service the debt. Similarly, if the creditor has made a loan partly on the basis of the difference between the market (liquidation) value of the borrower's assets less other liabilities, he will have to make certain that the borrower will not dissipate his assets or pledge them to another creditor.

Figure 4–4. Actual Rate of Return to Borrower.

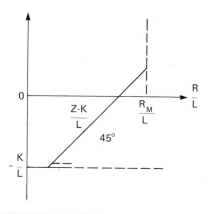

riskiness of the investment will be altered in such a way as to maximize the borrower's expected return.

If the expected return, R, remains constant, increases in riskiness, w, represent a mean-preserving spread—a shift from the center to the tails of the density function (see Rothschild and Stiglitz 1970). In this case, the cumulative distribution function $F(R,w)$ must satisfy two conditions:

$$\int_{o}^{R_M} \frac{\partial F}{\partial w}(R,w)dR = 0 \tag{4.9}$$

and

$$\int_{0}^{R} \frac{\partial F}{\partial w}(R,w)dR \geq 0 \text{ for all } R \tag{4.10}$$

If the increases in w do not affect the expected return on the investment, the creditor should assume that the borrower will chose the highest possible w, without any concern for the interest charge on the loan. But if at some point increases in w reduce the expected return on the investment, the degree of risk the borrower elects may depend on the contract rate of interest. The higher the contract rate, the smaller the range of high investment outcomes that will yield a postive return to the borrower and the greater the likelihood that the borrower will choose a riskier project with a lower total expected return.[6]

A creditor who cannot control the risk of an investment project must anticipate the borrower's choice of risk characteristics. Differentiating the expression for the borrower's expected return, equation (4.7), with respect to the risk index, w, we obtain:

$$\frac{\partial r_b}{\partial w} = \frac{-(1-\pi)}{L} \int_{Z-K}^{R_M} \frac{\partial F}{\partial w}(R,w)dR \qquad (4.11)$$

Given the terms of the loan contract, a marginal increase in the risk of the investment will alter the borrower's expected return. Given Z and K, the optimal degree of riskiness for the borrower $\hat{w}$, is

6. Keeton (1979): 199–203) has developed a set of restrictions on the cumulative distribution function that imply that increases in the contract rate will necessarily lower the creditor's expected rate of return on the loan. In the context of our model, these assumptions may be restated as follows:

1. For each w, there exists an $\bar{R}$ such that $\dfrac{\partial F(R,w)}{\partial w} > 0 \; for \; 0 < R < \bar{R}$ and $\dfrac{\partial F(R,w)}{\partial w} < 0$ for $\bar{R} <$
    $R < R_M$. This assumption implies that an increase in risk shifts probability densities from the center to the tails of the distribution and that the cumulative distribution associated with level of risk w_j, $F(R,w_j)$ can cut the cumulative distribution associated with a marginally lower level of risk w_i, $F(R,w_i)$ only once from above as in Figure A.

Figure A.

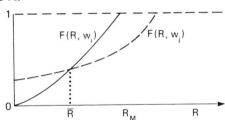

2. For all w, the minimum possible investment outcome is less than Z-K. This assumption insures that default is possible and that a conflict between borrower and creditor may therefore arise.
3. $R = 0$ at $w = w_{min}$ and $\bar{R} = R_M$ at $w = w_{max}$. This assumption insures that the borrower will choose neither the least risky nor the most risky investment possibility. In order to insure that the borrower's choice of w is unique given the loan terms, Keeton (1979: 205) has developed two alternative additional restrictions on the cumulative distribution function:
    * $\bar{R}$ is a continuous function of w and is nondecreasing in w for all w such that $\bar{R} < R_M$; or
    *   If $w_j > w_i$, $F(R',w_j) = F(R',w_i)$ implies $F(R,w_j) > F(R,w_i)$ for $0 < R < R'$ and $F(R,w_j) < F(R,w_i)$ for $R' < R < R_M(w_i)$.

the $\hat{w}$ that satisfies the condition that:

$$\frac{\partial r_b}{\partial w} = \frac{-(1-\pi)}{L} \int_{Z-K}^{R_M} \frac{\partial F}{\partial w}(R,\hat{w})dR = 0 \qquad (4.12)$$

Differentiating this condition with respect to the contract rate we get:

$$\frac{\partial^2 r_b}{\partial r \partial w} = (1-\pi)\frac{\partial F}{\partial w}(Z-K,w) > 0 \qquad (4.13)$$

As the contract rate rises, so does the optimal riskiness of the investment project to the borrower.

In contrast, as the borrower's capital position increases the optimal degree of investment risk decreases. Differentiating equation (4.11) with respect to the borrower's capital position yields:

$$\frac{\partial^2 r_b}{\partial K \partial w} = \frac{-(1-\pi)}{L}\frac{\partial E}{\partial w}(Z-K,w) < 0 \qquad (4.14)$$

Thus, increases in the borrower's capital position limit the scope for a conflict of interest between the creditor and the borrower. Indeed, where $K = Z$, the moral hazard problem disappears, since under these conditions the expected return to the borrower becomes:

$$r_b = \frac{-\pi K}{L} + \frac{(1-\pi)}{L}\int_0^{R_M}(R-Z)f(R,w)dR \qquad (4.15)$$

and $\partial r_b/\partial w|_{K=Z} = 0$. When the borrower's capital position equals the contractual amount due, the borrower cannot increase his expected return by shifting to riskier projects. In contrast, when the borrower's capital position is zero, the borrower will get the maximum benefit from increases in the riskiness of the investment and the lender is most vulnerable to moral hazard (see equation 4–11).

Arithmetic Illustrations of Moral Hazard

To illustrate the concept of moral hazard, assume potential borrowers have a choice of the investments given in Table 4–1, where the alternative to earning the specified amount is to lose everything.

Table 4-1. Investment Alternatives.

Project	Termination Value per $100 Invested	Probability	Expected Value
A	$110	.99	$109
B	$200	.50	$100

These outcomes are deliberately stacked so that expected value is lower on the high risk investment.

Now assume that two firms with different amounts of capital can both borrow $100 to invest in one of the two projects (interest is ignored for the moment). We calculate the expected value of each investment to the two firms in Table 4–2.

For the borrower with capital of $100, the conservative investment project A has the highest expected value, whereas for the borrower with $10 of capital, investment B has the highest expected value.

Note that the addition of interest on the loan increases the relative attractiveness of the high risk venture, since interest merely adds to the terminal debt that must be repaid and is equivalent to a lower capital ratio. For example, when the interest rate is zero, investments A and B have expected returns of $119 and $100 respectively for the firm with capital of $100, but if an interest rate of 50 percent is imposed, the expected returns become $68 and $75 respectively. The investment with the lower expected value now has the highest expected return for this firm.

Nor is there necessarily an interest rate that will compensate the creditor for the risk of moral hazard. Consider the extreme case where the borrower has no capital and the lender knows that the borrower's venture has the following payoff for each $100 invested.

Terminal Value	Probability
$225	0.5
0	0.5

With a 0.5 probability of loss the interest rate to cover the lender's risk would have to be over a 100 percent—for example, 115 percent—which would reduce the borrower's return to a 0.5

Table 4-2. Expected Return to Borrower Using $100 of Borrowed Funds.

	Capital of Borrower	
Project	$10	$100
A	$21	$119
B	$55	$100

probability of gaining $10. With these terms, the borrower would prefer the following venture.

Terminal Value	Probability
$300	.3
0	.7

While this venture has a lower expected value ($90 as compared to $112.50), to the borrower faced with an interest rate of 115 percent, it is a better deal, since it provides a 0.3 probability of earning $85, with an expected value of $25.50, as opposed to a 0.5 probability of earning $10, which has an expected value of $5. But of course the lender's risk in the second venture is now no longer covered by the 115 percent rate.

As a general matter, if a weakly capitalized borrower can choose from a sufficiently wide menu of risk-return ventures and if the lender cannot control the borrower's choices, the borrower can always stay ahead of the game by choosing a venture that is to his own advantage and to the disadvantage of the lender.

Rationing as a Response to Moral Hazard

Given the distribution of investment returns, there is a contract rate that maximizes the lender's expected return. Differentiating equation (4.6) with respect to the contract rate, we find that:

$$\frac{\partial r_c}{\partial r} = (1 - \pi)(1 - F(Z - K, w)) - (1 - \pi)\frac{1}{L}\int_0^{Z-K} \frac{\partial F(R,w)}{\partial w}\frac{\partial w}{\partial r}dR \quad (4.16)$$

The creditor maximizes his expected return at the point at which the expected value of the increase in the contract rate when the borrower does not default precisely offsets the expected loss due to the induced increase in the probability of default.[7] If the creditor's expected return at this optimal contract rate $\hat{r}$ is less than the opportunity cost of funds, the borrower will be rationed, since raising the contract rate beyond $\hat{r}$ will reduce the expected return to the creditor. In effect, rationing arises from the lenders concern with the moral hazard that, at a higher contract rate, the borrower will employ the funds in a riskier venture that will reduce the expected return to the lender.

Note that if the borrower cannot increase the riskiness of the investment, raising the contract rate raises the expected return to the creditor until the rate reaches the level where it completely exhausts the expected return from the investment under the most favorable outcome plus the borrower's capital. No borrower would knowingly enter such a contract. The introduction of bankruptcy cost, which makes the borrower's capital position less valuable to the creditor than to the borrower, will result in an optimal contract rate to the lender that is lower than the contract rate that would bankrupt the borrower.[8]

Risk Premiums in Competitive Equilibrium

If (risk-neutral) lenders are in perfectly competitive markets, creditors will be forced to set contract rates so that they yield an expected return equal to the opportunity cost of funds, which we assume is the risk-free rate, r^*. Thus, in competitive equilibrium:

$$r_c = r^* = \frac{\pi K}{L} + (1 - \pi)r - \frac{(1 - \pi)}{L} \int_0^{Z-K} F(R, \hat{w}) dR \qquad (4.17)$$

Solving for the contract rate, we obtain

$$r = \frac{r^*}{(1 - \pi)} - \frac{\pi K}{(1 - \pi)L} + \frac{1}{L} \int_0^{Z-K} F(R, \hat{w}) dR \qquad (4.18)$$

7. If $\dfrac{\partial^2 F(R, \hat{w})}{\partial^2 w} < 0$, $\partial w/\partial r$ will be > 0.

8. See Barro (1976) for a model that analyzes the impact of bankruptcy costs in a setting in which the borrower's collateral is treated as a stochastic variable.

and the risk premium is:

$$r - r^* = \frac{\pi r^*}{(1 - \pi)} - \frac{\pi K}{(1 - \pi)L} + \frac{1}{L} \int_0^{Z-K} F(R,\hat{w})dR \qquad (4.19)$$

The risk premium depends on the subjective probability of a disaster, the borrower's capital position, and the cumulative distribution governing investment outcomes during normal times.

As the borrower's capital position increases, the risk premium declines:

$$\frac{\partial(r - r^*)}{\partial K/L} = \int_0^{Z-K} \frac{\partial F}{\partial w}(R,\hat{w}) \frac{\partial w}{\partial K} dR - \frac{-\pi}{(1 - \pi)} + F(Z - K) < 0 \qquad (4.20)$$

The borrower's capital position affects the risk premium through two channels. First, larger capital may lead the borrower to reduce the riskiness of the investment project. Second, larger capital is a buffer against loss to the creditor. In contrast to the first effect, the strength of the second effect depends on how the borrower's capital is used. If the borrower's capital is pledged as collateral, the creditor gets the full benefit of the buffer effect and equation (4.19) describes the risk premium exactly. But if the borrower is permitted to invest his capital in the project and if $\pi > 0$, some of the buffer effect may be lost, and the risk premium will be correspondingly higher.

CLASSIFICATION OF BORROWERS BY CAPITAL POSITIONS

We find it useful to distinguish two critical capital positions—K_s, the safe capital position, and K_m, the minimum acceptable capital position. If the borrower has a capital position equal to or greater than K_s, he will not be charged a risk premium. We term such borrowers "prime" borrowers. We can derive an explicit expression for the safe capital position (where $\pi > 0$) by setting the risk premium in equation (4.19) at zero and solving for K_s:

$$\frac{K_s}{L} = r^* + \frac{(1 - \pi)}{\pi L} \int_0^{Z^*-K_s} F(R,\hat{w})dR \qquad (4.21)$$

If $\pi = 1$, $K_s = Z^*$—that is, K_s must be sufficient to repay the loan and yield a return equal to the risk-free rate. If $\pi = 0$, then K_s is that value of K for which

$$0 = \frac{1}{L} \int_0^{Z^* - K_S} F(R, \hat{s}) dR \tag{4.22}$$

This condition is satisfied if $K_s = Z^*$, but it may also be satisfied by a much lower K, if there is a very low probability of the investment returns falling below the default point. The prime status of borrowers is determined by the risk characteristics of their investment projects as well as by their capital positions.

It is axiomatic that the more capital one has, the more one can borrow. The other side of this is that given a borrower's loan requirement, there is a minimum capital requirement (K_m). Borrowers with capital positions less than K_m are termed "rationed" borrowers.

What is troublesome in the concept of a minimum capital requirement is the possibility of trading off capital (or loan size) against interest rate. If there were no constraints on interest rates, there should be no minimum capital requirement. However, as we have shown, there are constraints on interest rates. The ultimate constraint arises when the lender exhausts all the conceivable returns from the borrower's investment, plus the borrower's capital, in order to earn a satisfactory return. At that point, no further trade-off between capital and interest rate is possible, and a minimum acceptable capital position, K_m, is defined.

In practice, K_m will be fixed well below this level. The minimum capital position may be set to limit the lender's risk of insolvency. This "insolvency constraint" may arise if the lender maximizes expected profits subject to the constraint that his risk of bankruptcy not exceed some probability, p^*.[9] Using K_c to represent the creditor's capital position, we can write the constraint as:

$$Pr(R < z - K - K_c) = \pi + (1 - \pi)F(z - K - K_c) \leqslant p^* \tag{4.23}$$

Given the subjective probability of a disaster, the creditor's capital, the distribution of investment outcomes for the borrower, and the contractual repayment due, this relationship determines a minimum acceptable capital position. If the borrower's K is less than

---

9. This "safety first" formulation of a financial intermediary's objective function can be traced back to an article by Roy (1952). More recently, Blackwell (1976) has developed an elaborate version of the model to explain credit rationing.

this minimum, the creditor will refuse to lend to the borrower because it would expose the creditor to an unacceptable risk of insolvency.

Although it is not clear that a creditor's shareholders are best served by an insolvency risk constraint, it is likely to be in the interest of the managers of the creditor institution. Managers who preside over the failure of a financial institution are tarnished by the association and seldom will find another position as good. In addition, the regulators and supervisors of the financial institution may impose an insolvency risk constraint on the institution for reasons of public policy.

Alternatively, the minimum capital requirement may be fixed to protect the lender against the moral hazard associated with the borrower's selection of investment projects after the loan is drawn down. The moral hazard constraint reflects an attempt by the lender to assure that the expected return on a loan will be at least equal to the opportunity cost of making the loan, in the face of some ability of the borrower to alter the project returns after the loan is made. If project returns could not be altered by borrowers, it would always be in the lender's interest to charge as high a loan rate as can be negotiated (up to the maximum possible rate where the lender would take everything, as noted above). If there is a probability greater than zero that the borrower can earn enough to cover the higher rate, the lender's expected return will be higher, even though the probability of a shortfall from the promised return will also be higher. But if the borrower can change the project returns in a way that increases risk to the lender, higher rates may not be in the interest of the lender because they provide the borrower with an incentive to make this type of adjustment. Hence, moral hazard may lead to an optimal rate of interest for a given prospective borrower. At contract rates above the optimum, the loss to the lender from higher default rates exceeds the gains from higher promised contractual returns; at rates below the optimum, the opposite is the case. The optimal contract rate, $\hat{r}$, given L, π and the distribution of investment returns, defines a minimum acceptable capital position, K_m:[10]

$$\pi \frac{K_m}{L} = \pi r^* - (1 - \pi)(r - r^*) + (1 - \pi) \frac{1}{L} \int_0^{Z-K_m} F(R, \hat{w}) dR \qquad (4.24)$$

10. K_m will be zero if the subjective probability of a disaster is zero, if the investment project is perfectly safe, and if it can be effectively monitored so that it remains perfectly safe after the loan is extended.

At the optimum rate, the borrower cannot trade off a lower capital position against a higher contract rate.

It is evident from equation (4.24) that K_m depends on π (as well as on the distribution of investment returns). If $\pi = 1$, then $K_m = Z^*$, the same as K_s, and the minimum acceptable capital position will equal the capital position that will qualify the borrower for the risk-free rate. In this case the contract return makes no difference, since creditors are certain the investment will yield no returns. As the value of π drops below one, K_m falls relative to K_s. K_m must be large enough so that the difference between the optimal contract rate and the expected rate of loss in the event of a default equals the risk-free rate.

If the borrower's capital position is less than K_m, he will be rationed. Note that he cannot adequately compensate the creditor by offering a higher contract rate, because K_m is defined for the contract rate that maximizes the expected return to the creditor.

Borrowers with capital positions greater than or equal to K_m and less than K_s are termed "risky" borrowers. These borrowers pay a risk premium proportional to their capital positions as shown in equation (4.19). As a borrower's capital position rises toward K_s, the risk premium declines—both because larger capital reduces default risk and because the borrower may reduce the riskiness of the investment.

CLASSIFYING FINANCIAL CONDITIONS

A financial disorder or crisis is a pathological condition that has occasionally characterized financial markets. The central feature is that borrowers who in other states were able to borrow without difficulty become unable to borrow at any terms. In this section we attempt a taxonomy of financial conditions that will assist our understanding of exactly what a crisis is and how it differs from other conditions. (How these conditions come into being is another question that is discussed later.) The conditions described are perceived conditions based on prevailing expectations, whether or not these expectations are justified.

As noted in the preceding section, economic units are prime borrowers when their capital positions, K, are $> K_s$, they are rationed borrowers, when $K < K_m$, and they are risky borrowers when $K < K_s$ and $\geq K_m$. Three financial states of the world can be characterized largely in terms of different mixes in the proportions of these three categories of borrowers. In "benign" financial conditions, capital positions are high, $\pi = 0$, and subjective shock probabilities are low, so that a large proportion of units have capital positions above K_s. Rationed borrowers are limited to the irreducible "fringe of unsatisfied borrowers." We would also expect liquidity positions to be strong, partly because high capital positions make most units highly creditworthy and also because the economic conditions that are conducive to high capital positions are also conducive to large holding of liquid assets.

In "vulnerable" financial conditions, shock probabilities are higher, π is significantly greater than zero, and capital positions are lower than in benign conditions. Hence, the capital positions of a substantial proportion of units fall below K_s—they pay risk premiums. In addition, a larger proportion of units have capital positions marginally less than K_m and are rationed. Liquidity positions are more dependent on the ability to borrow ("liability management") than on liquid asset holdings, making borrowers' capital positions a strategic determinant of liquidity position. Greater vulnerability implies a wider range of risk premiums for risky borrowers having capital ratios within the K_m–K_s range, as discussed below.

In "crisis" conditions, a significant proportion of economic units have capital positions well below K_m. (This reflects either a sharp increase in the subjective probability of a disaster, π, or the occurrence of a shock that has reduced capital positions.) Since outstanding loans to such borrowers are above the level lenders find acceptable, no new loans are made, and creditors take all possible steps to reduce their outstanding loans. When many lenders do this who had previously adopted a strategy of dealing with low probability hazards by making short commitments, crisis states involve "runs", that is, attempts by creditors to convert their claims quickly before others do so and before the resources of the debtor are exhausted. Units subject to runs encounter major liquidity problems that may spill over to other units that may be viewed as suspect. Weak liquidity positions are a pervasive characteristic of crisis states.

Some observers find it difficult to understand why it is not always possible to dampen a run by offering to pay higher interest rates. The answer is, of course, implicit in our case for K_m. If because of moral hazard the rate is already at the point where it maximizes the lender's return or if the insolvency probability is already at the maximum level the lender will tolerate, an offer to pay a higher rate will not find a taker. Indeed, the offer to pay higher rates is likely to reinforce rather than dampen any tendency for lenders to run. The reason is that when borrowers come under suspicion and other sources of information are unreliable, interest rates are viewed as a risk indicator.[11]

THE SUBJECTIVE PROBABILITY OF A DISASTER

Our hypothesis regarding subjective expectations of a disaster is based on the literature on natural disasters, which in some respects are analagous to financial disasters. A segment of the literature on natural disasters focuses on the issue of how people deal with low probability events that carry high potential losses (Kunreuther, et al. 1978). A major finding is that when subjective disaster probabilities fall below some threshold level, people behave as if they were zero. In their study of disaster insurance, Ginsberg and Kunreuther (1977) cite experiments that support this concept:

> Subjects were presented with a series of gambles each of which involved the possibility of losing a given amount with a specified probability.... Subjects showed a strong tendency to buy insurance only for high probability, low loss events...and rejected insurance in situations where the probability of loss was low and the potential losses high.
>
> The subject's behavior can be explained (Slovic, et al., 1977) in

11. Our one-period model assumes that the lender knows the investment opportunities faced by the borrower and that the borrower will choose the opportunity that is most advantageous, which might be one with high risk—especially if the borrower's capital position is weak. In a multiperiod model, however, the borrower may find it advantageous to forego risky projects that are most attractive in the short run if their selection would violate their understanding with the lender and prejudice their long-run relationship. When the lender extends credit on the basis of this type of understanding, he is said to base his loan decision on the borrower's character. In long-standing relationships the lender usually knows the rate a borrower can afford to pay when loan funds are used in accordance with their understanding. If the borrower suddenly expresses a willingness to pay a rate well above this level, it is likely to be interpreted by the lender as a signal that the borrower intends to violate their agreement and go for a high risk opportunity.

The interest rate may serve a similar signaling role when borrowers who look to the open market for funds come under suspicion. The cost of funds to such borrowers rises, but not because they pay higher rates. Rather, it is because they must expend greater effort to convince their customary sources that they remain sound and, failing that, to find new sources. But the judgment of bankers who have been in this situation is that an offer to pay a higher rate would be interpreted by the market as an acknowledgment by the bank of its weakness, and it would therefore be self-defeating.

terms of a probability threshold, the level of which may vary from individual to individual and situation to situation. Events with probabilities below the threshold are simply dismissed from further consideration. This heuristic-ignore low probability events—is given by subjects themselves and can easily be rationalized in terms of economizing on attention. (1977: 21–22)

Elsewhere, Kunreuther and Slovic note that "[s]uch a strategy is understandable in view of the fact that limitations of people's time, energy and attention capacities create a 'finite reservoir of concern.' Unless we ignored many low-probability threats we would become so burdened that any sort of productive life would become impossible" (1978: 67).

It is very likely that the same behavioral strategy would apply to firms as to individuals. The normal decision process within a firm does not create any pressure to charge a premium to cover a very low probability contingency that is very unlikely to generate any losses within the conventional period covered by income statements. (This is in contrast to losses that occur on a continuing basis, which are a charge on current income, so that there is direct pressure from the budgetary process to charge an interest rate high enough to cover them.) And since very low probabilities are also very imperfectly formulated probabilities, there is a natural tendency to resist charging a risk premium. If markets are competitive, furthermore, even firms that are prepared to expend the resources needed to formulate a reasonable judgment on probabilities may not be able to charge a risk premium if other firms ignore them.

This tendency to ignore low probability contingencies is reinforced by the incentive system in many institutions and the high rate of job mobility among managers. The performance of decisionmakers is often evaluated over a relatively short period of time. If the hazard does occur, it most likely will be long after the decisionmaker has moved to another position within the same institution or to another institution.

Indeed, our view is that protective behavior by lenders against low probability hazards is less likely than protective behavior by individuals against natural hazards. Hazards of both types can often be anticipated before they occur. This is little help to an individual who has built a house on a flood plain or along an earthquake fault line (the types of decisions explored by Kunreuther and his colleagues), but it may help a lender, depending on the nature of his commitment. The lender may view his behavior as more akin to parking a mobile home on the flood plain, retaining the capacity to get out when the waters start to rise. This reinforces the predisposition to ignore the hazard when the waters are low.

A strategy of dealing with low probability hazards by keeping commitments short and with the expectation of bailing out if storm clouds appear can only work for isolated shocks, and it may not work then, if there is a "run"—that is, if everyone tries to get off the financial flood plain at the same time. (See above for a more rigorous definition of "run.") Capital positions particularly cannot be strengthened at short notice. Attempting to sell shares when a major credit shock looms on the horizon would be akin to a homeowner attempting to buy flood insurance when the flood waters are lapping at his doorstep. Individual lenders can always improve their liquidity positions, however, and all lenders can do so at the same time if the central bank is accommodative (see below).

We thus postulate that there is a threshold probability π^* that a major shock will occur. Any probability below π^* is too low to be operationally significant and is treated as if it were zero. No risk premiums are collected to cover this contingency.

INCREASING VULNERABILITY

The important questions concern how and why an economy moves from one condition to another. A comprehensive answer would far exceed our capacities at this stage, but we will offer some fragments of an answer.

The causes of increasing vulnerability can be classified broadly as those increasing the probability that shocks will occur and those reducing the capacity to withstand shocks. The probability of a shock can rise either because of an unfavorable shift in the distribution governing investment returns or because the capital positions of borrowers decline relative to their contractual debt service obligations. Our efforts have focused on explaining why, during an economic expansion, borrowers' capital positions tend to decline. There may also be an endogenous process that generates unfavorable shifts in the distribution of investment returns, but in this chapter, we assume that credit shocks are stochastic, subject to a stable but very low probability. This is the usual assumption made regarding natural disasters. We argue that the economy's vulnerability to a shock increases during a period of economic expansion because borrowers' capital positions and creditors' capital positions fall in response to a decline in the subjective probabilities of a major shock.

Subjective Shock Probabilities

Our postulate, drawn from the natural disaster literature, is that the subjective probability of a major shock is a negative function of the length of time that has elapsed since the last such shock. As the period from the last shock lengthens, the subjective probability of another one declines.[12] This is illustrated by Figure 4–5. Note that below some threshold level π^*, the probability of a disaster is regarded as if it were zero.

Figure 4–5.   Probability of a Disaster.

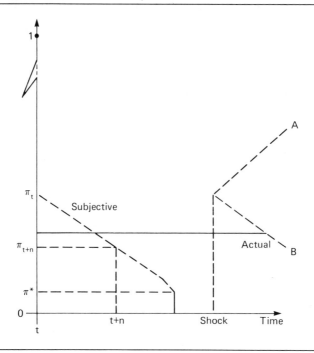

12. Tversky and Kahneman (1974) have described this phenomenon as a cognitive bias that stems from reliance on the availability heuristic for estimating the probability of an event. They note (p. 26) that "recent occurrences are likely to be relatively more available than earlier occurrences. It is a common experience that the subjective probability of traffic accidents rises temporarily when one sees a car overturned by the side of the road." Note that declining subjective probabilities may also be consistent with a Bayesian approach to formulating possibilities.

The decline in the subjective probability of a disaster may lead to a decline in capital positions. Creditors can lend to borrowers with lower capital positions, or permit loans outstanding to rise, or allow their own capital to fall, without increasing the subjective probability of their own insolvency. In Figure 4–6 the lender's subjective insolvency risk is the same at point B as at point A, even though capital positions are weaker or loan commitments larger, because the subjective probability of a disaster has fallen from π_t to π_{t+n}.

In an expanding economy, growing confidence that is associated with expansion strengthens the tendency for subjective shock probabilities to decline merely through the passage of time. If the real probability of a major shock has not fallen, this decline in capital positions makes the system more vulnerable.

A very similar line of argument can be applied to declining liquidity positions during a period that does not contain a major

Figure 4–6.   Probability of Lender Insolvency.

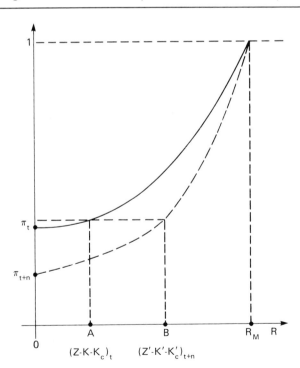

liquidity shock. As subjective probabilities of such a shock decline, the presumed need to hold liquid assets to meet unexpected contingencies ("precautionary needs") also declines. This process is reinforced during a period of economic expansion by the euphoria accompanying the expansion and by rising interest rates that raise the opportunity cost of being liquid.

We view the process by which declining subjective shock probabilities lead to reduced capital positions and liquidity positions as involving largely implicit decisions associated with an expanding economy. We need not assume that firms make explicit decisions to reduce capital and liquidity positions in response to declining subjective shock probabilities. It is only necessary to assume that they will accept without resistance declines that occur from forces associated with expansion that are outside of their immediate control.

In an expanding economy, asset growth tends to exceed growth in retained earnings, which for financial institutions especially is always the major source of capital growth. Similarly, the composition of assets shifts from liquid to illiquid categories. For example, a bank sells liquid assets "temporarily" in order to accommodate loan demands of valued customers, but it never has a good opportunity to replenish the liquid assets, and when it looks around it finds that other banks are in much the same situation; hence, it redefines what constitutes an "acceptable" liquidity position.

We would expect that declining subjective shock probabilities would affect portfolio risk in the same way that they affect capital position and liquidity position. Just as lower capital positions are accepted because they are presumed to provide the same degree of safety as higher positions at an earlier time (see Figure 4–6), assets are acquired that at an earlier time would have been considered too risky. (Except in extremis, firms rarely change their policies deliberately to take more risk. What they change are their perceptions of the risk associated with different courses of action.) But if in fact real shock probabilities have not declined, they have increased their risk of insolvency.

In adjusting their asset portfolios, lenders will extend their reach into areas where information is not as good or is more costly to acquire or both. (The underlying presumption is that good information is not as badly needed as before.) They may enter new product lines or expand into geographical areas where they have not operated before—and they may cross political and currency boundaries.

Actual and Perceived Financial Conditions

The taxonomy of financial conditions described above referred to perceived conditions, but subjective and actual probabilities of a disaster need not correspond. A long period of declining subjective shock probabilities that lead to reduced capital positions and liquidity positions that increase real vulnerability will not cause an increase in perceived vulnerability until something happens to jar perceptions—a nontrivial shock of less than crisis proportions. When this occurs, the perceived π may jump very quickly, increasing K_m and K_s. Suddenly some firms are rationed out of the market, and others must pay risk premiums for the first time.

We can derive an explicit expression for the increase in the risk premiums by taking the partial derivative of equation (4.19) with respect to an increase in the subjective probability of a major shock:

$$\frac{\partial(r - r^*)}{\partial \pi} = \frac{r^* - K/L}{(1 - \pi)^2} \tag{4.25}$$

Note that the change in the risk premium depends on the initial level of π. The higher the initial subjective probability of disaster, the larger the change in the risk premium associated with a given change in that probability. Note also that an increase in π will lead to a larger increase in the risk premium the lower the borrower's capital position. Thus, since a rise in π has a greater effect on risk premiums paid by weakly capitalized borrowers than on the premiums paid by strongly capitalized borrowers, the range of risk premiums paid by risky borrowers widens. This phenomenon is termed "tiering." In recent times, it was observed in the Eurocurrency interbank market in the aftermath of the failure of the Herstatt Bank in 1974 and in the U.S. certificate of deposit (CD) market in the wake of the collapse of the Franklin National Bank in 1974. In both instances, the tiering was in response to a sharp upward revision in expectations of a major banking crisis.

Capital Position and Liquidity Position as Determinants of Vulnerability to Financial Crises

Liquidity position is a much less important determinant of systemic vulnerability than capital position. In general, an illiquid firm with strong capital can withstand interest rate and credit shocks and (assuming an effective central bank) can ride out a liquidity shock by borrowing at high rates. But an insolvent firm with a strong liquidity position, while it may continue operations for a period, will probably be forced to close sooner or later. This (oversimplified) typology is shown in Table 4–3.

There is another sense in which capital position is much more important then liquidity position in determining systemic vulnerability. If π increases suddenly and firms decide they want to strengthen their capacity to meet all types of shocks, they can strengthen their liquidity position to whatever degree the central bank wishes to be accommodative. Since central banks are not equity investors, however, they can do little to help firms increase their capital positions except to offer superfluous advice regarding the virtues of slowing growth, cutting dividends, or selling shares. The first two measures can do little to help in the short run, and the third is not available to firms without access to credit markets. In the United States this would include all except the very largest financial institutions. Since the developments that cause firms to want more capital are very likely also to cause the price of equity capital to rise sharply, even firms with access to the market may be deterred from raising capital in this way.

By a similar line of argument of the three shocks identified in this chapter, credit shocks represent the greatest danger. Interest rate and liquidity shocks are at least partly controllable by the central

Table 4–3. Liquidity and Solvency as Determinants of Failure.

	Solvent	Insolvent
Liquid	Survival	Delayed failure
Illiquid	Probable survival	Immediate failure

bank. While the central bank may choose as a matter of policy not to control them in the ordinary course of affairs and may in fact take actions that generate or intensify such shocks, in an emerging crisis it can shift gears and moderate their force. In the case of credit shocks, however, there is not much the central bank can do except to see that solvent units are not dragged under along with insolvent ones.

Institutional Developments and "Go for Broke" Strategies

Institutional developments during a period of expansion may either intensify or dampen tendencies toward increases in vulnerability, but on balance the first is more likely. Regulation of financial institutions aimed at protecting solvency tends to become more restrictive during periods of contraction and more liberal during periods of expansion, as legislatures and regulators get caught up in the prevailing expectations of the period. New financial institutions that are formed to exploit the entrepreneural opportunities that arise during expansion are likely to be less risk averse and more weakly capitalized (and therefore more vulnerable to shock) than older institutions that have "memories." Real estate investment trusts are a good example.

The development of forward and futures markets in financial instruments, which is largely a reaction to growing interest rate instability and the demand for low cost methods of hedging the risk associated with such instability, might appear to be a counterexample. Such markets facilitate risk shifting and thereby soften the burdens imposed by market instability. However, forward and futures markets can be used to gamble as well as to hedge, and under conditions of stress they become a convenient way for firms in distress to play "go for broke."

A "go for broke" strategy is an extreme form of moral hazard that arises when the borrower's capital position has been depleted so that he has nothing to lose from low investment returns. Under these circumstances, the borrower will prefer the investment with the highest possible investment returns, even if the expected return for the investment is lower than for less risky options.

For example, suppose a firm has liabilities to creditors totaling $20 billion, that it can choose between two operating strategies that yield different end of period asset positions, and that there are two

Table 4-4. A Go-for-Broke Example.

	STATE 1 (p = 0.9)	STATE 2 (p = 0.1)	Expected Values of Assets
Strategy A	$20b	$20b	$20b
Strategy B	$10b	$30b	$12b

possible future states of the world (see Table 4–4). Strategy Ā will yield a return of $20 billion in both states of the world, which is just large enough to cover the bank's obligation to its creditors but with nothing left over for the shareholders. Strategy B̄ will yield a very low return, $10 billion, if the first state of the world occurs (a probability of 0.9) and a very high return, $30 billion, if the second state of the world occurs (a probability of 0.1).

Even though strategy B has a lower expected value, the bank's management may nonetheless adopt it. Under strategy B there is one chance in ten that the bank's shareholders will earn $10 billion, and they cannot be worse off than under strategy Ā. The firm's creditors, employees, and society, however, are much worse off under strategy B̄.

Firms playing go for broke look for action and cover. To such a player, the wider the potential swings in values (the action) the better, since they pocket the gain but do not take the losses. But they also seek cover—that is, a seemingly legitimate reason for playing the game. Otherwise, creditors or regulators will catch on to what they are doing and shut them down. Forward and future markets provide both action and cover to all types of financial institutions. Foreign exchange markets perform a similar role for large commercial banks, and the amount of action they offer increases with greater interest rate instability. Thus, institutional developments designed to reduce vulnerability to interest rate instability may have the unintended effect of increasing the risk of insolvency.

The Issue of Inevitability

In a model where the actual probability of a disaster π is fixed, where subjective probabilities decline as the period since the last disastrous shock lengthens, and where the capacity to withstand shock tracks subjective probabilities, crises are inevitable, since a low probability event must occur sooner or later. Furthermore, since vulnerability will continue to increase until a major shock occurs, a crisis is bound to get worse the longer it is delayed. This model, however, fails to allow for the impact of nontrivial shocks of less than crisis magnitude on subjective probabilities regarding disastrous shocks. Does the system "learn from experience"?

Reference was made above to rapid adjustments in K_m, K_s, and risk premiums when such a shock occurs. But these adjustments do not significantly affect the capacity to withstand future shocks unless the shift in shock probabilities is long lasting.

The problem is illustrated in Figure 4–5, which shows a sharp jump in subjective shock probabilities on the occurrence of a nontrivial shock following a long period without any shocks. Viewing this from the perspective of the individual firm, we can assume that this shock is larger than the firm expected but smaller than the one for which the firm was prepared. Does the firm assume that a larger shock is more likely than it thought before? If so it will maintain or even strengthen its capital position as shown in branch A of the subjective probability line in Figure 4–5. Or does the firm assume that the unexpected shock is the worst that can happen, in which case it might allow its capital position to run down as illustrated by branch B. This is an empirical question of great importance, but in the current state of knowledge we must take an agnostic stance.

CRISIS SCENARIOS AND THE LENDER OF LAST RESORT

A "crisis scenario" is a sequence of events over a relatively short time that includes at least one major shock and culminates in a financial crisis. An illiquidity scenario originates with a liquidity shock—an unexpected increase in the severity of credit rationing due to a marked increase in either the demand or supply of loanable funds. The rationing that arises is of the disequilibrium type,[13] but if it generates a cumulative process involving mounting expectations of a

---

13. The possibility of disequilibrium rationing has never been seriously challenged by economists, and virtually all the literature (and controversy) has been concerned with equilibrium rationing. On this point see Baltensperger (1978).

credit shortage, a crisis could run its course before equilibrium was restored.

One possible cause of a liquidity shock is an attempt by the central bank to combat strong excess demand with an extremely tight monetary policy.[14] An explosive rise in interest rates could cause dealers suddenly to become apprehensive regarding the possible downside risk in holding securities and to refuse to increase their positions. At this point dealer markets would cease to function, and what were considered to be "liquid assets" would be transformed into illiquid assets. This would result in extraordinary demands for bank loans and might possibly lead commercial banks to renege on their loan commitments, and this in turn would simulate even more demand—a "run" on bank loans in order to stockpile cash. For a short period in the fall of 1966 such a scenario developed in the United States, but it was aborted before cash stockpiling began (see Guttentag 1969 and the sources cited there). If not checked, a scenario of this sort would at some point trigger an insolvency scenario, as firms unable to discharge their debts begin to fail.

An insolvency scenario originates with a credit shock or an interest rate shock. In the past the most important type of credit shock was caused by a deflation that resulted in borrower failures and credit losses to lenders. This may not be the most important type of credit shock in the future. Where loans contracts call for floating rates, as in Eurocurrency markets, interest rate shocks are converted into credit shocks. If debt service burdens are already heavy, the effects of marked increases in interest rates could be much the same as a credit shock caused by deflation.[15] (Of course, if lenders assume interest rate risk themselves by writing fixed rate loan contracts of markedly different duration than their liabilities, their capital could be eroded directly by an interest rate shock, which was what happened to the thrift institutions in the United States in 1980 and 1981.) If losses to lenders are large relative to their capital, threats to lender solvency will arise. Banks suspected of being in a precarious position because of heavy losses may find it difficult to borrow, creating an illiquidity problem.

While insolvency scenarios eventually become illiquidity

14. Another cause would be a blockage of convertibility of governments of one or more countries in which major banks had large positions, as noted in Guttentag and Herring (1982).

15. For a discussion of how this might happen in Eurocurrency markets, see Guttentag and Herring (1980).

scenarios and vice versa, it is useful to distinguish them because of their different implications for policy. In general, central banks find it easier to deal with illiquidity scenarios (which they may have been instrumental in initiating) than with insolvency scenarios. The appropriate remedy for the first is to flood the financial markets with money on the presumption that so long as the creditworthiness of borrowers is unimpaired, the money will go where it is needed. Given such a policy,[16] any failure of illiquid but solvent firms would be isolated (and probably limited to small firms), and there would be little danger of contagion via a spreading loss of confidence of creditors.

Insolvency scenarios are much more difficult to deal with. It is neither possible nor desirable to have all firms that are headed toward failure. What the central bank must try to do is to prevent the insolvency of some firms from creating severe illiquidity problems for other firms who would otherwise be solvent. Hence, the central bank must ease credit generally, in the hope that the banks will lend freely to solvent firms. If they do not, the central bank must decide whether to lend directly to such firms.

Under its lender of last resort responsibilities, the central bank has a clear responsibility to lend directly to solvent banks and to give banks the benefit of the doubt if solvency is at issue. As noted earlier, however, the central bank cannot provide capital to insolvent firms, and traditionally central banks do not assume responsibility for disposing of insolvent banks. Yet major social costs can arise from failure of some official agency to make a prompt and effective disposition of insolvent banks—either through liquidation, merger, or government intervention (see Guttentag and Herring 1982). In short, a central bank can deal with an illiquidity scenario, but not an insolvency scenario, on its own.

SUMMARY AND CONCLUSION

Our analysis began with a consideration of the micreconomics of lending behavior. We showed how risk premiums were set in

---

16. We do not take effective central bank performance for granted. For a discussion of why a central bank might blunder during an illiquidity scenario, see Guttentag (1972).

competitive markets in response to subjective probabilities of credit shocks, and we demonstrated how moral hazard could lead to credit rationing and the imposition of minimum capital requirements. These results enabled us to classify borrowers according to their capital positions and the risk premiums they are charged. Prevailing financial condition were then categorized as benign, vulnerable, or crisis according to whether the preponderance of borrowers were classified as prime, risky, or rationed.

The dynamics of our analysis stems from a cognitive bias that has been emphasized in the analysis of economic behavior with regard to natural disasters and observed and verified in the empirical literature on decisionmaking under uncertainty: The subjective probability of a major shock is a negative function of the length of time that has elapsed since the last such shock. To the extent that subjective probabilities decline even though actual probabilities remain constant or increase, the system becomes more vulnerable to financial disorder. As subjective probabilities decline, risk premiums diminish, and the capital ratios of both borrowers and lenders are allowed to run down. Financial conditions shift from benign to vulnerable. When some unfavorable event causes a sharp revision of subjective probabilities or reduces capital positions, there will be a sudden, substantial increase in the number of borrowers who are rationed. This event will jolt the system into a crisis state in which the newly rationed borrowers find they cannot get new loans. Nor can they roll over maturing debt, since creditors will make every effort to reduce outstanding exposure. Borrowers with short-term liabilities will find themselves subject to runs as creditors rush to redeem their claims before others do so and before the borrower's assets are exhausted.

Since this has been an exploratory essay, it should not be surprising that we have raised as many questions as we have answered. For example, does an economic expansion tend to cause an unfavorable shift in the distribution of investment returns? Do institutional developments designed to reduce uncertainty, such as futures markets, increase or reduce the vulnerability of the system to financial disorder? Are financial crises inevitable or can borrowers and lenders learn from close calls? And to what extent is our conceputal framework useful in analyzing historical episodes of financial disorder? These and other questions raised in the course of our analysis are under study.

APPENDIX: GLOSSARY OF SYMBOLS

f the density function governing the returns on investment

F the cumulative distribution of returns on investment

K the capital position of the borrower

K_c the capital position of the creditor

K_m the minimum capital position that the creditor considers acceptable

K_s the capital position that is large enough to enable the debtor to borrow at the risk-free rate

L the loan size

π the subjective probability that nature will draw from the disastrous distribution where all investment returns are zero

π^* threshold probability of π, below which it is treated as if it were zero

r one plus the contractual interest rate

r^* one plus the risk-free rate of return

$\hat{r}$ one plus the contractual interest rate that maximizes the expected return to the creditor

r_b one plus the expected rate of return to the borrower

r_c one plus the expected rate of return to the creditor

R the gross return on investment

R_M the maximum possible return on investment

w an index of the riskiness of the investment; higher values of w imply increasing riskiness in the Rothchild-Stiglitz sense of greater weight in the tails of the density function governing investment outcomes

$\hat{w}$ the degree of risk that maximizes the expected return to the borrower given L, r, and K

Z the total payment due from the borrower at the end of the loan contract period (Lr)

Z^* the total payment due on a risk-free loan at the end of the contract period (Lr^*)

REFERENCES

Baltensperger, Ernst. 1978. "Credit Rationing: Issues and Questions." *Journal of Money Credit and Banking* 10, (May): 170–81.

Barro, Robert. 1976. "The Loan Market, Collateral, and Rates of Interest." *Journal of Money Credit and Banking* 8, (November): 439–56.

Blackwell, Norman R. 1976. "An Investigation of the Theory of Credit Rationing." Ph.D. dissertation, University of Pennsylvania, Department of Finance.

Ginsberg, Ralph, and Howard Kunreuther. 1977. *Insurance and Market Failure.* Wharton School, Department of Decision Sciences, December.

Guttentag, Jack. 1969. "Defensive and Dynamic Open Market Operations, Discounting, and the Federal Reserve System's Crisis-Prevention Responsibilities." *Journal of Finance* 24, (May): 249–63.

——. 1972. "Discussion." In *Controlling Monetary Aggregates II: The Implementation.* Federal Reserve Bank of Boston Conference Series No. 9, September.

Guttentag, Jack, and Richard Herring. 1980. "Financial Disorder and Eurocurrency Markets." In *Proceedings,* Conference on Bank Structure and Competition, Federal Reserve Bank of Chicago.

——. 1981. "The Lender of Last Resort Function in an International Context," unpublished manuscript.

Keeton, William R. 1979. *Equilibrium Credit Rationing.* New York: Garland Publishing Inc.

Kunreuther, Howard et al. 1978. *Disaster Insurance Protection.* New York: John Wiley.

Kunreuther, Howard, and Paul Slovic. 1978. "Economics, Psychology and Protective Behavior." *American Economic Review* 68, (May): 64–69.

Minsky, Hyman. 1977. "A Theory of Systemic Fragility." In *Financial Crises,* edited by E.A. Altman and A.W. Sametz. New York: Wiley Interscience.

Rothschild, Michael, and Joseph E. Stiglitz. 1970. "Increasing Risk: I, A Definition." *Journal of Economic Theory* 2, (September): 225–43.

Roy, A.D. 1952. "Safety First and the Holdings of Assets." *Econometrica* 20, no. 3, (July): 431–49.

Slovic, P.; B. Fischhoff; S. Lichtenstein; B. Corrigan; and B. Combs. 1977. "Preference for Insuring Against Probable Small Losses: Implications for the Theory and Practice of Insurance." *Journal of Risk and Insurance* 44, no. 2, (June): 237–58.

Stiglitz, Joseph, and Andrew Weiss. 1980. "Credit Rationing in Markets with Imperfect Information, Part 1," Econometric Research Program, Research Memorandum No. 267, Princeton University, August.

Tversky, A., and D. Kahnerman, 1974. "Judgement Under Uncertainty: Heuristics and Biases." *Science* 185, (Sept): 1124–31.

5 DISCUSSION OF "A FRAMEWORK FOR THE ANALYSIS OF FINANCIAL DISORDER"

James Tobin
Yale University

The story Guttentag and Herring tell has both convincing and unconvincing aspects. Yes, Eurocurrency and other international banks could get into trouble if LDC borrowers, sovereign governments in many cases, defaulted on loans. Some banks might have difficulty meeting their short-term liabilities. Domino effects could occur because of interbank deposits; and in anticipation of them, runs on some institutions might occur.

Because of confusion and disagreement about jurisdiction and responsibility, Guttentag and Herring report, no reliable lender of last resort facilities are in place to deal with these contingencies. Anyway, the classic dilemma inhibits the arrangement and announcement of such facilities. On the one hand, assurances to banks and depositors encourage them to take excessive risk. On the other, the absence of assurances increases the system's vulnerability to runs and domino effects. As the authors argue, lender of last resort facilities must be conjoined with supervision and regulation, which are even more difficult in international and expatriate banking. Banks' standards of prudence are relative to peer behavior. Absolute standards drift down in the absence of supervision and regulation, leaving the lenders of last resort in a "no win" situation.

But beyond the effects on Eurobanks themselves, the Guttentag-Herring crisis scenario is not convincing. When their depositor-

199

lenders run away from Eurobanks, where do they run to? Presumably not to currencies, as in the great national panics of history. Do they run home, to deposits in the same currency, in less internationally tangled domestic banks? If so, there is no aggregative danger to national banking systems, which can even take over some of the lending business of the suspect Eurobanks. Since the problems originate with LDC loans, there is no reason to expect flight from any major currency to others.

The obvious and most likely remedy is that lenders of last resort buy or guarantee the loans, enabling the banks to meet their liabilities or to replace bad loans with good. With respect to LDC and sovereign loans, the IMF and the World Bank would be heavily involved on a borrower-by-borrower basis, which makes more sense than a bank-by-bank pattern. If the resources of the IMF and the World Bank do not suffice, maybe we need an international Reconstruction Finance Corporation.

Although Guttentag and Herring give the impression that international lending has endangered private banks, there seems no generic a priori reason that this should be so. Presumably worldwide loan portfolios are better diversified, not worse. Private international banks seem to have concentrated on the cream of LDCs—the Gang of Four, Mexico, Brazil.

Although exchange risk causes much anxiety, this is often an optical illusion. Exchange fluctuations simply mirror or offset other changes that would cause trouble in a regime of pegged rates.

As I have argued elsewhere (Tobin 1978), the problem is not the exchange rate regime, but the technical perfection and efficiency of international money markets. They have outrun the central banking institutions and controls. Given the impossibility of an international central banking authority or even of substantial policy coordination among national authorities, I advocated throwing some sand in the wheels, specifically by imposing an internationally agreed tax on currency exchanges. Guttentag and Herring have now provided me with another argument, the absence of international lenders of last resort and bank regulators.

In Chapter 4, Guttentag and Herring go back and forth between general and specific and between theory and real world. I find the connections pretty loose. I have trouble with their concept of a "disastrous distribution." Where loans to a particular borrower or project are in peril, I fail to see the macro problem, the "disorder" and "crisis" they warn us against. The preventives and the remedies are fairly obvious. What if the dice throw up a worldwide disaster? The only example I can see is nuclear war. In contingencies of that scope and depth, all bets are off. The real catastrophe is so much more serious than its financial implications that both private agents and public authorities may be excused for ignoring it in their plans and decisions, as all of us do every day.

I wish the authors would be specific about the shocks they have in mind. A taxonomy would include credit crunches, accelerations of inflation, cyclical recessions, OPEC and other real shocks to terms of trade, wars, and natural disasters. Effects and remedies will presumably differ.

I have no complaint about the authors' micro model of credit—the reasons for credit rationing and the reasons some borrowers are denied loans at any interest rate. I do have trouble tracking the macro (economywide or global) implications they draw from the micro model.

One technical quibble about the typical loan transaction they model: The borrower's capital, available to the lender if the project goes bad, is not itself at risk. It appears to be in escrow. I would have expected a project financed partly by borrowed funds and partly by the borrower's capital, with the lender having title to the contracted amount or to the value of the whole project, whichever is smaller.

In conclusion, Guttentag and Herring perform a valuable service by calling our attention to the unregulated world of international banking and the possibility that competitive pressures there can lead to defaults and "disorder." They do not make a convincing case that the disorder will extend to large-scale financial crises beyond the control of national central banks, whatever may happen to individual institutions. Their attempt to develop a general theory of credit crisis, linking macroeconomic events to the microeconomics of banking and credit markets, is a laudable ambition. At the moment, however, it has a long way to go.

REFERENCES

Tobin, James. 1978. "A Proposal for International Monetary Reform." *Eastern Economic Journal* 4, no. 3–4, (July-October).

PART
III

6 AN ANALYSIS OF THE PREDICTIVE ACCURACY OF ECONOMETRIC MODELS
The Case of the WEFA Model

INTRODUCTION

This work was originally conceived as a sequel to *Forecasts with Quarterly Macro-Econometric Models* by Y. Haitovsky, G. Treyz, and V. Su (HTS); it formed part of the National Bureau of Economic Research's (NBER) program of studies on economic fluctuations in the United States.

In an attempt to avoid some of the difficulties of HTS, the approach was designed to rely as much as possible on the records of the organizations responsible for the macromodels under consideration. The latter were, of course, Wharton Econometric Forecasting Associates Inc. (WEFA) and the Bureau of Economic Analysis (BEA) of the U.S. Department of Commerce.

The design of the research called for them to provide us with the computer tape modules actually used to produce a given forecast. We were then to reproduce their forecasts for the period under

The research on which this paper is based was in part supported by NSF grant SOC 74–18671. I wish to express my appreciation to my research assistants, Ates Dagli and Stavros Peristiani, without whose excellent assistance this work would not have been completed.

study (1972–74) to be sure that we are able to recreate the model and informational context under which the model operators were functioning. Once we were assured of that, we could conduct various experiments (simulations) in an effort to disentangle from the forecast error that part which was due to unavoidable data inaccuracies or revisions as well as ignorance of the correct values of the exogenous variables during the forecast period. On the assumption that ignorance of the correct values of the exogenous variables should induce an error component which is independent of the sampling error involved in estimation as well as the structural error, we could, in principle, isolate the component of the forecast error due to the basic properties of the model. Precisely the remaining error would reflect the sampling, structural, and misspecification errors. This procedure would have necessitated reestimating each model module with revised data every time a revision affected the sample period over which the two models were estimated.

One might interject that the misspecification error is not independent of the component due to parameter uncertainty and structural errors. That is quite true, but if we state as *a null hypothesis that the model is correctly specified* and if we obtain the (estimated) variance of a given forecast, the difference between this and the component isolated above would give us the net impact of the misspecification error on the mean squared error of the forecast.

As is known, however, the Mark III version of the Wharton model and several of the versions of the BEA model are not estimated by consistent methods. In particular, all equations of the Mark III version used to generate the forecasts over the period of interest (1972–73) were estimated by least squares. Thus, it was not really possible to estimate reliably something like a forecast variance.

Consequently, we are reduced to considering various measures of forecast accuracy with and without the correct values of the exogenous variables, and with and without constant adjustments. In this article we shall examine the WEFA Mark III model. In a subsequent article we shall examine the BEA model.

Finally, I ought to note with great appreciation the cooperation extended to us by the staff at WEFA and BEA. Despite their cheerful cooperation, the task of documenting and reproducing their forecasts has been extremely demanding of resources and time.

FORECASTING WITH LINEAR AND NONLINEAR ECONOMETRIC MODELS

The question of efficiency of forecasts from econometric models has been treated in a technical sense elsewhere (Dhrymes 1973, 1978). Here we shall analyze the nature of the errors inherent in forecasts based on estimated econometric models. For completeness we note that the general linear structural econometric model (GLSEM) is given by

$$YB^* = XC + U \qquad (6.1)$$

where Y, X, U are, respectively, Txm, TxG, Txm containing T observations on the current endogenous, predetermined, and random variables of the model. The matrices B^*, C contain the unknown structural parameters. The rows of U, say u_i: $t = 1, 2, \ldots, T$ are m-element random vectors.

A priori restrictions usually require that some elements in each column, say b^*i, $c \cdot i$, of B^* and C, respectively, are zero although more general linear restrictions may be entertained. A normalization convention requires that in the ith equation the coefficient of y_{ti} be unity. In particular, this implies that the mxm matrix B^* may be written as

$$B^* = I - B, \; b_{ii} = 0, i = 1, 2, \ldots, m. \qquad (6.2)$$

From (1) we obtain the *reduced form*

$$Y = X\Pi + V \qquad (6.3)$$

where

$$\Pi = CD, \; V = UD, \; D = (I - B)^{-1}. \qquad (6.4)$$

If the model contains lagged endogenous variables, we may partition the matrix X as

$$X = (Y_{-1}, Y_{-2}, \ldots Y_{-k}, W) \qquad (6.5)$$

where W is the Txs matrix of exogenous variables. For simplicity of exposition take

$$k = 1.$$

Then, given estimates $\tilde{C}, \tilde{B}$ based on a sample of size T, and given the vector w_{T+1}, a forecast is simply

$$\tilde{y}_{T+1\cdot} = y_{T\cdot} \, \tilde{\Pi}_1 + w_{T+1\cdot} \, \tilde{\Pi}_0 \qquad (6.6)$$

where we have conformably partitioned

$$\Pi = \frac{\Pi_1}{\Pi_0}, \; X = (Y_{-1}, W). \qquad (6.7)$$

Note that

$$\Pi_1 \text{ is } mxm, \; \Pi_0 \text{ is } sxm \; (m + s = G).$$

In general, a τ-period forecast is $(\tau \geq 1)$

$$\tilde{y}_{T+\tau\cdot} = y_{T\cdot} \, \tilde{\Pi}_1^\tau + \sum_{i=1}^\tau w_{T+i\cdot} \, \tilde{\Pi}_0 \tilde{\Pi}_1^{\tau-1}. \qquad (6.8)$$

Notice, further, that provided the model is stable, the longer the forecast horizon (that is, the larger the τ), the smaller the influence of the initial conditions $y_{T\cdot}$ and the forecast simply becomes a weighted sum of the exogenous variables asserted to prevail over the forecast horizon. Now, if the estimation procedure is a consistent one, Π_0, Π_1 are estimated consistently, and the *forecast will be consistent* and what I shall call *conditionally unbiased.*

To explain what is meant by this, consider the forecast error

$$\tilde{y}_{t+\tau\cdot} - y_{T+\tau\cdot} = -v_{T+\tau\cdot}^* + y_{T\cdot} \, (\tilde{\Pi}_1^\tau - \Pi_1^\tau)$$

$$+ \sum_{i=1}^\tau w_{T+\tau\cdot} \, \tilde{\Pi}_0 \tilde{\Pi}_1^{\tau-i} - \Pi_0 \Pi_1^{\tau-i} \qquad (6.9)$$

If the sample is sufficiently large, the second and third members of the right member of (9) can be made arbitrarily small, in probability. But then the conditional mean of the forecast error, conditional on $(Y_{t\cdot}, w_{t\cdot})$: $t = T, T-1, T-2, \ldots$ will also obey

$$P \, \{E[\tilde{y}_{t+\tau\cdot} - y_{T+\tau\cdot} | w_{T+i\cdot}, i = 1, 2, \ldots, t(y_{t\cdot}, w_{t\cdot}):$$

$$t = T, T-1, T-1 \ldots)] < \delta\} > 1 - \epsilon \qquad (6.10)$$

if the sample size is large enough.

The expression in (10) defines conditional unbiasedness. In general the forecast error in (9) is not an unbiased estimator of zero, given the manner in which we have estimated Π. Even if Π were estimated by least squares, it would not be unbiased given that the model contains lagged endogenous variables. Thus, in the ordinary sense of the term, unbiased forecasts from dynamic econometric models do not exist. However, conditionally unbiased forecasts do exist.

We next examine the variability of such forecasts in terms of the mean squared error of $\tilde{y}_{T+\tau}$. considered as a forecast of $E(y_{T+\tau}.)$. The tools for addressing this issue have essentially been provided in Dhrymes (1973) and have been elaborated upon by Schmidt (1974) and others.

In particular, the problem is to provide some distribution theory for $\tilde{\Pi}_1^\tau - \Pi_1^\tau$ and $\tilde{\Pi}_0\tilde{\Pi}_1^{\tau-1} - \Pi_0\Pi_1^{\tau-1}$; we have

$$\tilde{\Pi}_1^\tau - \Pi_1^\tau = \tilde{\Pi}_{*\tau}(\tilde{\Pi}_1 - \Pi_1), \; \tilde{\Pi}_{*\tau} = \sum_{j=1}^{\tau-1} \tilde{\Pi}_1^{\tau-1-j}\Pi_1^j \tag{6.11}$$

and

$$\begin{aligned}\tilde{\Pi}_0\tilde{\Pi}_1^{\tau-i} - \Pi_0\Pi_1^{\tau-i} &= \tilde{\Pi}_0\tilde{\Pi}_1^{\tau-i} - \tilde{\Pi}_0\Pi_1^{\tau-i} + \tilde{\Pi}_0\Pi_1^{\tau-i} - \Pi_0\Pi_1^{\tau-i} \\ &= \tilde{\Pi}_0\tilde{\Pi}_{*\tau-i}(\tilde{\Pi}_1 - \Pi_1) + (\tilde{\Pi}_0 - \Pi_0)\Pi_1^{\tau-i}.\end{aligned} \tag{6.12}$$

thus,

$$\begin{aligned}\text{vec}\,(\tilde{\Pi}_1^\tau - \Pi_1^\tau) &= (I \boxtimes \tilde{\Pi}_{*\tau})(\tilde{\Pi}_1 - \Pi_1) \\ \text{vec}\,(\tilde{\Pi}_0\tilde{\Pi}_1^{\tau-i} - \Pi_0\Pi_1^{\tau-i}) &= (I \boxtimes \tilde{\Pi}_0\tilde{\Pi}_{*\tau-i})(\tilde{\pi}_1 - \Pi_1) \\ &\quad + (\Pi_1^{'\tau-i} \boxtimes I)(\tilde{\Pi} \quad \boxtimes I)(\tilde{\Pi}_0 - \Pi_0)\end{aligned} \tag{6.13}$$

and consequently,

$$e'_{T+\tau}. = \tilde{y}'_{T+\tau}. - y'_{T+\tau}. = -v^{*'}_{T+\tau}. + [(I \boxtimes y_T. \Pi_{*\tau}) + \sum_{t=1}^{\tau}$$

$$(I \boxtimes w_{T+i}. \, \tilde{\Pi}_0\tilde{\Pi}_{*\tau-i})]\,(\tilde{\pi}_1 - \pi_1)$$

$$+ \sum_{i=1}^{\tau} (\Pi_1^{'\tau-i} \boxtimes W_{T+I}.)(\tilde{\pi}_0 - \pi_0)$$

or, more compactly,

$$e'_{T+\tau \cdot} = \tilde{y}'_{T+\tau \cdot} - y'_{T+\tau \cdot} = -v^{*'}_{T+\tau \cdot} + Z_{T(\tau)}(\tilde{\Pi} - \Pi) \tag{6.14}$$

where

$$Z_{T(\tau) \cdot} = \sum_{i=1}^{\tau} (\Pi_1'^{\tau-1} \otimes w_{T+i \cdot}), (I \otimes y_{T \cdot} \tilde{\Pi}_{* \tau})$$

$$+ \sum_{i=1}^{\tau} (I \otimes w_{T+i \cdot} \tilde{\Pi}_0 \tilde{\Pi}_{* \tau-i})$$

$$(\tilde{\Pi} - \Pi) = (\tilde{\Pi}_0' - \Pi_0', \tilde{\Pi}_1' - \Pi_1')'.$$

With this notation, we find that approximately the mean squared error matrix is given by

$$MSE(e'_{T+\tau \cdot})\ \Omega^* + Z_{T(\tau)} \underset{T}{G} Z'_T(\tau) \tag{6.15}$$

where G is the covariance matrix of the limiting distribution of $\tilde{\Pi}$, given for example in Dhrymes (1973) for a variety of restricted and unrestricted reduced form estimators.

Notice, incidentally, that when the *model does not contain lagged endogenous variables*, then $\Pi_1 = 0$; defining by convention

$$\Pi_1^0 = I$$

we see that the expression in (14) reduces to

$$e'_{T+\tau \cdot} = \tilde{y}'_{T+\tau \cdot} - y_{T+\tau \cdot} = -v^{*'}_{T+\tau \cdot} + (I \otimes w_{T+\tau \cdot})(\tilde{\pi}_0 - \pi_0)$$

$$Z_{T(\tau)} = [I \otimes w_{T+\tau \cdot}, 0], v^*_{T+\tau \cdot} = u_{T+\tau \cdot} C_0(I - B)^{-1} \tag{6.14a}$$

which is the situation encountered in the standard exposition of such matters.

It is seen, therefore, that the situation is not materially different as between the cases where the model does and does not contain lagged endogenous variables. Thus, in examining the properties of forecasts generated ex ante and ex post, we shall use the simpler form; our discussion, then, as is reflected in our notation implicitly assumes that the model is not dynamic. However, in view of the preceding discussion, it is an entirely trivial matter to allow for lagged endogenous variables.

The ex post forecast error is given by

$$e_{T+\tau \cdot} = \tilde{y}_{T+\tau \cdot} - y_{T+\tau \cdot} = -v_{T+\tau \cdot} + x_{T+\tau \cdot} (\tilde{\Pi} - \Pi) \qquad (6.16)$$

where the model considered now is that of (1), (2), and (3) *with the understanding that it is not dynamic;* thus $x_{T+\tau \cdot}$ is the vector of exogenous variables, and

$$V_{T+\tau \cdot} = u_{T+\tau \cdot} D. \qquad (6.17)$$

Hence

$$MSE(e'_{T+\tau \cdot}) \; \Omega + (I_{\text{Ø}} \, x_{T+\tau \cdot}) \, \frac{G}{T} \, (I_{\text{Ø}} x'_{T+\tau \cdot}) \qquad (6.18)$$

where Ω is the covariance matrix of the reduced form error and G is the covariance matrix of the limiting distribution of the (restricted) reduced form.

The ex ante forecast is given by

$$\hat{e}_{T+\tau \cdot} = -v_{T+\tau \cdot} + \hat{x}_{T+\tau \cdot} \; \tilde{\Pi} - x_{T+\tau \cdot} \; \Pi$$

$$= -v_{T+\tau \cdot} + x_{T+\tau \cdot} (\tilde{\Pi} - \Pi) + (\hat{x}_{T+\tau \cdot} - x_{T+\tau \cdot}) \; \tilde{\Pi}. \qquad (6.19)$$

On the *assertion that the error committed in forecasting the exogenous variables is independent of the structural error process,* we find

$$MSE(\hat{e}'_{T+\tau \cdot}) \; \Omega + (I_{\text{Ø}} \, x_{T+\tau \cdot}) \, \frac{G}{T} \, (I_{\text{Ø}} \, x'_{T+\tau \cdot}) + (\tilde{\Pi}' _{\text{Ø}} I)$$

$$MSE(\hat{x}'_{T+\tau \cdot})(\tilde{\Pi}_{\text{Ø}} I) = MSE(e'_{T+\tau \cdot}) + \tilde{\Pi}' MSE(\hat{x}'_{T+\tau \cdot}) \tilde{\Pi} \qquad (6.20)$$

Model operators are also in the habit of introducing constant adjustments, which are usually justified as due to data revisions or possibly unusual events such as strikes that may take place during the forecast period. In any event, the justifications produced here are unrelated both to structural errors and to the evolution of the exogenous variables. If the data revisions affect only the sample period, then they affect only the numerical values work we shall use the model only in the form estimated by its operators, this occasions no particular problems. If the revisions affect also data over the forecast horizon, then since we shall be using only the revised form of the data we would usually expect "the constant adjustment version" to do better both with and without the correct values of the exogenous variables—that is, in both the ex ante and ex post form.

On the other hand, if the constant adjustments reflect "strikes" and other unusual events, we would again expect both in the ex post and ex ante form that the constant adjustment will do worse to the extent that the unusual event did not materialize and better if it did materialize. But in any event, the constant adjustment is not related to the structural error or the process generating the exogenous variables or the model operators' estimate of them, at least not invariably.

Now a constant adjustment is of the form

$$\tilde{\Pi}^* = \tilde{\Pi} + \Delta\tilde{\Pi}, \quad \Delta\tilde{\Pi} = \Delta\tilde{C}(I - \tilde{B})^{-1} \Delta\tilde{C} = {}^{\Delta\tilde{c}}_0 1 \cdot \tag{6.21}$$

since by definition the procedure adjusts the constant term of a given (each) equation, and this corresponds to the coefficient of the fictitious variable

$$x_{t1} = 1, \text{ for all } t. \tag{6.22}$$

The forecast error, ex post, with constant adjustment is

$$e^*_{T+\tau \cdot} = \tilde{y}^*_{T+\tau \cdot} - y_{T+\tau \cdot}$$

$$= -v_{T+\tau \cdot} + x_{T+\tau \cdot}(\tilde{\Pi} - \Pi) + x_{T+\tau \cdot}\Delta\tilde{\Pi} \tag{6.22a}$$

and consequently,

$$MSE(e^{*\prime}_{T+\tau \cdot}) = \Omega + (I_{\boldsymbol{N}} x_{T+\tau \cdot}) \frac{G}{T} (I_{\boldsymbol{N}} x'_{T+\tau \cdot}) + \Delta\tilde{\pi}'_1 \cdot \Delta\tilde{\pi}'_1 \cdot \tag{6.23}$$

where

$$\Delta\tilde{\pi} = \Delta\tilde{c}_1 \cdot \tilde{D} \tag{6.24}$$

and $\tilde{\pi}_1 \cdot$ is evidently the first *row* of $\tilde{\Pi}$, corresponding to the reduced form coefficient of the fictitious variable x_{t1} of equation (22).

Finally, the ex ante forecast error in this context is

$$\hat{e}^*_{T+\tau \cdot} = \tilde{y}^*_{T+\tau \cdot} - y_{T+\tau \cdot} = -v_{T+\tau \cdot} + \hat{x}_{T+\tau \cdot}\tilde{\Pi} - x_{T+\tau \cdot}\Pi + \hat{x}_{T+\tau \cdot}\Delta\tilde{\Pi}$$

$$= -v_{T+\tau \cdot} + x_{T+\tau \cdot}(\tilde{\Pi} - \Pi) + (\hat{x}_{T+\tau \cdot} - x_{T+\tau \cdot})\tilde{\Pi} + \Delta\tilde{\pi}_1 \cdot \tag{6.24a}$$

Hence, on the assertion that the constant adjustment is not correlated with the error process or the error committed by the operator in forecasting the exogenous variables, we find

$$MSE(\hat{e}^{*\prime}_{T+\tau \cdot}) MSE(e^{*\prime}_{T+\tau \cdot}) + \tilde{\Pi}' MSE(\hat{x}'_{T+\tau \cdot})\tilde{\Pi}. \tag{6.25}$$

Thus we have the relations

$$MSE(\hat{e}^{*\prime}_{T+\tau\cdot})\quad MSE(e^{\prime}_{T+\tau\cdot}) + \Delta\tilde{\pi}^{\prime}_{1\cdot}\,\Delta\tilde{\pi}_{1\cdot} + \tilde{\Pi}^{\prime}\,MSE(\hat{x}^{\prime}_{T+\tau\cdot})\tilde{\Pi} \quad (6.26a)$$

$$MSE(e^{*\prime}_{T+\tau\cdot})\quad MSE(e^{\prime}_{T+\tau\cdot}) + \Delta\tilde{\Pi}^{\prime}_{1\cdot}\,\Delta\tilde{\Pi}_{1\cdot} \quad\qquad\qquad (6.26b)$$

$$MSE(\hat{e}^{\prime}_{T+\tau\cdot})\quad MSE(e^{\prime}_{T+\tau\cdot}) + \tilde{\Pi}^{\prime}\,MSE(\hat{x}^{\prime}_{T+\tau\cdot})\tilde{\Pi} \qquad\qquad (6.26c)$$

$$MSE(e^{\prime}_{T+\tau\cdot}) = \Omega + (I\!\!N\,x_{T+\tau\cdot})\,\frac{G}{T}\,(I\!\!N\,x^{\prime}_{T+\tau\cdot}). \qquad\qquad (6.26d)$$

Hence, on the assertion that the constant adjustment process is independent of the structural error process and the process generating the exogenous variables, we would expect (26d) to be the smallest matrix and (26a) to be the largest; no particular ordering can be established between (26b) and (26c).

Consider now the possibility that constant adjustments may be related to the error process realization for $t < T+\tau$, but not for $t \geq T+\tau$. This would correspond to the assertion that there have been data revisions since the model has been estimated, and thus the parameter estimators are not consistent. Consequently, the limiting distribution of $\tilde{\Pi}$ is not centered on Π but on, say, $\bar{\Pi}$. In this case the expression in (16) is modified to

$$e_{T+\tau\cdot} = \tilde{y}_{T+\tau\cdot} - y_{T+\tau\cdot}$$

$$= -v_{T+\tau\cdot} + x_{T+\tau\cdot}\,(\tilde{\Pi} - \bar{\Pi}) + x_{T+\tau\cdot}\,\Delta\Pi \qquad (6.27)$$

where

$$\Delta\Pi = \bar{\Pi} - \Pi \qquad\qquad (6.28)$$

is the inconsistency of the estimator $\tilde{\Pi}$.

In this context (26d) is modified to

$$MSE(e^{\prime}_{T+\tau\cdot}) = \Omega + (I\!\!N\,x_{T+\tau\cdot})\,\frac{\bar{G}}{T}\,(I\!\!N\,x^{\prime}_{T+\tau\circ})$$

$$+ \Delta\Pi^{\prime}\,x^{\prime}_{T+\tau\cdot}\,x_{T+\tau\cdot}\,\Delta\Pi \qquad\qquad (6.29)$$

and (26b) is modified to

$$MSE(e^{*\prime}_{T+\tau\cdot})\;\Omega + (I\!\!N\,x_{T+\tau\cdot})\,\frac{\bar{G}}{T}\,(I\!\!N\,x^{\prime}_{T+\tau\cdot}) + \Delta\bar{\Pi}^{\prime}\,x^{\prime}_{T+\tau\cdot}\,x_{T+\tau\cdot}\,\Delta\tilde{\Pi}$$

$$+ {''E''}(\Delta\tilde{\pi}^{\prime}_{1\cdot}\,\Delta\tilde{\pi}_{1\cdot}) + {''E''}(\tilde{\Pi} - \Pi)^{\prime}\,x^{\prime}_{T+\tau\cdot}\,\Delta\tilde{\pi}_{1\cdot}$$

$$+ {''E''}\,\Delta\tilde{\pi}^{\prime}_{1\cdot}\,x_{T+\tau\cdot}\,(\tilde{\Pi} - \Pi) \qquad\qquad (6.29a)$$

where "E" is meant to signify the expectation obtained by the approximation of the relevant by the limiting distribution of $\tilde{\Pi}$ and $\Delta\tilde{\Pi}_1\cdot$.

Consequently, we may write

$$MSE(e^*_{\to_{\iota T}\cdot}) = MSE(e^{'}_{\to_{\iota T}\cdot}) + {''E''}\,\Delta\tilde{\pi}^{'}_\omega \cdot \Delta\tilde{\pi}_1\cdot$$
$$+ (\tilde{\Pi} - \bar{\Pi})' x^{'}_{T+\tau}\cdot \Delta\tilde{\Pi}_1\cdot + \Delta\tilde{\Pi}^{'}_1\cdot x_{T+\tau}\cdot (\tilde{\Pi} - \Pi). \qquad (6.30)$$

Here, if $\Delta\tilde{\pi}_1\cdot$ is chosen properly then we would expect that

$$MSE(e^*_{T+\tau}\cdot) - MSE(e^{'}_{T+\tau}\cdot) \geqslant 0.$$

A similar analysis can be carried out with ex ante forecasts.

As to the case where constant adjustments are meant to reflect strikes and other unusual events, the procedure is, of course, quite reasonable. On the other hand, strikes of consequence do not occur frequently, and hence this explanation could not be a serious one in view of the fact that every forecast embodies a series of constant adjustments. There remains a possibility that constant adjustments and forecasts of exogenous variables are good substitutes for each other and for expressing the model operators' personal views as to the evolution of the economy. In this case we may expect the constant adjustment to be uncorrelated with the correct exogenous variables but to be correlated with $\hat{x}_{T+\tau} - x_{T+\tau}\cdot$. In addition, constant adjustments will not be correlated with the error process. Thus, the forecast error is now (ex post)

$$e^*_{T+\tau}\cdot = \tilde{y}^*_{T+\tau}\cdot - y_{T+\tau}\cdot = -v_{T+\tau}\cdot + x_{T+\tau}\cdot (\tilde{\Pi} - \Pi) + x_{T+\tau}\cdot \Delta\tilde{\Pi} \qquad (6.31)$$

while ex ante it is

$$\hat{e}^*_{T+\tau}\cdot = \tilde{y}^*_{T+\tau}\cdot - y_{T+\tau}\cdot = -v_{T+\tau}\cdot + x_{T+\tau}\cdot (\tilde{\Pi} - \Pi)$$
$$+ (\hat{x}_{T+\tau}\cdot - x_{T+\tau}\cdot)\tilde{\Pi} + \Delta\tilde{\pi}_1\cdot. \qquad (6.32)$$

Consequently,

$$MSE(e^*_{T+\tau}\cdot)\,\Omega + (I_{\boldsymbol{\mathfrak{w}}}\, x_{T+\tau}\cdot)\, \frac{G}{T}\, (I_{\boldsymbol{\mathfrak{w}}}\, x^{'}_{T+\tau}\cdot) + \Delta\tilde{\pi}^{'}_1\cdot \Delta\tilde{\pi}_1\cdot. \qquad (6.33)$$

$$MSE(e^{*\prime}_{T+\tau \cdot}) \, \Omega + (I_{\textbf{N}} \, x_{T+\tau \cdot}) \overset{G}{-} (I_{\textbf{N}} \, x^{\prime}_{T+\tau \cdot}) + \Delta \tilde{\pi}^{\prime}_1 \cdot \Delta \tilde{\pi}_1 \cdot$$

$$+ \, \tilde{\Pi}^{\prime} \, MSE(\hat{x}^{\prime}_{T+\tau \cdot}) \tilde{\Pi} + \tilde{\Pi}^{\prime} \, E \, [(\hat{x}_{T+\tau \cdot} - x_{T+\tau \cdot})^{\prime} \, \Delta \tilde{\pi}_1 \cdot]$$

$$+ \, E \, [\Delta \tilde{\pi}^{\prime}_1 \cdot (\hat{x}_{T+\tau \cdot} - x_{T+\tau \cdot})] \, \tilde{\Pi} = MSE(e^{*\prime}_{T+\tau \cdot})$$

$$+ \, \tilde{\Pi}^{\prime} MSE(\hat{x}^{\prime}_{T+\tau \cdot}) \tilde{\Pi} + \tilde{\Pi}^{\prime} \, E \, [(\hat{x}_{T+\tau \cdot} - x_{T+\tau \cdot})^{\prime} \, \Delta \tilde{\pi}_1 \cdot]$$

$$+ \, E \, [\Delta \tilde{\pi}^{\prime}_1 \cdot (\hat{x}_{T+\tau \cdot} - x_{T+\tau \cdot})] \Pi. \tag{6.34}$$

Thus, to summarize this development: if the model is well specified and constant adjustment is an arbitrary activity of the model builders, unrelated to the structural error process and the errors made in forecasting the exogenous variables, then we have the situation in (26) and thus:

$$MSE(\hat{e}^{\prime}_{T+\tau \cdot}) - MSE(e^{\prime}_{T+\tau \cdot}) \geqslant 0$$

$$MSE(\hat{e}^{*\prime}_{T+\tau \cdot}) - MSE(e^{*}_{T+\tau \cdot}) \leqslant 0$$

$$MSE(\hat{e}^{*\prime}_{T+\tau \cdot}) - MSE(\hat{e}^{\prime}_{T+\tau \cdot}) \gtrless 0$$

On the other hand, if constant adjustment is related to data error over the period of estimation and then if the model operators are successful in this attempt (that is, if they succeed in neutralizing data errors),

$$MSE(e^{\prime}_{T+\tau \cdot}) - MSE(e^{*\prime}_{T+\tau \cdot}) \geqslant 0$$

$$MSE(\hat{e}^{\prime}_{T+\tau \cdot}) - MSE(\hat{e}^{*\prime}_{T+\tau \cdot}) \geqslant 0.$$

Finally, if the constant adjustment process is related to the way exogenous variables are forecast by model operators, then:

$$MSE(e^{*\prime}_{T+\tau \cdot}) - MSE(e^{\prime}_{T+\tau \cdot}) \geqslant 0$$

$$MSE(e^{*\prime}_{T+\tau \cdot}) - MSE(\hat{e}^{*\prime}_{T+\tau \cdot}) \geqslant 0$$

since the constant adjustment will be inappropriate with the correct exogenous variables. This explains the first inequality. The second states that model builders "do better" in an ex ante constant adjustment framework than in an ex post constant adjustment one.

In common parlance the relations above are implications of the view that model builders "know what they are doing and their models are basically good."

A negation of the inequalities above would mean that "model builders don't know what they are doing" or that "their models are not basically good." Of course, we can never observe the mean squared error matrices. We could approximate them, however, by

$$\sum_{\tau=1}^{N} MSE(\epsilon'_{T+\tau.}) \frac{1}{N} \sum_{\tau=1}^{N} \epsilon'_{T+\tau.} \epsilon'_{T+\tau.} \tag{6.35}$$

where $\epsilon_{T+\tau.}$ denotes a generic forecast error for period $T+\tau$.

This concludes the discussion of the linear models. We examine now the case of nonlinear models. Both the WEFA and BEA models are of the form

$$f(y_{t.}, x_{t.})B^* + x_{t.} C = u_{t.} \tag{6.36}$$

where f is a vector valued function containing the auxiliary functions of the model. The number of such auxiliary functions is n. Adhering to the conventions introduced earlier, we have in (36) the following dimensions: f is $1 \times n$, B^* is $n \times m$ $(n > m)$, x_t is $1 \times G$, C is $G \times m$, and u_t is $1 \times m$. It is assumed that f is such that

$$J(y)B^*$$

is nonsingular almost everywhere, where

$$J(y) = \frac{\partial f''}{\partial y} \, .$$

An example will clarify this and subsequent issues. Consider the simple nonlinear (in variables) model:

$$\begin{aligned} y_{t1} & & + c_{11}x_{t1} & & = u_{t1} \\ y_{t2} + b^*_{12}y^4_{t1} & & + c_{22}x_{t2} & = u_{t2} \end{aligned} \tag{6.37}$$

and for simplicity assume that the error terms are normally distributed. Here the auxiliary functions are contained in

$$f(y_{t.}, x_{t.}) = (y_{t1}, y^4_{t1}, y_{t2}) \tag{6.38}$$

Moreover

$$B^* = \begin{matrix} 1 & 0 \\ 0 & b_{12}^* \\ 0 & 1 \end{matrix}, \quad C = \begin{matrix} c_{11} & 0 \\ & \\ 0 & c_{22} \end{matrix} ,$$

$$u_{t\cdot} = (t_{t1}, u_{t2}), \quad (u'_{t\cdot}) = \Sigma > 0$$

$$J(y) \quad \begin{matrix} 1 & 4y_{t1}^{3t} & 0 \\ & & \\ 0 & 0 & 1 \end{matrix} \qquad J(y)B^* = \begin{matrix} 1 & 4b_{12}^* y_{t1}^3 \\ & \\ 0 & 1. \end{matrix} \qquad (6.39)$$

An important property of such models is that, in general, *conditionally unbiased forecasts do not exist*. What this statement means, in a strict logical sense, is that the statement "conditionally unbiased forecasts for such models exist provided the parameters have been estimated unbiasedly" is false.

Generally, a forecast from such a model is obtained, *mutatis mutandis* in exactly the same way as in linear models, that is, given a (generally) consistent estimator for B^* and C and the values of the exogenous variables, say, $x_{T+\tau}$. the forecast of the endogenous variables is the vector, say $\tilde{y}_{T+\tau}$, which solves the system

$$f(y_{T+\tau}, x_{T+\tau})\tilde{B}^* + x_{T+\tau} \cdot \tilde{C} = 0 \qquad (6.40)$$

—that is, the specific vector $\tilde{y}_{T+\tau}$. such that[1]

$$f(\tilde{y}_{T+\tau}, x_{T+\tau})\tilde{B}^* + x_{T+\tau} \cdot \tilde{C} = 0. \qquad (6.40a)$$

The important property of nonlinear models is that no matter how accurate estimators for B^* and C we obtain, we will not have, in general, conditionally unbiased forecasts of $E(y'_{t}\cdot)$.

To demonstrate this, it is sufficient to produce one example where this is so. To that effect, return to the model of (37) and consider the extreme case where B^* and C are known.

First, solve the system in (37) to obtain

$$y_{t1} = u_{t1} - c_{11}x_{t1}$$
$$y_{t2} = u_{t2} - c_{22}x_{t2} - b_{12}^*(u_{t1}^4 - 4u_{t1}^3 c_{11}x_{t1}$$
$$+ 6u_{t1}^2 c_{11}^2 x_{t1}^2 - 4u_{t1} c_{11}^3 x_{t1}^3 + c_{11}^4 x_{t1}^4). \qquad (6.41)$$

---

1. Often in this discussion y will be used both in the sense of a generic variable symbol (an indeterminate) or a specific value assumed by that indeterminate. The context will usually make clear what the precise meaning is.

Thus,

$$E(y_{t1}) = -c_{11}x_{t1}$$
$$E(y_{t2}) = -c_{22}x_{t2} - b^*_{12}c^4_{11}x^4_{t1} - 3b^*_{12}\sigma^2_{11}$$
$$- 6b^*_{12}\sigma_{11}c^2_{11}x^2_{t1}. \tag{6.42}$$

Now, a forecast from this model yields

$$\bar{Y}_{T+\tau,1} = -c_{11}x_{T+\tau,1}$$
$$\bar{Y}_{T+\tau,2} = -c_{22}x_{T+\tau,1} - b^*_{12}c^4_{11}x^4_{T+\tau,1}$$
$$= -c_{22}x_{T+\tau,1} - b^*_{12}\bar{Y}^4_{T+\tau,1}. \tag{6.43}$$

A comparison of (43) with (42) will show that

$$\bar{Y}_{T+\tau,1} = E(y_{T+\tau,1})$$
$$\bar{Y}_{T+\tau,2} = E(y_{T+\tau,2}) + 3b^*_{12}\sigma^2_{11} + 6b^*_{12}\sigma_{11}c^2_{11}x^2_{T+\tau,1} \tag{6.44}$$

so that, indeed, it does not yield an unbiased forecast of the vector y *even if the parameters of the model are known.* It is also clear from the preceding that the extent of bias incidence is structurally dependent and may well depend on the assumed exogenous variables over the forecast period.

This feature of nonlinear (in variables) models is certainly a more plausible explanation for the behavior of model builders' constant adjustment procedures. Of course, it may not be the only or a complete explanation, since model misspecification may equally lead to constant adjustments in order to counter the effect of misspecification and thus improve the accuracy of forecasts.

Leaving the misspecification issues as a residual of this analysis, we may proceed to analyze the mean squared error properties of forecasts, essentially in the same way that we did for linear models. We stress again that in this phase the model is taken as a satisfactory specification of the real world processes it purports to describe.

In order to obtain an expression for the forecast error, we must proceed in a roundabout way since in nonlinear models a closed form expression for the reduced form does not exist. To this effect, note that the forecast is a solution to (40)—and moreover given the realization of the error process

$$\{u'_{t\cdot}: t = 1,2,\ldots T\}$$

and the exogenous variables $x_{T+\tau}$. is a vector of "constants." On the other hand, the actual observation, $y_{T+\tau}$., will be a solution of (36) and as such will depend explicitly on $u_{T+\tau}$.. In any event, we have

$$f(\tilde{y}_{T+\tau}.,x_{T+\tau}.)\tilde{B}^* - f(y_{T+\tau}.,x_{T+\tau}.)B^* + x_{T+\tau}. \, (\tilde{C} - C) = -u_{T+\tau}. \quad (6.44)$$

Expanding $f(y_{T+\tau}., x_{T+\tau})$ by the mean value theorem, about $\tilde{y}_{T+\tau}$ we find

$$f(y_{T+\tau \circ},x_{T+\tau}.) = f(\tilde{y}_{T+\tau}.,x_{T+\tau}.) + (y_{T+\tau}. - \tilde{y}_{T+\tau}.) \, J(\tilde{y}_{T+\tau}^*.) \quad (6.45)$$

where

$$J(y) = \frac{\partial f'}{\partial y} \quad (6.46)$$

and is evaluated at $y = \tilde{y}_{T+\tau}$. where

$$|\tilde{y}_{T+\tau}^*. - \tilde{y}_{T+\tau}.| < |y_{T+\tau}. - \tilde{y}_{T+\tau}.|. \quad (6.47)$$

Thus, (44) may be rewritten as

$$\tilde{y}_{T+\tau}. - y_{T+\tau}. = -u_{T+\tau}. \, J(\tilde{y}_{T+\tau}^*.,x_{T+\tau}.)B^{*^{-1}}$$

$$- f(\tilde{y}_{T+\tau}.,x_{T+\tau}.),x_{T+\tau}. \begin{matrix} B^* - B^* \\ \tilde{C} - C \end{matrix}$$

$$J(\tilde{y}_{T+\tau}^*.,x_{T+\tau}.)B^{*^{-1}} \quad (6.48)$$

A comparison with (14) and (14a) shows that the structure of the problem is basically similar, except that in the nonlinear case,

$$E \, u_{T+\tau}. \, [J(\tilde{y}_{T+\tau}^*.)B^*]^{-1} \neq 0 \quad (6.49)$$

and thus conditionally unbiased forecasts do not exist. The second term in the right-hand member of (48) can be made arbitrarily small in probability by suitably increasing the size of the sample from which we estimate the unknown parameters in B^* and C.

Otherwise the same considerations apply as in the case of linear structural models, and the discussion given earlier need not be repeated.

Thus, the basic tool for judging the forecasting performance of nonlinear (in the variables) models such as that of WEFA and the role played by improper exogenous variables and constant adjustments will be the comparison of the various mean squared error quantities just discussed.

SIMULATION RESULTS

General Framework

In order that we examine the consequences of the issues raised in the previous section, we have carried out eight sets of simulations, corresponding to the permutations of three categories that each take two possible values.

1. Data: original and updated (revised)
2. Tampering with model: constant adjustment, and no constant adjustments
3. Exogenous variables: forecasts of exogenous variables by model operators; correct values of exogenous variables

The simulations were carried out, as is the practice of WEFA, for eight periods. In terms of the data provided us it was possible to simulate only five such forecasts—for 1972.4 through 1974.3; 1973.1 through 1974.4; 1973.2 through 1975.1; 1973.3 through 1975.2; and 1973.3 through 1975.4. In constructing the updated (revised) data matrix, we have used the 1977.3 WEFA tape which, in principle, ought to contain the routinely revised national income accounts (NIA) data through 1975.3—the last period for which we have generated forecasts.

In view of various changes in definitions in the NIA, considerable effort was devoted to a reconciliation process so that all data were put on a consistent basis—that is, consistent with the definitions in effect when the forecasts in question were made by WEFA and over the period covered by such forecasts.

Although, in principle, it is possible to provide a set of summary statistics for all the endogenous variables of the WEFA model, the computer software made available to us was not sufficiently flexible to permit it. We have, therefore, selected fourteen variables for which we have provided statistics like Root Mean Squared Error (PRMSE), Mean Error (MEAN), Mean Absolute Error (MABSLT), Mean Percent Error (MPE), and Mean Absolute Percent Error (MAPE). These statistics are available from the author upon request; in Tables 1 through 8 in the Appendix we give only the percent root mean squared error (PRMSE) for each eight-quarter forecast. This is done to conserve space.

In another experiment whose results will be studied later, we have constructed a "time series" model—ARIMA (4,0,0)—for each of the fourteen variables in question. We view such models as the natural succession to the "naive" models to which structural models were compared in the past. Interestingly enough, recent macro-economic fashions have reverted to this naive practice. Hence the comparison of the forecasting performance of such models (in comparison to WEFA's model) gain added significance. The results of this experiment are also available from the author upon request. In Table 9 of the Appendix we give the results only for PRMSE.

The Role of Data Revisions

Since we have not re-estimated the WEFA model, the impact of data revisions on the accuracy of forecasts is felt only through the lagged endogenous and exogenous variables contained in the model's equations.

If, as often claimed, constant adjustments in part reflect the impact of data revisions which are, then, informally taken into account by the model operator, we would expect that forecasts with *revised data and constant adjustments would do worse than those using original data* and *constant adjustments.*

Comparing, in pairs, Tables 1 and 5, 3 and 7, 2 and 6, 4 and 8, it is easily seen that in the overwhelming majority of cases forecasts with original and revised (updated) data do not yield appreciable differences. The most dramatic differences occur for the forecasting period 1973.4 through 1975.3, where with updated data (Table 5), the percent root mean squared error (PRMSE) is. .038, .083, .075 for nominal GNP (GNP$), Unemployment and Nominal Gross Private Domestic Investment (I$), original data are .057, .143, .041. Although for this period we record the largest discrepancies in these two forecasts, it is not the case that the one with revised data does, on the whole, appreciably better or worse than the one with original data unless we use a capricious weighting scheme.

Thus, whatever the motivation for constant adjustments, it is not plausible to argue that they account for data revisions since the two sets of forecasts (in Tables 1, 2, 3, and 4 and 5, 6 7, and 8) cannot, on a (suitable) pairwise comparison, provide us with a consistent ranking. Indeed, on the whole the differences in PRMSE are not sufficiently large to justify close investigation. We are left, therefore, with the conclusion that, other things being equal, data revisions do not account for much of the observed accuracies or inaccuracies of WEFA's forecasts.

Constant Adjustments

Here we shall compare forecasts with a view to determining the impact of constant adjustments on the accuracy of forecasts generated by the WEFA model.

In the second section our analysis showed that if the constant adjustment process is independent of the structural error process and of the process generating the exogenous variables, then we could expect that

$$MSE(e^{*'}_{T+\tau \cdot}) - MSE(e'_{T+\tau \cdot}) \geqslant 0.$$

In Tables 2 and 4, and Tables 6 and 8, we have some evidence bearing on this issue. Tables 2 and 4 (based on original data but correct exogenous variables) yield the startling conclusion that the No Constant Adjustment version of the model tends to dominate (in terms of smaller PRMSE), generally for nominal GNP, P (the implicit GNP deflator), consumption (C$) and occasionally fixed investment (IF$), nonresidential structures (IP$) and imports (M$).

The version with constant adjustments tends to dominate invariably for unemployment (UN), residential structures investment (IHT$) and occasionally for exports (FE$). Turning to Tables 6 and 8, which utilize the updated version of the data bank we see exactly the same situation except that here it is more typical to have real investment (I) consistently better forecast by the constant adjustment version. Thus we must conclude that the constant adjustment process is either related to attempts to correct, on an ad hoc basis, model misspecification or that it is related to the manner in which the required exogenous variables are forecast. To shed some light on this aspect we examined the same versions as above but in an ex ante sense, that is, using the forecast values of the required exogenous variables.

If the constant adjustment process is chosen in such manner so as to counter errors in forecasting the exogenous variables, we could expect that

$$MSE(\hat{e}'_{T+\tau \cdot}) - MSE(\hat{e}^{*'}_{T+\tau \cdot}) \geqslant 0.$$

Evidence on this issue is provided in Tables 1 and 3 (versions using the original data) and Tables 5 and 7 using the updated version of the data bank. In both versions the frequency of better performance is tilted in favor of the constant adjustment version—while in the previous set of comparisons it was tilted in favor of the no constant adjustment version. Nonetheless it remains a fact that almost always the PRMSE for GNP$ (nominal GNP) and C$ (consumption) are smaller in the No Constant Adjustment Version. The PRMSE are invariably smaller—by large factors—for UN (unemployment) and often for I$ (nominal gross private investment) and its various components in the case of the Constant Adjustments version.

The impression is, therefore, overwhelming that the WEFA model in general does reasonably well except for unemployment and (less frequently) some components of investment, and that the constant adjustment process is more related to an attempt to provide ad hoc corrections for these characteristics rather than data revisions, errors in forecasting the requisite exogenous variables, or the autoregressive character of the error terms. The latter is, in fact, not even an argument since the proper response to such a situation is to incorporate this feature of the model in the estimation phase. On the other hand, we had shown in the previous section that even in a properly specified and consistently estimated nonlinear model, there is room for constant adjustments, owing to the fact that conditionally unbiased forecasts of the endogenous variables do not exist if, as is common, in forecasting we set the error terms of the model equal to their assumed mean (zero). This explanation will potentially admit of constant adjustment, which depends on the forecast values of the relevant exogenous variables.

In terms of the criteria set forth in section 2 it only remains for us to examine systematically the ex post-ex ante versions of the forecast *without constant adjustments*. The results relevant for this comparison are contained in Tables 3 and 4 (original data) and Tables 7 and 8 (updated data).

The most noteworthy feature of this comparison is that it is lacking in the dramatic contrasts we observed earlier. Instances are indeed rate where the ex post-ex ante comparison yields PRMSE which differ by an order of magnitude of two. Using the original data version (Tables 3 and 4), we note that the model does consistently better ex post for real GNP, almost always (73.2, 73.3, 73.4) better for P (implicit GNP deflator) and unemployment, and as frequently as not for investment as well. The results are appreciably the same when the updated version is used (Tables 7 and 8), although in this case using the "old exogenous" variables, on balance, yields somewhat better forecasts for investment and its components and invariably better forecasts for nominal GNP.

The results constitute evidence of considerable misspecification or appreciable correlation between the error terms of the model and those variables termed by the model operators, "exogenous."

Finally, in this section it is useful to ask: is the model on its own as good as the model *cum* its operators? In other words, if we compare the ex ante forecasts with constant adjustments (and "old exogenous" variables) with *ex post forecasts without constant adjustments,* will we find that one invariably dominates the other? The relevant comparisons here involve Tables 1 and 4 and possibly Tables 5 and 8.

An examination of Tables 1 and 4 reveals that for the forecast beginning in 1972.4 the model itself (that is, ex post no constant adjustment) does better in every respect except for investment and unemployment; in subsequent forecasts its advantage diminishes so that *on balance the model* cum *operators* does substantially better—that is, the constant adjustments not only overcome the "handicap" of not knowing the correct values of the exogenous variables but also the intrinsic "weakness" of the model in "explaining" unemployment and the various components of investment—particularly investment in residential structures.

The conclusion is, therefore, inevitable: the model contains substantial misspecifications, particularly with regard to its investment and unemployment equations although the latter is understandable, given that unemployment is determined residually. The constant adjustment process may be viewed with justification more as a means of coping with this problem than as a means of coping with data revisions, ignorance of correct exogenous variables, and similar matters.

Comparison with Naive Forecasting Schemes

Of late it has become fashionable in empirical macroeconomics to argue that we do not know anything about the structure of the economy and because of that it is preferable to rely on autoregressive models in describing the behavior of economic variables of interest. Of course, this is a retrogressive step and does represent a reaction (some would say overreaction) to the plethora of various "structural" models that have been proliferating over the past two decades. Has this reaction gone too far in claiming too much for itself and ignoring the contributions of structural models? A partial answer to this question is provided by a number of experiments whose results are reported in this section.

The naive model to which we compare WEFA's model is an ARIMA (4,0,0) process which is reestimated prior to each forecast. To be precise, for the fourteen variables chosen for analysis we estimate the parameters of the process from 1955.1 through 1972.3; we then generate the eight-period forecast for 1972.4, 1973.1 through 1974.3; then we reestimate over the period 1955.1 through 1972.4 and forecast from 1973.1 through 1974.4, and so on. In this exercise we use only updated data. The relevant results from this activity are contained in Table 9 of the Appendix.

In the end we compare the PRMSE from this naive model to WEFA's PRMSE for each eight-period forecast, variable by variable. The detals of this comparison are given in Tables 6–1 and 6–2. The entries in both of these tables, W, B, and so on, have the following meanings:

S	ARIMA forecasts have approximately the same PRMSE as WEFA's forecasts.
B	ARIMA's forecasts have PRMSE that is smaller but not less than one-half of WEFA's forecast.
BB	ARIMA's forecasts have PRMSE which are between one-quarter and one-half of those of WEFA's forecasts.
BBB	ARIMA's forecasts have PRMSE which are, at most, one-quarter of those of WEFA's forecasts.
W	ARIMA's forecasts have PRMSE which are larger, at most twice that of WEFA's forecasts.
WW	ARIMA's forecasts have PRMSE which are between two and four times those of WEFA's forecasts.
WWW	ARIMA's forecasts have PRMSE which are more than four times larger than those of WEFA's forecasts.

In Table 6–1 we compare ARIMA with the basic WEFA model, that is, the version involving updated data, no constant adjustments, and the correct values of the exogenous variables. The entries in Table 6–1 show that ARIMA does better for unemployment, nominal investment in residential structures as well as nominal fixed investment (plant and equipment) and nominal housing investment; its dominance is generally marginal, except for unemployment where it is overwhelming. We had occasion to remark in an earlier context that WEFA's basic model is very weak in its unemployment and investment specifications. In every other respect WEFA's model, however, is overwhelmingly dominant; it is particularly so in forecasting real GNP and the implicit GNP deflator; on balance the model does appreciably better than the ARIMA process—especially if unemployment is not considered. We note, in particular, that in WEFA's model unemployment is a residual obtained from forecasts of employment and labor force. Evidently WEFA's model could easily be modified so as to obtain unemployment and employment through "estimating" equations and determine civilian labor force through an identity. This will no doubt improve the forecasting performance of WEFA's model, since small errors in large variables (like employment and the labor force) often translate into large errors for small variables (like unemployment which, over the range of samples considered in this study, has fluctuated well within the limits of .01 and .09).

In Table 6–2 we present a comparison with WEFA's forecasts as generated at the relevant time—that is, using the basic WEFA model with original data, constant adjustments, and incorrect exogenous variables. Hence, here the question is: could WEFA's operators have done better using the ARIMA structure? In this comparison we give the ARIMA version an edge, since we have estimated its parameters with updated data, and the PRMSE *for all forecasts* are computed relative to the updated data. Nonetheless, Table 6–2 is much more favorable to WEFA. The only variable for which ARIMA dominates—though be it weakly—is unemployment; it has a rather slight edge for nominal fixed investment and nominal investment in residential structures (housing investment). In all other aspects it is decidedly dominated by WEFA's forecasts.

Thus, not only does it appear that structural models contain substantial information but that WEFA's model operators have insights over and above those they have incorporated in their model!

Table 6-1. Comparison of PRMSE of Eight-Quarter Forecasts: WEFA Model Ex Post, No Constant Adjustments Versus ARIMA (4, 0, 0) Re-estimated Up to Quarter Immediately Preceding Forecast (Updated Data).

Variables		Forecast Beginning in Quarter			
		1972.4	1973.1	1973.2	1973
1. Nominal GNP	(GNP$)	WWW	B	S	W
2. Real GNP	(X)	WW	W	WWW	WW
3. Implicit GNP Deflator	(P)	WWW	WWW	WW	WW
4. Unemployment	(UN)	BBB	BBB	BBB	BBB
5. Personal Consumption Expenditures	(C$)	WWW	B	WWW	WW
6. Non Auto Durables	(CDEA$)	W	B	WWW	WWW
7. Nominal, Gross Private Domestic Investment	($)	S	B	WW	WW
8. Nominal, Fixed Investment	(IF$)	B	B	B	B
9. Nominal, Nonresidential Investment	(IP$)	B	BBB	WWW	W
10. Nominal, Investment in Residential Structures	(IHT$)	B	B	B	BB
11. Exports	(FE$)	WW	W	W	W
12. Imports	(M$)	WW	WW	W	W
13. Nominal, Government Purchases of Goods and Services	(G$)	W	W	W	S
14. Real Gross Private Domestic Investment	(I)	B	WW	WWW	WWW

Note: Key to symbols is provided in the text.

Table 6-2. Comparison of PRMSE of Eight-Quarter Forecasts: WEFA Public Forecasts (Post Meeting); Ex Ante Constant Adjustments Original Data Versus ARIMA (4, 0, 0) Re-estimated up to Quarter Immediately Preceding Forecast (Updated Data).

Variables		Forecast Beginning in Quarter			
		1972.4	*1973.1*	*1973.2*	*1973*
1. Nominal GNP	(GNP$)	WW	BB	S	W
2. Real GNP	(X)	W	W	WWW	WWW
3. Implicit GNP Deflator	(P)	W	W	WW	WW
4. Unemployment	(UN)	B	B	B	W
5. Personal Consumption Expenditures	(C$)	WW	BB	WWW	W
6. Non Auto Durables	(CDEA$)	B	B	WWW	WWW
7. Nominal, Gross Private Domestic Investment	(I$)	WWW	WW	WW	WW
8. Nominal, Fixed Investment	(IF$)	S	W	B	B
9. Nominal, Nonresidential Investment	(IP$)	WW	S	WWW	WW
10. Nominal, Investment in Residential Structures	(IHT$)	S	B	W	B
11. Exports	(FE$)	W	WW	WW	WW
12. Imports	(M$)	WW	WW	WW	WW
13. Nominal, Government Purchases	(G$)	WW	WW	WW	Ww
of Goods and Services	(G$)	WW	WW	WW	W
14. Real Gross Private Domestic Investment	(I)	W	WWW	WWW	WWW

Note: Key to symbols is provided in the text.

The conclusion is thus inescapable. "Time series" models much advocated by those who find innumerable faults with structural models do demonstrably worse in describing the evolution of the fourteen variables chosen here for analysis. Even given every advantage, the ARIMA (4,0,0) version does on balance worse than WEFA's basic model. Thus, as a modeling tool, ARIMA is dominated by a structural model—even one with many faults.

We arrive at this conclusion without even examining the possibility that the ARIMA coefficients, when estimated with successively more observations, disclose instabilities that may lead us to doubt its usefulness irrespective of other considerations; we also are not examining the fact that a stable autoregressive process will generally not predict turning points.

Conclusion

We have sought in this article to appraise the forecasting performance of WEFA's model over the period 1972.4 through 1975.3, one of the most turbulent periods in recent economic history.

The strategy was to conduct a number of experiments in which the accuracy of WEFA's model forecasts was explored in connection with the process of constant adjustments, also taking into account and the facts of data revisions and the unavailability of information on exogenous variables over the forecasting horizon when forecasts were made.

Finally, we compared the accuracy of WEFA's model forecasts to those of a continuously estimated ARIMA (4,0,0) process for a select group of fourteen key macroeconomic variables.

We found no plausible theoretical explanation for constant adjustments consistent with the assertion of no misspecification, save the one given in the second section that when we deal with a nonlinear (in the dependent variables) model, we cannot obtain conditionally unbiased forecasts even if we know the structural parameters of the model. In the example adduced, the bias is due to the fact that in forecasting, we set the value of the error terms to zero[2] and depends on the covariance structure of the error and the exogenous variables over the period of the forecast. The constant

---

2. Evidently, forecasting by random shocks *inter alia* may offer a possibility of overcoming this problem.

adjustment process used in connection with WEFA's model does not appear, however, to have any such systematic basis.

The major findings of the study are: (1) data revisions do not appear to matter very much, or at any rate they are not a significant factor in the accuracy (or inaccuracy) of WEFA's forecasts; (2) the constant adjustment process is more related to ad hoc attempts to correct appreciable misspecification in the unemployment and investment behavior built into WEFA's model than to any other factor; (3) the WEFA model with revised data, correct exogenous variables (ex post) and no constant adjustment produces forecasts of unemployment and various components of investment which are useless; (4) with all its faults, WEFA's basic model as in (3) above, on balance, decidedly dominates the performance of the ARIMA (4,0,0) forecasts except for unemployment; (5) WEFA's public forecasts, that is, with original data, constant adjustments and incorrect values of exogenous variables (ex ante) decidedly dominate the ARIMA forecasts although the latter do marginally better on unemployment and some components of investment.

REFERENCES

Brissimis, S.N. 1976. "Multiplier Effects for Higher than First-Order Linear Dynamic Econometric Models." *Econometrica:* 593–600.

Dhrymes, P.J. 1973. "Restricted and Unrestricted Reduced Forms: Asymptotic Distribution and Relative Efficiency." *Econometrica:* 119–134.

Dhrymes, P.J. 1978. *Introductory Econometrics.* New York: Springer Verlag.

Evans, Michael K.; Yoel Haitovsky; and George I. Treyz, assisted by Vincent Su. 1972. "An Analysis of the Forecasting Properties of U.S. Econometric Models." In B.G. Hickman (ed.), *Econometric Models of Cyclical Behavior,* pp. 949–1139. New York: Columbia University Press.

Feldstein, M.S. 1971. "The Error of Forecast in Econometric Models when the Forecast Period Exogenous Variables are Stochastic." *Econometrica:* 556–573.

Fromm, Gary, and Lawrence R. Klein. 1976. "The NBER/NSF Model Comparison Seminar: An Analysis of Results." *Annals of Economic and Social Measurement* (Winter): 1–28.

Fromm, Gary; Lawrence R. Klein; and George R. Schink. 1972. "Short-and Long-Term Simulations with the Brookings Model." In B.G. Hickman (ed.), *Econometric Models of Cyclical Behavior,* pp. 201–292. New York: Columbia University Press.

Goldberger, A.S.; A.L. Nagar; and H.S. Odeh. 1961. "The Covariance Matrices of Reduced Form Coefficients and Forecasts for a Structural Econometric Model." *Econometrica:* 556–573.

Haitovsky, Yoel, and George Treyz. 1972. "Forecasts with Quarterly Macroeconometric Models: Equation Adjustments, and Benchmark Predictions: The U.S. Experience." *Review of Economics and Statistics* (August): 317–325.

Haitovsky, Yoel; George Treyz; and Vincent Su. 1974. *Forecasts with Quarterly Macroeconometric Models* New York: National Bureau of Economic Research, Columbia University Press.

NcNees, Stephen K. 1973. "The Predictive Accuracy of Econometric Forecasts." *New England Economic Review* (September/October):3–22.

McNees, Stephen K. 1975. "An Evaluation of Economic Forecasts." *New England Economic Review* (November/December):3–39.

McNees, Stephen K. 1976. "An Evaluation of Economic Forecasts: Extension and Update." *New England Economic Review* (Sepember/October): 30–44.

Schmidt, P. 1974. "The Asymptotic Distribution of Forecasts in the Dynamic Simulation of an Econometric Model." *Econometrica:* 303–309.

Schmidt, P. 1978. "A Note on Dynamic Simulation Forecasts and Stochastic Forecast-Period Exogenous Variables." *Econometrica:* 1227–1230.

APPENDIX

Table 1. Percent Root Mean Squared Error (PRMSE) for Eight-Quarter Forecasts Beginning in the Indicated Quarter WEFA Model, Original Data, Constant Adjustments "Old" Exogenous Variables.

	Variable	1972–4	1973–1	1973–2	1973–3	1973–4
GNP$	Gross national product	0.045401	0.041987	0.040666	0.038207	0.057628
X	Real gross national product	0.017905	0.023981	0.015483	0.007805	0.014470
P	Implicit price deflator	0.052095	0.060513	0.053782	0.038201	0.046771
UN	Unemployment	0.113251	0.166634	0.110355	0.094255	0.143059
C$	Personal consumption expend.	0.050252	0.045201	0.042636	0.037176	0.056332
CDEA$	Non-auto durables	0.073843	0.046267	0.021990	0.011634	0.042783
I$	Gross domestic investment	0.022485	0.040733	0.044081	0.051367	0.040711
IF$	Fixed investment	0.181936	0.194765	0.195889	0.197282	0.215763
IP$	Nonresidential investment	0.029273	0.014107	0.009459	0.023781	0.059940
IHT$	Residential structures inv.	0.093492	0.084120	0.060599	0.104763	0.159569
FE$	Exports	0.213716	0.163318	0.116624	0.064502	0.084153
M$	Imports	0.151142	0.082425	0.066725	0.055197	0.035053
G$	Govt. purchases of goods & svcs.	0.102140	0.088123	0.096413	0.095509	0.121410
I	Gross private domestic invest.	0.051774	0.072057	0.083943	0.034596	0.044013

Table 2. Percent Root Mean Squared Error (PRMSE) for Eight-Quarter Forecasts Beginning in the Indicated Quarter WEFA Model, Original Data, Constant Adjustments "Correct" Exogenous Variables.

	Variable	1972–4	1973–1	1973–2	1973–3	1973–4
GNP$	Gross national product	0.048080	0.042853	0.060461	0.072101	0.086851
X	Real gross national product	0.007045	0.014675	0.025593	0.052942	0.075473
P	Implicit price deflator	0.044532	0.054115	0.038322	0.021360	0.013560
UN	Unemployment	0.290409	0.356188	0.130173	0.103539	0.198540
C$	Personal consumption expend.	0.041056	0.036743	0.044481	0.050380	0.065896
CDEA$	Non-auto durables	0.051655	0.030694	0.020998	0.024558	0.068930
I$	Gross domestic investment	0.073561	0.095282	0.082105	0.106459	0.157139
IF$	Fixed investment	0.212744	0.219913	0.222992	0.223078	0.226719
IP$	Nonresidential investment	0.020936	0.030127	0.040870	0.059876	0.104291
IHT$	Residential structures inv.	0.148871	0.136254	0.131966	0.087091	0.121503
FE$	Exports	0.234670	0.179474	0.159314	0.095764	0.089294
M$	Imports	0.151800	0.100764	0.118493	0.143376	0.243268
G$	Govt. purchases of goods & svcs.	0.136428	0.126239	0.146336	0.166758	0.177306
I	Gross private domestic invest.	0.090129	0.113779	0.081629	0.090176	0.133490

Table 3. Percent Root Mean Squared Error (PRMSE) for Eight-Quarter Forecasts Beginning in the Indicated Quarter WEFA Model, Original Data, No Constant Adjustments "Old" Exogenous Variables.

	Variable	1972-4	1973-1	1973-2	1973-3	1973-4
GNP$	Gross national product	0.019806	0.028229	0.028392	0.025472	0.031516
X	Real gross national product	0.014494	0.015516	0.032131	0.031257	0.039674
P	Implicit price deflator	0.007618	0.015425	0.051935	0.047988	0.050605
UN	Unemployment	0.475419	0.576882	0.606167	0.554375	0.579868
C$	Personal consumption expend.	0.023341	0.026882	0.025244	0.023683	0.036970
CDEA$	Non-auto durables	0.041288	0.038229	0.029643	0.027809	0.054008
I$	Gross domestic investment	0.124608	0.181450	0.042878	0.039605	0.090854
IF$	Fixed investment	0.200906	0.209237	0.162567	0.169919	0.183229
IP$	Nonresidential investment	0.086235	0.130732	0.050761	0.070482	0.113267
IHT$	Residential structures inv.	0.139692	0.143220	0.154336	0.221652	0.209878
FE$	Exports	0.165058	0.146120	0.158566	0.148626	0.145177
M$	Imports	0.128476	0.087227	0.093921	0.057567	0.022362
G$	Govt. purchases of goods & svcs.	0.192140	0.088123	0.096413	0.095509	0.102438
I	Gross private domestic invest.	0.080539	0.117764	0.068074	0.043757	0.069767

Table 4. Percent Root Mean Squared Error (PRMSE) for Eight-Quarter Forecasts Beginning in the Indicated Quarter WEFA Model, Original Data, No Constant Adjustments "Correct" Exogenous Variables.

	Variable	1972–4	1973–1	1973–2	1973–3	1973–4
GNP$	Gross national product	0.011028	0.020319	0.042806	0.053075	0.068413
X	Real gross national product	0.007796	0.022300	0.012648	0.025331	0.035183
P	Implicit price deflator	0.010227	0.016394	0.038906	0.035819	0.045135
UN	Unemployment	0.754994	0.858478	0.592361	0.477231	0.442127
C$	Personal consumption expend.	0.017493	0.031374	0.022400	0.027419	0.045297
CDEA$	Non-auto durables	0.043199	0.059351	0.019726	0.020072	0.037260
I$	Gross domestic investment	0.174079	0.231059	0.043686	0.069322	0.096653
IF$	Fixed investment	0.212784	0.212178	0.180636	0.191218	0.191518
IP$	Nonresidential investment	0.082792	0.119216	0.028896	0.058930	0.056740
IHT$	Residential structures inv.	0.107011	0.111446	0.133563	0.177326	0.247671
FE$	Exports	0.194246	0.167997	0.197831	0.177704	0.149524
M$	Imports	0.122622	0.095404	0.144229	0.151528	0.160890
G$	Govt. purchases of goods & svcs.	0.136428	0.126239	0.146336	0.166758	0.177306
I	Gross private domestic invest.	0.153358	0.198028	0.054391	0.066311	0.089738

Table 5. Percent Root Mean Squared Error (PRMSE) for Eight-Quarter Forecasts Beginning in the Indicated Quarter WEFA Model, Updated Data, Constant Adjustments "Old" Exogenous Variables.

	Variable	1972-4	1973-1	1973-2	1973-3	1973-4
GNP$	Gross national product	0.044481	0.043890	0.039341	0.039561	0.036738
X	Real gross national product	0.21319	0.029372	0.013850	0.003415	0.021319
P	Implicit price deflator	0.055833	0.066697	0.049381	0.038229	0.025486
UN	Unemployment	0.122035	0.155100	0.087661	0.089874	0.083167
C$	Personal consumption expend.	0.050005	0.048241	0.011803	0.037680	0.034359
CDEA$	Non-auto durables	0.071318	0.047980	0.022723	0.011592	0.026765
I$	Gross domestic investment	0.029419	0.042777	0.033665	0.063203	0.073718
IF$	Fixed investment	0.186268	0.194411	0.200143	0.198577	0.188344
IP$	Nonresidential investment	0.014312	0.021415	0.021169	0.023076	0.044097
IHT$	Residential structures inv.	0.090612	0.075175	0.058785	0.106417	0.077047
FE$	Exports	0.215473	0.168956	0.113480	0.004524	0.076186
M$	Imports	0.153891	0.091989	0.079398	0.057434	0.124418
G$	Govt purchases of goods & svcs	0.100431	0.087723	0.096030	0.095509	0.102438
I	Gross private domestic invest	0.066415	0.086221	0.075872	0.042209	0.041004

Table 6. Percent Root Mean Squared Error (PRMSE) for Eight-Quarter Forecasts Beginning in the Indicated Quarter WEFA Model, Updated Data, Constant Adjustments "Correct" Exogenous Variables.

	Variable	1972–4	1973–1	1973–2	1973–3	1973–4
GNP$	Gross national product	0.047453	0.043890	0.059642	0.039561	0.087493
X	Real Gross national product	0.006926	0.029372	0.026986	0.008415	0.077106
P	Implicit price deflator	0.047695	0.066697	0.034900	0.038229	0.012438
UN	Unemployment	0.298049	0.155100	0.122330	0.089874	0.215154
C$	Personal consumption expend.	0.041041	0.048241	0.044243	0.037680	0.066439
CDEA$	Non-auto durables	0.048853	0.047980	0.023605	0.011592	0.071579
I$	Gross domestic investment	0.076199	0.042777	0.072366	0.063203	0.150861
IF$	Fixed investment	0.217634	0.194411	0.228109	0.198577	0.225014
IP$	Nonresidential investment	0.029650	0.021415	0.048045	0.023076	0.104879
IHT$	Residential structures inv.	0.143825	0.075175	0.130968	0.106417	0.122925
FE$	Exports	0.236376	0.166956	0.156991	0.064524	0.088722
M$	Imports	0.154496	0.091989	0.130585	0.057434	0.247120
G$	Govt. purchases of goods & svcs.	0.135153	0.087723	0.146084	0.095509	0.177306
I	Gross private domestic invest.	0.101129	0.086221	0.067527	0.042239	0.132159

Table 7. Percent Root Mean Squared Error (PRMSE) for Eight-Quarter Forecasts Beginning in the Indicated Quarter WEFA Model, Updated Data, No Constant Adjustments "Old" Exogenous Variables.

	Variable	1972–4	1973–1	1973–2	1973–3	1973–4
GNP$	Gross national product	0.020582	0.024850	0.027994	0.028553	0.032550
X	Real gross national product	0.016426	0.020720	0.030130	0.030829	0.036910
P	Implicit price deflator	0.006529	0.010464	0.047597	0.048312	0.050380
UN	Unemployment	0.479345	0.544337	0.580711	0.550206	0.561539
C$	Personal consumption expend.	0.022467	0.022246	0.022897	0.023849	0.033953
CDEA$	Non-auto durables	0.039018	0.033716	0.027449	0.027373	0.048257
I$	Gross domestic investment	0.135911	0.177618	0.053053	0.055374	0.088822
IF$	Fixed investment	0.207145	0.210331	0.165571	0.170914	0.178792
IP$	Nonresidential investment	0.102799	0.136891	0.059717	0.070329	0.107966
IHT$	Residential structures inv.	0.143432	0.152956	0.160270	0.220252	0.210714
FE$	Exports	0.166858	0.150293	0.155718	0.148626	0.144835
M$	Imports	0.130757	0.097728	C.107488	0.059518	0.024633
G$	Govt. purchases of goods & svcs.	0.100431	0.087723	C.096030	0.095509	0.102438
I	Gross private domestic invest.	0.097685	0.130979	0.064195	0.049416	0.063146

Table 8. Percent Root Mean Squared Error (PRMSE) for Eight-Quarter Forecasts Beginning in the Indicated Quarter WEFA Model, Updated Data, No Constant Adjustments "Correct" Exogenous Variables.

	Variable	1972–4	1973–1	1973–2	1973–3	1973–4
GNP$	Gross national product	0.011333	0.015384	0.042580	0.054246	0.069889
X	Real gross national product	0.011397	0.026321	0.012407	0.025470	0.035292
P	Implicit price deflator	0.013408	0.019200	0.036061	0.036133	0.044957
UN	Unemployment	0.760923	0.833832	0.576205	0.472384	0.426587
C$	Personal consumption expend.	0.016382	0.024660	0.020948	0.028184	0.046293
CDEA$	Non-auto durables	0.041949	0.051709	0.018999	0.021914	0.040464
I$	Gross domestic investment	0.180583	0.222362	0.033189	0.053660	0.071645
IF$	Fixed investment	0.218495	0.211774	0.182797	0.191633	0.189376
IP$	Nonresidential investment	0.096180	0.122306	0.038964	0.057477	0.052307
IHT$	Residential structures inv.	0.109218	0.120835	0.140734	0.175466	0.247650
FE$	Exports	0.196187	0.173208	0.196755	0.177804	0.149143
M$	Imports	0.124989	0.107121	0.157711	0.153452	0.164400
G$	Govt. purchases of goods & svcs.	0.135153	0.137000	0.146847	0.166758	0.177306
I	Gross private domestic invest.	0.168193	0.208010	0.042051	0.057596	0.076043

Table 9. Percent Root Mean Squared Error (PRMSE) for Eight-Quarter Forecasts Beginning in the Indicated Quarter ARIMA (4,0,0) Model, Reestimated Before Each Forecast, Updated Data.

	Variable	1972–4	1973–1	1973–2	1973–3	1973–4
GNP$	Gross national product	0.197049	0.010574	0.041903	0.062426	0.090293
X	Real gross national product	0.026930	0.044754	0.064248	0.054878	0.060403
P	Implict price deflator	0.093096	0.087754	0.125274	0.112996	0.101419
Un	Unemployment	0.101336	0.096526	0.101210	0.104395	0.114822
C$	Personal consumption expend.	0.198536	0.016512	0.167974	0.062999	0.087801
CDEA$	Non-auto durables	0.054895	0.036779	0.130822	0.104567	0.119779
I$	Gross domestic investment	0.179069	0.141122	0.119122	0.121101	0.107508
IF$	Fixed investment	0.186850	0.171998	0.163715	0.163375	0.164866
IP$	Nonresidential investment	0.063082	0.011363	0.178622	0.070784	0.098638
IHT$	Residential structures inv.	0.092099	0.067291	0.077346	0.079634	0.072143
FE$	Exports	0.390104	0.329799	0.276450	0.220844	0.184687
M$	Imports	0.308726	0.267889	0.214562	0.183176	0.162341
G$	Govt. purchases of goods & svcs.	0.228985	0.221206	0.198679	0.171908	0.164090
I	Goss private domestic invest.	0.903577	0.598542	0.576174	0.574545	0.580127

INDEX

Age, xxiv, xxvi, 85. *See also* Demographic variables
Allocation of resources, efficiency of, xiv, xviii
Arbitrage Pricing Theory (APT), 153–55
Assessment, diverse
  and CAPM, 146–47, 148
  in other security-pricing models, 151–57

Barro, Robert, 3
Black, Fischer, 130–31, 141, 143, 145
Blume, Marshall, 4, 11–12, 148
Borrowers
  capital position of, xxix–xxx, 163–65, 177–80, 195, 201
  expected return to, 169–70, 175
  and "go for broke, " 190–91
  moral hazard and, xxix, 170–75
  natural hazards and, 185, 195
  and shocks, 165, 195
Boskin, Michael, 6
Bradley, Richard, 134, 137
Brigham, Eugene, 137
British household budget data, 113, 116
Bureau of Economic Analysis (BEA)
  model, xxviii, 25, 33, 55–57, 63–65, 75–76, 205–206
Bureau of Labor Statistics, xi

Capital asset pricing model (CAPM), xxii, xxx–xxxii, 129–30
  and cost of information, 147
  diverse information sets in, 146–47, 148
  and human capital, 147–48
  market efficiency in, 129–30
  market portfolios and, 146–51
  new tests on, 129–33
  and OPM, 140–45
  riskless asset version, 130, 147
  and short selling positions, 146, 148
  "two-parameter" version, 130–31
Capital asset pricing model-Modigliani Miller (CAPM-MM), 133–40
Capital gains, xii–xv, 10–11, 17, 27
Capital markets, xvi, 14–19
Capital position of borrowers, xxix, 164, 177–80, 185
  during benign financial conditions, 181, 195
  and financial conditions, 181, 189–90, 195
  during financial crisis, 181, 195
  and subjective shock probability, 185–88, 195
  during vulnerable financial conditions, 181, 195
Capital stock, 28–29

Capital structure, xxxi, 12, 133–40
Central bank, role during financial crisis, 164, 190, 192–94, 199–201
Chase model, 25, 47, 56–57, 65–67, 75–76
Chen, Andrew H., 137
Chirinko, Robert S., xxvi–xxvii
"Clientele effect," xv
Cohn, Richard, 13–19
Consumption patterns
in demand analysis, xxiv–xxvi, 85–86, 89, 95, 102, 104, 109
and interest rates, 4
in WEFA model, xxxiii, 222–23
vs. welfare analysis, 113, 116–17
Consumption theories, xi–xii, xxi
Constant elasticity of substitution (CES) function, 28. See also Generalized CES demand system
Contract rates, xxix, 163–90. See also Capital position of borrowers
Copeland, Thomas E., 137
Corporate financing, 133–40
Corporate profits tax rate, xxvii, 25, 27, 51
in BEA model, 33, 51
in Chase model, 51, 56
in DRI model, 51, 70
in Michigan model, 51–53, 70
in MPS model, 51
Corporate saving, 2–4
Costs
in econometric models of investment equations, 26–27
of equity capital, xiv–xv, xxvi, xxviii, 133–36, 139
of information, 147, 151–57
user, xxvii–xxviii, 10, 26, 30, 33
Cost of capital, xxix–xxx
in BEA model, 55, 75
in Chase model, 56–57, 75
in DRI model, 58, 75
in inflation, 10–11
in MPS model, 75
effect of tax parameters on investment, 32, 47, 50, 53–54, 75
in Wharton model, 61
Creditors. See Lenders
Credit shock, 163, 164–67, 189, 193
Crockett, Jean, 148

David, Paul, 2
Debt, corporate, xvii, xxxi, 133, 135–37, 139
-equity relationship, xxxi, 135–37
effect of inflation on, 15
Debt service variable, 47, 57–58

Default risk, 163, 168
Demand analysis
conditional equivalence scales in, 86, 108–109
and demographic scaling, 90–93
and demographic translating, 88–90
demographic variables in, xxiii xxvi, 85–86, 87–100, 102–104, 109, 116
and Gorman specification, 93–94
and modified Prais-Houthakker, 94–99, 119
Demand for investment goods, 10–13
Demographic scaling, 87, 90–93, 100, 105, 108–109, 116
Demographic translating, 87–90, 99–100, 106, 109, 116
Demographic variables, xxiii–xxvi
in demand analysis, 85–86, 102–104, 109, 116
general procedures for, 87–100, 116
in welfare analysis, 108–17
Dhrymes, P.J., xxxii–xxxiii, 207, 210
Distribution of income, 3–4, 8–9
Distribution of wealth, 2
Dividend, xiv, xxvii. See also Earnings; Stock prices
-stock price ratio, 54–55, 60, 76
Dolde, Walter, 7
Donaldson, Gordon, 138
Douglas, George W., 131
DRI model, xxvii, 25, 47–48, 51–53, 55, 57–59, 67–70, 75–78

Earnings, xv, xxvii–xxviii, 14–17. See also Dividends; Stock prices
-price ratio, 47, 58
Econometric models, 205–206
forecasting with, xxxii–xxxiii, 207–219
investment functions in, xxvi–xxviii, 25–26, 30, 53–62
simulation results, 220–30
Economic earnings, xv, 14–17
Economies of scale in consumption, 87, 99–100, 108
Eisner, Robert, xxvi–xxvii
Equity, xv, xxx–xxxi, 140–45. See also Cost of equity capital
Equivalence scales, 86, 95, 108–14, 116–18
conditional, 86, 108–109, 116–17
unconditional, 86, 110–14, 116–18
Expected earnings, xv, xxvii–xxviii, 14–17
Expenditures, 88, 91, 104, 106–108
and consumption, 109–10
Eurobanks, 199–200

Fama, Eugene F., 2, 8, 12, 14, 16, 19, 131–32
Family Expenditure Survey (FES) series, 101
Family size. *See also* Demagragraphic variables
  and consumption, 85–86, 89, 95
  in welfare analysis, 113–15
Federal Home Loan Bank Board (FHLBB), xix, xx
Federal Housing Administration, xx
Federal Reserve Board Survey of Financial Characteristics of Consumers (1962–63), xx
Feldstein, Martin, 2–3, 16
Financial assets, effect of inflation on, 17
Financial conditions, 180–82
  actual and perceived, 188
  benign, 181, 195
  capital/liquidity position and, 187, 189–90
  crisis, 181, 192–94, 195
  issue of inevitability, 191–92
  vulnerable, 181, 184–92, 195
Financial crisis, 164, 181, 184–92, 195, 201
Financial disorder, xxviii–xxx, 163–64, 194–95
  analysis of, 197–201
  borrower's capital, classification by, 164, 177–80
  crisis scenarios and central banks, 164, 192–94
  financial conditions, classification by, 180–82
  financial crisis, increasing vulnerability to, 184–92
  lending decisions in response to default risk and moral hazard, 168–77
  shocks and capacity to withstand, 164–67
  subjective probability of disaster, 182–84
Financial markets, xi, xvi, xxviii–xxx
  financial disaster in, xxviii–xxx, 163–64, 194–95
  moral hazard in, xxix, 163–64, 170–76, 179, 181
Forecasting, in econometric models, xxxii–xxxiii, 207–219, 221–22, 222–24, 229–30
Forecasts with Quarterly Macro-Econometric Models, 205
Friend, Irwin, xi–xxv, xxxi, 4, 7–8, 11–12, 14–15, 17, 19, 132, 148

Galai, Dan, 141–42, 144

Generalized CES demand system, 85, 100–108, 116, 120
General linear structural econometric model (GLSEM), 207
Gibson, William, 12
Ginsberg, Ralph, 182
"Go for broke" strategy, 190–91
Gorman procedure, 87, 93–94, 105–106, 116
Government saving, 2–4
Grossman, Sanford F., 155–56
GNP (Gross national product), xiv, xxxii–xxxiii, 221–23
Gullikin, N. Bulent, 18–19
Guttentag, Jack, xxviii, 194, 199–201

Haitovsky, Y., 205
Haley, Charles W., 137
Hamada, Robert S., 134, 144
Hasbrouck, Joel, 7–8, 11, 14–15, 17, 19
Herring, Richard, xxviii, 194, 199–201
Home construction industry, xix, 11
Home equity, xxi
"Homogeneous expectations" assumption, 130
Household behavior, xxiv–xxv, 2–4
Housing and Urban Development Act of 1968, xx
Houthakker, H.S., 94
Howard, David, 9
Howrey, Philip, 2, 6
Hymans, Saul H., 2, 6

Identification by assumption, 112–13
Income levels, xii–xiii, 101
  and risk aversion, xxi
  -saving relationship, 2–5, 7–8, 10
Inflation, xv, xxi
  effect on capital markets, 14–19
  hedge against, 17–18
  effect on investment, 10–13
  effect on saving, 1–10
  effect on stock prices, 13–19
Information sets, 146–47, 149, 151–57
Insolvency scenarios, 193–94
Institutional developments, for vulnerability, 190–91
Interest costs, 55, 57, 60
Interest rates, xix–xx, xxvi, 181
  effect on capital, 178
  and financial crisis, 181–182
  effect on moral hazard, 174–75
  effect on saving, 4–7
Interest rate shock, 164, 189, 191, 193
Internal Revenue Service (IRS), xiii
International Monetary Fund (UMF), 200

Investment, xiv–xv
  and capital stock, 28–29
  income ratio, 10
  effect of inflation on, 1, 10–13
  effect of tax incentives on, xxi, xxvi–
    xxviii, 25, 27, 30–33
  in WEFA model, xxxiii, 223–24, 230
Investment functions, in econometric models, xxvi, xxxiii, 25, 26–30, 53–62
Investment tax credit, xxviii, 25, 27, 30,
  51, 75–76
  in BEA model, 33, 51, 63, 65, 75
  in Chase model, 47, 56, 65–67
  in DRI model, 51, 69, 75
  in Michigan model, 49, 51, 75
  in MPS model, 49, 51, 74–75
  in Wharton model, 61

Jaffe, Jeffrey, 12
Jensen, Michael C., 131, 138
Jones, Emerson Philip, 5
Juster, Thomas, 9

Kim, E. Han, 137
Kunreuther, Harold, 182–83

Labor/nonlabor income, uncertainty of,
  7–8
Lease, Ronald C., 148
Leimer, Dean, 3
"Lender of last resort," 192–94,
  199–201
Lenders, xxix–xxx. See also Capital posi-
  tion of borrowers
  expected return to, 168–69, 175
  and "go for broke", 190–91
  moral hazards and, 170–75
  and natural hazards, 183–85, 195
  and shocks, 167, 195
Lending decisions, 168–77, 194–95
  and moral hazard, 163–64, 170–76,
    195
Lesnoy, Selog, 3
LDC loans, 200
Levered equity, xxxi–xxxii, 145
Levy, Haim, 12, 150
Lewellan, Wilbur, 148
Liability management, 181
Lieberman, Charles, 7
Life-cycle hypothesis, xii
Linear expenditure system (LES), 109, 113
Linter, John, xxx–xxxii, 131, 138, 147,
  150
Liquidity position, and financial conditions,
  187, 189–90
Liquidity shock, 164, 189, 193–94
Litzenberger, Robert H., 136–37

Losq, Etienne, 5, 7

MacBeth, James D., 131–32
Makin, 000, 12
Mandelker, Gershon, 12
"Marginal budget share," 88, 106
Market behavior, xiv–xv
Market efficiency, xvi, xx, 129–30,
  151–57
Market portfolios, xviii
  and CAPM, 146–51
  diversification of xiii–xiv
  in security-pricing models, 151–57
  tests of, 130–32, 134–35
Market prices, 155
Market value of firm, and OPM, 141–45
Market values of the fund's assets (NAV),
  136
Masulis, Ronald W., 136, 141–42, 144
Mayers, David, 147
McClure, Charles, 6
McKibben, Walt, 151
Meckling, William H., 138
Merton, Robert C., 5, 7, 141–42, 145,
  149, 152
Mexico, 200
Michigan model, 25, 48–49, 51–53,
  59–60, 70, 75–76
Miller, Merton H., 131, 133–40
Modest, David, 6–7
Modified Prais-Houthakker procedure, 87,
  94–99, 100, 105–106, 108, 116,
  119–20
Modigliani, Franco, 13–19, 133–40
Monetary policy, effect on saving, 7
Moral hazard, xxix, 163–64, 170–76,
  179, 181, 190, 195
Mortgage market, xx
MPS models, xxvii, 7, 25, 49–53, 60–
  61, 72–76
Muellbauer, J., 95
Mutual funds, xvii–xix
Myers, Stewart, 134, 137–38

National Bureau of Economic Research
  (NBER), 205
Natural hazards, 163, 182, 183–85, 195
New issues market, xvi–xvii
New York Stock Exchange, xxi, 11
Nonhuman wealth, 1, 6–7
Number of children, 87, 100–101, 108–
  109. See also Family size

Occupation, and stock ownership, xiii
OPEC (Organization of Petroleum Export-
  ing Countries), 201
Opportunity cost of capital, 26–27, 32,
  47–49, 61, 78–80

OPM (Options pricing model), xxxi–xxxii, 133, 140–45
Over-the-market (OTC), xvi–xvii

Permanent income hypothesis, xii, xxi–xxii, 2, 8–9
Plant/equipment outlays, xv, 10–13
Pollack, R.A., xxiii–xxvi, 113, 119–20
Portfolios. *See* Market portfolios
Prais, S.J., 94
Present value of financial distress (PVFD), 138
Price changes, xxiv–xxv, 88, 91, 104, 106, 110
Price-expenditure-demographic, 106, 110
Propensity to save, 3–5, 8–9
Proportional risk aversion, xxi, xxiv–xxv

Rate of return,
   in CAPM, xxii–xxiii, 12
   in option pricing model, xxxi–xxxii, 140–45
   and security-pricing models, 151–52
Reagan administration, 1, 4
Real cost of capital, 11–12
Real cost of equity, 12
Real economic earnings, xv, 15–17
Real investments, 10
Real national income, 1
Real plant and equipment, 13
Real rates of return, xv–xvi
Rental price. *See* User cost of capital
Retained earnings, effect on stock prices, xiv–xv
Reverse Gorman, 93–94, 105–106, 116
Risk, xxviii–xxx
   in CAPM, xxxi, 130–31, 134, 138–40
   in OPM, 141–45
Risk aversion, xiv, xx–xxi, 5, 156
Risk premiums, 164
   and borrower's capital position, 177, 194–95
   in capital asset pricing model, xxii–xxiii, 130–31, 134, 138–40
   and financial conditions, 188, 195
   and inflation, 12
   and shocks, 192, 195
Risky assets, xxi, 146–47
Robichek, Alexander, 138
Roll, Richard, 151, 153–54, 156
Rosenberg, Barr, 144–45, 151
Ross, Stephen A., 153–54
Rubenstein, Mark E., 134
"Run," 181, 184, 193, 195. *See also* Financial crisis

Saving
   corporate, xi, 2–4

personal, xi–xiii, xxi–xxii, 2–4
   -income ratio, xii–xiii, 2–4, 7–8, 10
   effect of inflation on, 1–10
   substitution between household and nonhousehold, 2–4
Savings and Loans industry, xix
Scadding, David, 2
Schlarbaum, Gary C., 148
Scholes, Myron, 131, 137, 141, 143
Scott, James, 137–38
Securities and Exchange Commission (SEC), xiv, xvii, 146
Security market line (SML), 148–50, 151–52, 157
Security-pricing models, 151–57
Sharpe, William, 150
Shocks
   definition of, 164
   probability of, 165–67, 185–88, 192, 195, 201
   types of, 164
Short selling on CAPM, 146, 148
Size of family. *See* Family size
Slovic, P., 182–83
Sociodemographics, and consumption, xii–xiii
Sosin, Howard, 136
Stiglitz, Joseph E., 155–56
Stock, xiii, 17–18, 141–45
   capital gains from, xii–xiii, 10–11, 17
   effect of inflation on, 17–18
   and OPM, 141–45
Stock market, xvi–xvii, xvii–xx
Stock prices, xiv, xxvii–xxviii, 145
   -dividend ratio, xiv, 54–55, 60, 76
   impact of mutual funds on, xviii–xix
   and inflation, 13, 14–19
   and profits, 76
Su, V., 205
Subjective probability of disaster, 166, 178, 182–84, 195
Subjective shock probabilities, 185–88, 192, 195
Substitution, between household/nonhousehold saving, 2–3

Tanner, J. Ernest, 2
Taste differences, 114–16
Tax advantage of corporate debt, 135–37, 139
Tax depreciation charges, xxvii, 25, 27, 30–31, 51
   in BEA model, 33, 51
   in Chase model, 47, 51, 56
   in DRI model, 51–53, 69
   in Michigan model, 48–49, 51, 70
   in MRS model, 49
   in Wharton model, 61

Tax parameters, effect on investment in models, xxvii, 25, 30–32, 33–50, 50–53
Tax policies, effect of, xv, xxi–xxii
  on inflation, 17–18
  on investment, xxvi–xxviii, 25, 27, 30–33
  on saving, 3–7, 9
Tiering, 188
"Time series" model, 221
Tobin, James, 7, 200
Transitory income, xii–xiii
Treyz, G., 205
"Two-parameter," 130–32

Unemployment, in WEFA model, xxxiii, 221–24, 230
U.S. Department of Commerce, 205
User cost of capital, xxvii–xxviii, 10, 26–27, 30, 33, 47–50, 75–76
  in BEA model, 33, 55, 78
  in Chase model, 47, 56–57, 79
  in DRI model, xxvii, 26, 47, 75, 79
  in Michigan model, 48–49, 70, 79
  in MPS model, xxvii, 49, 75

Van Horne, James C., 137
Veterans Administration, xx

Wachtel, Paul, 9

Wales, T.J., xxiii–xxvi, 113
Wealth level. *See also* Income levels in demand analysis, xxiv, xxv, 2, 6–7
  and risk aversion, xx–xxi
Weber, Warren, 6
WEFA model (Wharton Econometric Forecasting Associates, Inc.), xxxii–xxxiii, 205–206
  vs. ARIMA model, 225–30
  comparisons with naive forecasting schemes, 224–29
  and constant adjustments, 222–24, 229–30
  forecasting with, 207–19, 229–30
  MARK III model, 206
  role of data revisions in, 221–22, 230
  simulation results, 220–30
Weiner, 000, 130, 142, 145, 152
Welfare analysis
  role of demographic variables in, 86, 108–17
  with taste differences, 114–15
  and unconditional equivalence scales, 86, 110–14
Westerfield, Randolph, xxvi, 11–12, 132
Weston, J. Fred, 137
Wharton model, 25, 50–51, 61, 74–76
Williams, Joseph, xxxii, 148–50, 153, 154
World Bank, 200

LIST OF CONTRIBUTORS

Robert S. Chirinko, Northwestern University
Phoebus Dhrymes, Columbia University
Robert Eisner, Northwestern University
Irwin Friend, University of Pennsylvania
Jack Guttentag, University of Pennsylvania
Richard Herring, University of Pennsylvania
John Linter, Harvard University
Robert A. Pollak, University of Pennsylvania
James Tobin, Yale University
Terence J. Wales, University of British Columbia

About the Editors

Marshall E. Blume is Howard Butcher Professor of Finance at the University of Pennsylvania's Wharton School and is associate director of Wharton's Rodney L. White Center for Financial Research. Blume, who received his Ph.D. from the University of Chicago, has been a visiting professor in Belgium, Sweden, and Portugal, and has held teaching positions at the University of Chicago. He was also managing editor of *The Journal of Finance.*

Dr. Jean A. Crockett is chairman and professor of finance at the Wharton School, chairman of the board of directors of the Federal Reserve Bank of Philadelphia, and a member of the board of directors of the American Finance Association and the Pennwalt Corporation. She received her Ph.D. from the University of Chicago. Her research interests and empirical studies are related to consumption and saving, composition of household portfolios, interest rates, and business investment decisions.

Paul Taubman is chairman and professor of economics at the University of Pennsylvania. Taubman received his Ph.D. from the University of Pennsylvania and has taught at Harvard. He is a fellow of the Econometric Society and of the International Society for Twin Studies.